Financial Markets and Trading

Founded in 1807, John Wiley & Sons is the oldest independent publishing company in the United States. With offices in North America, Europe, Australia, and Asia, Wiley is globally committed to developing and marketing print and electronic products and services for our customers' professional and personal knowledge and understanding.

The Wiley Finance series contains books written specifically for finance and investment professionals as well as sophisticated individual investors and their financial advisors. Book topics range from portfolio management to e-commerce, risk management, financial engineering, valuation, and financial instrument analysis, as well as much more.

For a list of available titles, visit our web site at www.WileyFinance.com.

Financial Markets and Trading

An Introduction to
Market Microstructure
and Trading Strategies

ANATOLY B. SCHMIDT

WILEY

John Wiley & Sons, Inc.

Published by John Wiley & Sons, Inc., Hoboken, New Jersey.
Published simultaneously in Canada.

For general information on our other products and services or for technical support, please contact our Customer Care Department within the United States at (800) 762-2974, outside the United States at (317) 572-3993 or fax (317) 572-4002.

Wiley also publishes its books in a variety of electronic formats. Some content that appears in print may not be available in electronic books. For more information about Wiley products, visit our web site at www.wiley.com.

Library of Congress Cataloging-in-Publication Data:

Schmidt, Anatoly B.
  Financial markets and trading : an introduction to market microstructure and trading strategies / Anatoly B. Schmidt.
       p. cm.—(Wiley finance ; 637)
    Includes bibliographical references and index.
    ISBN 978-0-470-92412-9 (cloth); ISBN 978-1-118-09363-4 (ebk);
    ISBN 978-1-118-09364-1 (ebk); ISBN 978-1-118-09365-8 (ebk)
  1. Fixed-income securities. 2. Stock exchanges. 3. Microfinance. I. Title.
  HG4650.S36 2011
    332.64—dc22
                                                                              2011008890

10 9 8 7 6 5 4 3 2 1

Contents

Preface

The idea of writing this book came to me as a result of conversations with participants of meetings on quantitative finance and algorithmic trading, and with several generations of students doing internships in my group. I realized that there was a need for a single book that describes how modern financial markets work and what professional trading is about—a book devoted to the market microstructure and trading strategies.

The market microstructure theory has been an established field in finance. It has been thoroughly described in the graduate-level courses by O'Hara (1995), Hasbrouck (2007), and de Jong & Rindi (2009). Also, Harris (2002) has offered a detailed account on financial markets for practitioners. In the last decade, the landscape in this field has dramatically changed due to revolutionary changes in trading technology and the proliferation of electronic order-driven markets. The first goal of this book is to offer an overview of modern financial markets and the theoretical concepts of the market microstructure.

Trading is a process closely interwoven with the market microstructure. Indeed, in O'Hara's (1995) pioneering monograph, the market microstructure is defined in the following way: "While much of economics abstracts from the mechanics of trading, microstructure theory focuses on how specific trading mechanisms affect the price formation process." According to Harris (2002), market microstructure is "a branch of financial economics that investigates trading and the organization of markets." Also, de Jong & Rindi (2009) relate the market microstructure to the "process of financial price formation" and emphasize the importance of the market organization. Hence, while trading is widely discussed in the academic literature on the market microstructure, it is perceived primarily as a process of price formation. Yet, trading means much more for those who have ever traded for a living, for investing, or just for fun. The subject of trading strategies as a knowledge domain can be defined as studies of decision making on what, when, and how to trade. Much of its contents has been contributed by practitioners and may contain some subjective elements. Trading strategies have also received notable attention in academy, which has produced important methodological findings. Most of these results are scattered in periodical literature. The second goal of this book is to provide an overview of the main concepts and methods used in deriving and back-testing trading strategies.

This book is for any reader who is interested in the theoretical aspects of the market microstructure and trading. It can be used by students of undergraduate finance programs and may also be useful for masters-level courses in financial engineering and mathematical finance. I have tried to offer a balance between the theoretical aspects of the market microstructure and trading strategies that may be more relevant for practitioners. I have also included in the Appendix the basic elements of time series analysis and probability distributions, which are used in the presentation of the main material.

The book is organized into three parts:

Part I (Chapters 1 to 6) is an overview of modern financial markets for equities, FX, and fixed income. I start by introducing various types of traders, orders, and market structures, and then present the major market micro-structure models. Finally, I describe some important empirical properties of modern equity and FX markets.

Part II (Chapters 7 to 9) addresses the basics of market dynamics, in-cluding statistical distributions, dynamics, and volatility of returns. I discuss the efficient market hypothesis and possible predictability of returns. I also introduce the concept of agent-based modeling of financial markets.

Part III (Chapters 10 to 13) is devoted to trading. It offers a summary of the concepts used in technical analysis and statistical arbitrage as well as a more detailed description of trading performance criteria and back-testing strategies. Finally, I discuss the ideas used in optimal order execution, such as optimal order slicing and the taker's dilemma.

Specifically, the book is structured as follows:

Chapter 1 gives a general description of financial markets. I describe the different types of traders and orders. Then, I introduce different market structures including quote- and order-driven markets, and continuous and call auctions.

Chapter 2 provides an overview of modern U.S. and European equity markets including major exchanges and alternative trading systems. I also introduce institutional FX and U.S. fixed income market structures. Finally, I go over the popular and somewhat controversial (in 2010) topic of high-frequency trading.

Chapters 3 through 5 are devoted to the main market microstructure models. In particular, in Chapter 3, I describe the inventory models including the risk-neutral models—Garman's (1976) model and Amihud-Mendelson (1980) model—and the Stoll's (1978) model with risk aversion. I introduce the informational models—the Kyle's (1985) model and the Glosten-Milgrom

(1985) model—and their extensions in Chapter 4. Both inventory and informational models address the dealers markets. I review several models for limit-order markets—the Cohen-Maier-Schwartz-Whitcomb (1981) model, the Foucault (1999) model, the Parlour (1999) model, and their extensions—in Chapter 5.

Chapter 6 focuses on empirical market microstructure. First, I describe the Roll's (1984) model, the Glosten-Harris (1998) model, and the Hasbrouck's (1991, 2007) structural models, which are often used for interpreting empirical data. Then, I review intraday trading patterns, the specifics of order flows, and market impacts in equity markets and FX markets.

In Chapter 7, I provide an overview of statistical distributions and dynamics of returns. I address the problem of return predictability by reviewing the efficient market hypothesis and various types of the random walk. Then, I describe recent empirical data on statistical distributions of returns. Finally, I outline the concept of fractals and its applications in finance.

In Chapter 8, I focus on the volatility of returns. In particular, I provide an overview of various conditional heteroskedasticity models. Then, I describe current approaches to estimating the realized volatility. Finally, I outline the methods for measuring market risk.

In Chapter 9, I introduce the concepts of agent-based modeling of financial markets. I describe various trading patterns in terms of agent behavior and give an overview of two major families of agent-based models: (1) adaptive equilibrium models and (2) non-equilibrium price models.

Basic technical trading strategies are described in Chapter 10. I discuss the main concepts in chart trading, including trend-, momentum-, and oscillator-based trading strategies. I further introduce the head-and-shoulder pattern as an example of the complex geometric patterns that have gained popularity in technical trading.

Chapter 11 is devoted to arbitrage strategies. First, I give an overview of the main types of hedging strategies. Then, I focus on pair trading, which has a straightforward formulation in terms of the econometric concept of cointegration. Discussion of arbitrage risks concludes this chapter.

Back-testing of trading strategies is addressed in Chapter 12. First, I list the key performance criteria of trading strategies. Then, I provide an overview of the major resampling techniques (bootstrap and MCMC). I also introduce the random entry protocol that can be used for resampling coupled time series. Finally, I focus on the protocols for comparing trading strategies: White's (2000) bootstrap reality check and its extensions.

Chapter 13 is devoted to order execution strategies. First, I describe the benchmark-driven execution schedules (VWAP, TWAP, and other). Then, I focus on cost-driven execution schedules including the risk-neutral and risk-averse strategies. Finally, I describe the problem of choosing the order type (taker's dilemma).

There are two appendixes at the back of the book. Appendix A provides reference material on basic statistical notions and statistical distributions that are frequently used in finance. Appendix B describes the main concepts of time series analysis: autoregressive and moving average models, trends and seasonality, and multivariate models (vector autoregressive models).

The topics covered in this book are described using multiple sources. Though I made an effort to indicate the authors of new ideas in the field, most references are provided for further reading rather than for comprehensive chronological review. My choice of references to technical trading strategies and to time series analysis, which are extensively covered in the literature, is inevitably personal.

The following notations are used in the book interchangeably: $X(t_k) \equiv X(t) \equiv X_t$, $X(t_{k-1}) \equiv X(t-1) \equiv X_{t-1}$. $E[X]$ is used to denote the expectation of the variable X. The conditional probability of event Y given event X is denoted with $Pr(Y|X)$. Variables in the bold format refer to matrices and vectors.

The views expressed in this book are mine and may not coincide with the views of my former and current employers. I would greatly appreciate readers' comments, which can be sent to me at a_b_schmidt@hotmail.com.

ANATOLY B. SCHMIDT

Acknowledgments

Writing this book was my personal affair, about which few people knew. Craig Holder encouraged me to work on this project. Bill Falloon, Wiley's editor, took a risk by accepting it for publication.

I am grateful to members of the academic community for sharing with me their expertise. My special thanks go to Peter Hansen, Blake LeBaron, and Bruce Mizrach. Needless to say, all possible drawbacks of this book remain my sole responsibility.

Alas, my father Boris passed away before he could have seen this book. If I am able to crunch numbers, this comes from my dad. Boris did not have an opportunity to exploit his gift for math: He became an orphan while fleeing from Nazi-occupied Latvia to Russia and started working at the age of 16. My mother Ida taught literature for more than 40 years. I learned from her how to spend nights at my desk.

I am grateful to my wife Sofia and my children Mark and Sabina for their love and patience. I also constantly feel that they need me—and that's what helps me keep the pace.

Alec Schmidt

PART

One

Market
Microstructure

CHAPTER 1

Financial Markets: Traders, Orders, and Systems

This chapter describes a big picture of financial markets: who the traders are, what types of orders can be submitted, how these orders are processed, how prices are formed, and how markets are organized.

TRADERS

Let us start with the people who trade. They are called (well, you guessed it) *traders*. Those who trade for their own money (or their employer's money) are *proprietary traders*. Their ultimate goal is to make profits by buying low and selling high, whether it is long-term investment or day trading. Other traders execute orders for their clients. They are called *brokers* or *agency traders*. To denote the institutional character of a broker, the term *brokerage (firm)* is also used. For brokers, profits from trading may not be important since they receive commissions for trading and other services from their clients. Typical brokerage services include matching the clients' buy and sell orders, connecting to markets, *clearing* and *settlement*, providing market data and research, and offering credit. Most of the listed services are self-explanatory, but clearing and settlement may need some elucidation. Settlement is delivery of traded assets to the trading counterparts (buyers and sellers). The trading process (sometimes called the *transaction*) does not occur instantly. For example, settlement in the spot foreign exchange for most currencies takes two business days. Clearing denotes all brokerage actions that ensure settlement according to the market rules. These include reporting, credit management, tax handling, and so on.

The institutions that trade for investing and asset management (pension funds, mutual funds, money managers, etc.) are called the *buy-side*. The *sell-side* provides trading services to the buy-side. Besides brokers, the sell-side includes *dealers* who buy and sell securities upon their clients' requests. In contrast to brokers, dealers trade for their own accounts. Hence, they have a business model of proprietary traders. Namely, dealers make profits by selling an asset at a price higher than the price at which they simultaneously buy the same asset.[1] Providing an option to buy and sell an asset simultaneously, dealers are *market makers* who supply *liquidity* to the market (see more about liquidity below). Traders who trade with market makers are sometimes called *takers*. Many sell-side firms have brokerage services and are called *broker-dealers*.

Harris (2002) provides a detailed taxonomy of various trader types. Here I offer a somewhat simplified classification. There are two major groups: (1) *profit-motivated traders* and (2) *utilitarian traders*. Profit-motivated traders trade only when they rationally expect to profit from trading. Utilitarian traders trade if they expect some additional benefits besides (and sometimes even instead of) profits. Investors who trade for managing their cash flows are the typical example of utilitarian traders. Indeed, when an investor sells (part of) his equity portfolio to get cash for buying a house, or invests part of his income on a periodic schedule, his trades may be not optimal in the eyes of pure profit-motivated traders. *Hedgers* are another type of utilitarian traders. The goal of hedging is to reduce the risk of owning a risky asset. A typical example is buying put options for hedging equities. Put options allow the investor to sell stocks at a fixed price.[2] The immediate expenses of buying options may be perceived as a loss. Yet these expenses can protect the investor from much higher losses in case of falling stock price. In the economic literature, utilitarian traders are often called *liquidity traders* to emphasize that they consume the liquidity that is provided by market makers.

Profit-motivated traders can be partitioned into *informed traders*, *technical traders*, and dealers.[3] Informed traders base their trading decisions on information on the asset fundamental value. They buy an asset if they believe it is underpriced in respect to the fundamental value and sell if the asset is overpriced. Since buying/selling pressure causes prices to increase/decrease, informed traders move the asset price toward its fundamental value. Traders who conduct thorough fundamental analysis of the asset values, such as the company's profits, cash flow, and so on, are called *value investors* (Graham & Dodd 2006). Note that fundamental values do not always tell the entire story. New information that comes in the form of unexpected news (e.g., discovery of a new technology, introducing a new product by a competitor, CEO resignation, or a serious accident, etc.) can abruptly challenge the asset price expectations. Also, estimates of the fundamental value of an asset may vary across different markets. Traders who explore these differences are called *arbitrageurs* (see Chapter 11).

Technical traders believe that the information necessary for trading decisions is incorporated into price dynamics. Namely, technical traders use multiple patterns described for historical market data for forecasting future price direction (see Chapter 10).

As it was indicated above, dealers (market makers) supply liquidity to other traders. In some markets, traders who are registered as dealers receive various privileges, such as exclusive handling of particular securities, lower market access fees, and so on. In return, dealers are required to always provide at least a minimum number of securities (in which they make the market) for buying and selling. Dealers make profits from the difference between the selling price and buying price that they establish. This implies that there are takers in the market who are willing to buy a security at a price higher than the price at which they can immediately sell this security. It seems like easy money providing that the price does not change and there are equal flows of buying and selling orders. Obviously, there is always a risk that dealers have to replenish their inventory by buying security at a price higher than the price they sold this security in the near past. This may be caused by a sudden spike in demand caused by either informed or liquidity traders. Similarly, dealers' loss may ensue when takers exert selling pressure. We shall return to the dealers' costs in Chapters 3 and 4.

ORDERS

When traders decide to make a trade, they submit *orders* to their brokers. Order specifies the trading instrument, its quantity (*size*), market side (buy or sell), price, and some other conditions (if any) that must be met for conducting a trade. When orders find their counterparts in the markets, a transaction occurs and it is said that orders are *matched* (or *filled*). Orders are submitted upon some market conditions. If these conditions change before an order is matched, the trader can cancel and possibly resubmit an order with other properties. Here the *latency* problem may become important. Traders do not receive confirmations of their trades instantly. If a trader attempts to cancel the order while it is being transacted, the cancellation fails.

There are two major order types: *market orders* and *limit orders*. Price is not specified for market orders and these orders are executed at the best price available at the order arrival time (i.e., a bid/offer order is filled at the current best offer/bid price). Limit buy and sell orders are *quoted* in the market with their *bid* and *ask* (or *offer*) prices, respectively. Prices of limit orders are sometimes called *reservation prices*. The highest bid and lowest ask (offer) currently present in the market are called *best bid* and *best ask* (*offer*), respectively. The difference between the best ask and the best bid is the *bid/ask spread* (see the next section). The *bid/ask bounce* of transaction prices is caused by trades randomly initiated by buy and sell orders. As a result, sequential transaction prices fluctuate between the best ask and best bid prices. It is said that any price within the spread is *inside the market.* The half-sum of the best bid and best ask is called *mid-point price* (or just *mid-price*).

Limit orders specify the worst price (highest offer or lowest bid) at which traders agree to trade. If a better price is available for matching the limit order at the time of its arrival, the transaction is done at the better price. Limit orders are not guaranteed to be executed. For example, a limit buy order is placed below the best bid but the price does not fall that low. Limit orders that are not immediately filled are stored in the *limit order book* (LOB) until they are matched or cancelled (see more about the LOB below). It is important to remember that the aggregated order size at any price in the LOB is finite. Hence, a large market order may wipe out the entire LOB inventory at best price and get filled not at a single price but within some price range. As a result, the best price worsens—at least temporarily. It is said that large orders have *market impact.* Some markets do not permit market orders and limit orders are the only option.

In some markets, all limit orders are automatically cancelled at the end of trading day. To prevent such a cancellation, an option known as *good-till-cancelled* may be available. Usually, such an option has a limited duration (e.g., one month).

For a trader, the choice between a limit order and market order (when the latter order is permitted) may be non-trivial. For example, a trader assuming a *long position* can submit a market buy order and fill an order at current best offer price. In other words, the trader becomes a taker. Another option is to submit a limit order at a current best bid (or even at a lower) price—that is, become a maker. It is said that takers pay the spread, which is the price for immediacy. Indeed, there is a risk that the price will move in an adverse direction and the maker order will not be executed within the acceptable time horizon. We shall return to this problem in Chapter 13. As I have indicated above, taker order is always filled at the best available price. Namely, a bid/ask submitted with a price higher/lower than the best ask/bid is still filled at the current best ask/bid. In general, limit orders submitted across the market are called *marketable limit orders.* Why would anyone submit such an order? This may happen if a trader wants to make a sure shot with at least partial filling but not to pay beyond some limit price.

Some markets permit *hidden limit orders.* These orders have a lower priority in respect to visible orders at the same price but higher priority than the limit orders with worse price. Sometimes orders can be partially hidden. In the latter case, when the visible order part is filled, it is replenished with the hidden amount and the order position in the LOB is preserved.

Cancel and replace limit orders allow traders to change the order size without losing the order position in the LOB.

Limit orders can be *pegged* in some markets. There are three ways to define pegged order. The first definition involves primary (market)—peg to the best price on the same (opposite) side of the market. Also, orders can be pegged to the bid/ask mid-price. The price of unfilled (e.g., due to latency) pegged orders moves along with their peg.

Some markets have an option to submit *market-on-open* and *market-on-close* orders. These orders are submitted in advance for executing at a new market opening and closing, respectively.

Stop orders can be treated as limit orders since they, too, specify the execution price. However, price has a different role in stop orders: It constrains possible loss rather than yields the realized profit. Indeed, a trader sells an instrument using a limit order at a higher price for locking in the profit after buying an instrument at a lower price. On the contrary, the sell stop order is filled when price falls to (or below) the order price. Hence, traders submit stop orders for mitigating the risk of possible adverse price moves.

Some other instructions may be provided with orders. *Fill-or-kill orders* are filled at their arrival in the market. Any portion of such an order that cannot be immediately filled is cancelled. Another constraint is used in the *all-or-none orders*: These orders can be filled completely, or not at all.

So far, selling implies that the trader owns the selling asset (i.e., has a long position in it). *Short selling*, or acquiring a *short position*, means that the trader borrows an asset from his broker and sells it. This makes sense if there is expectation that the asset price will fall. Then the trader buys the same asset (presumably) at a lower price for returning it to the broker and pockets the difference. Two special order types are used to implement this strategy: *sell short* and *buy to cover*. Note that the so-called *uptick rule* forbids short selling unless a short order is submitted either at a price above the last traded price, or at the last traded price if that price was higher than the price in the previous trade. In the United States, the uptick rule was in effect for many years until it was canceled in 2007. However, discussions on the necessity of this rule resumed in 2009 in the context of introducing a stricter regulation of financial markets.

THE BID/ASK SPREAD

The size of the bid/ask spread is an important object of the microstructure theory, which shall be addressed in future chapters. Here is a list of common definitions and components of the spread (de Jong & Rindi 2009).

The *quoted spread* between ask A_t and bid B_t that is averaged over T periods equals

$$S^Q = \frac{1}{T}\sum_{t=1}^{T}(A_t - B_t) \qquad (1.1)$$

In terms of the asset fundamental price, P_t^*, the averaged spread is

$$S = \frac{1}{T}\sum_{t=1}^{T}2q_t(P_t - P_t^*) \qquad (1.2)$$

where q_t is 1 for buy orders and -1 for sell orders. Since the value of P_t^* is not observable, the *effective spread* in terms of mid-price $M_t = 0.5(A_t + B_t)$ is usually used:

$$S^E = \frac{1}{T}\sum_{t=1}^{T}2q_t(P_t - M_t) \qquad (1.3)$$

Sometimes the *realized spread* is applied in post-trade analysis:

$$S^R = \frac{1}{T}\sum_{t=1}^{T}2q_t(P_t - M_{t+1}) \qquad (1.4)$$

It was already indicated that the bid/ask spread from the point of the view of a taker is the price for immediacy of trading. Now, let's examine the main components of the bid/ask spread, which are determined by dealers (makers).

First, the spread incorporates the dealers' operational costs, such as trading system development and maintenance, clearing and settlement, and so on. Indeed, if dealers are not compensated for their expenses, there is no rationale for them to stay in this business.

Dealer's inventory costs, too, contribute into the bid/ask spread. Since dealers must satisfy order flows on both sides of the market, they maintain inventories of risky (and sometimes undesirable) instruments. The inventory microstructure models will be discussed in Chapter 3. Glosten & Harris (1988) combine the operational and inventory costs into a single *transitory* component, since their effect on security price dynamics is unrelated to the security value. Another spread component reflects the dealer's risk of trading with counterparts who have superior information about true security value. Informed traders trade at one side of the market and may profit from trading with dealers. Hence, dealers must recover their potential losses by widening the spread. Not surprisingly, dealers pass these losses to uninformed traders.[4] This component of the bid/ask spread is called the *adverse-selection* component since dealers confront one-sided selection of their order flow. The adverse selection will be discussed in Chapter 4.

LIQUIDITY

Liquidity is a notion that is widely used in finance, yet it has no strict definition and in fact may have different meanings. Generally, the term *liquid asset* implies that it can be quickly and cheaply sold for cash. Hence, cash itself (i.e., money) is the ideally liquid asset. Real estate and antique on the other hand are not very liquid.

In the context of trading, liquidity characterizes the ability to trade an instrument without notable change of its price. A popular saying defines liquidity as the market's *breadth, depth, and resiliency*. First, this implies that the buying price and selling price of a liquid instrument are close, that is, the bid/ask spread is small. In a deep market, there are many orders from multiple makers, so that order cancellations and transactions do not affect notably the total order inventory available for trading. Finally, market resiliency means that if some liquidity loss does occur, it is quickly replenished by market makers. In other words, market impact has a temporary character. As we shall see in Chapter 13, analysis of market impact dynamics is a rather complex problem.

Various liquidity measures are used in different markets. For example, Xetra's (the European electronic trading system) liquidity measure corresponds to the relative market impact costs for the so-called *round trip* (simultaneous buying and selling of a position) for a given order size (Gomber & Schweickert 2002). Barclays Capital derives the FX liquidity index using the notional amounts traded for a fixed set of FX spreads and aggregated using a weighting by currency pair (quoted by Bank of England 2009). Sometimes inverse liquidity (*illiquidity*), based on the price impact caused by trading volume, is used (Amihud 2002):

$$\text{ILLIQ} = \frac{1}{N} \sum_{k=1}^{N} |r_k| / V_k \qquad (1.5)$$

In (1.5), r_k and V_k are the return and trading volume for time interval k. The notion of liquidity is rooted in the Kyle's model (1985), which will be discussed in Chapter 4.

MARKET STRUCTURES

Markets differ in their organization and trading rules. Some markets that are highly organized and regulated by government agencies are called *exchanges* (or *bourses*). In the United States, the trading of stocks, bonds, and several other securities is regulated by the *Securities and Exchanges Commission* (SEC). However, trading of commodities (including spot, futures, and options) is regulated by another government agency, the *Commodity Futures Trading Commission* (CFTC).

Historically, exchanges were founded by their members (dealers, brokers) for trading among themselves. In our days, many exchanges have become incorporated. Still, in most cases only members can trade at exchanges. An alternative to exchanges is the *over-the-counter* (OTC) *markets* where dealers and brokers can trade directly.

Market structure is defined with specifics of execution systems and with the type of *trading sessions* (Harris 2002; de Jong & Rindi 2009). There are two major execution systems: *order-driven markets* and *quote-driven markets*. In terms of trading sessions, order-driven markets can be partitioned into *continuous markets* and *call markets*. Many order-driven markets are *auctions* in which trading rules ensure that trading occurs at the highest price a buyer is willing to pay and at the lowest price a seller is willing to sell at. The process of defining such a price is called *price discovery* (or *market clearing*).

Another form of order-driven markets is *crossing networks*. Price discovery is not implemented in crossing networks. Instead, prices used in matching are derived from other (primary) markets. Hence, the term *derivative pricing rules* is used.[5] Orders submitted to crossing networks have no price and are prioritized according to their arrival time. The first advantage of crossing networks is that trading in these systems is (or at least is supposed to be) completely confidential. Another advantage is that trading there does not have an impact on price in the primary markets. Hence, crossing networks are attractive to those traders who trade orders of large size (*blocks*). On the other hand, trading in the dark may encounter significant *order imbalance*. It is usually calculated as a difference between aggregated demand and aggregated supply and is also called *excess demand*. As a result, the portion of filled orders (*fill ratio*) may be rather small. Another drawback of crossing networks is the imperfection of the derivative pricing that may be subject of manipulations. More specifics on different market structures will be detailed in the following sections.

Continuous Order-Driven Markets

In continuous markets, traders can submit their orders at any time while the market is open. Trading hours vary in different markets. For example, the New York Stock Exchange (NYSE) and NASDAQ are open on Monday through Friday; they start at 9:30 A.M. EST and close at 4:00 P.M. EST. On the other hand, the global FX spot market is open around the clock during the workdays and is closed only for a few hours on weekends (see more on FX markets in Chapter 2).

In order-driven markets, traders trade among themselves without intermediary market makers (dealers). In other words, every trader can become a market maker by placing a limit order. Those limit orders that are not immediately matched upon arrival are entered into the LOB according to the price-time priorities. Price priority has the primary precedence, which means that an order with a better (or more aggressive) price is placed before orders with worse prices.

Time priority means that a new order is placed behind the orders that have the same price and entered the market earlier. Matching of a new taker order with maker orders present in the LOB occurs upon the *First In, First Out* (FIFO) principle—that is, older maker orders are filled first. It is said that the first order with the best price is on *top of the order book*. Hence, the higher/lower the bid/offer order price is, the closer this order is to the top of the LOB.

In some markets, size precedence rule is used. Sometimes the largest order is executed in case of a parity of several orders, but sometimes the priority is given to the smallest order. Another option is *pro rata* allocation. Say the aggregated bid size exceeds the aggregated offer size. Then all bid orders are partially filled proportionally to their size.

Consider a few examples of matching in an order-driven market. Let the LOB have the following bids:[6] B1 –100@10.25 (best bid), B2 – 200@10.23, and the following offers: O1 – 200@10.30 (best offer), O2 – 200@10.35. A market buy order of a size less or equal to 200 will be filled at the price $P = 10.30$. If the size of the market buy order equals 200, it completely matches O1 and the bid/ask spread increases from $s = 10.30 - 10.25 = 0.05$ to $s = 10.35 - 10.25 = 0.1$.

A market buy order of size 300 will be matched as 200@10.30 + 100@10.35. What if you want to buy 500 units, which is higher than the entire offer inventory? Then you can submit a limit order that will be stored in the LOB until a new seller decides to match it. For example, you may want to submit a bid of 500@10.35. This would result in the immediate matching of 300 units and the remaining 200 units becoming the new best bid.

If a bid is submitted inside the market, that is, $10.25 < P < 10.30$, it is placed before B1 and becomes the new best bid. The bid/ask spread then decreases from $s = 0.05$ to $s = 10.30 - P$. If a bid is submitted with a price in the range $10.23 < P \leq 10.25$, it is placed in the LOB between the bids B1 and B2. Finally, a bid with a price $P \leq 10.23$ is placed behind the bid B2.

Oral Auctions

In *oral auctions* (or *open-outcry auctions*), traders (brokers and dealers) gather in the same place (floor market). Traders are required to communicate (using shouting and hand signals) their trading intentions and the results of trading to all market participants. This ensures great transparency of the trading process.

In oral auctions, order precedence rules and price discovery are similar to those in continuous order-driven markets. However, there may be some additional secondary precedence rules. In particular, public order precedence gives priority to public traders in respect to floor traders.

Open-outcry auctions used to be the main trading venue in the past. In our days, most of floor markets have deployed electronic trading systems that have replaced or are used along with open outcry.

Call Auctions

In call auctions, trading occurs at predetermined moments in time. Call auctions can be conducted several times a day (so-called fixings) or at the openings and closings of continuous sessions. Orders submitted for a given call are batched and executed simultaneously at the same price. Prior to auction, all submitted orders are placed according to the price-time precedence rules. Aggregated demand and supply are calculated implying that a trader willing to buy/sell at price P will also buy/sell at a price lower/higher than P. The auction price is defined in such a way that yields a maximum aggregated size of matched orders. Consider an example of price discovery in a call market with the orders listed in Table 1.1.

The maximum trading volume here corresponds to the price of 10.80 (see Table 1.2). The aggregated supply at this price (with a size of 800) is matched completely. However, part of the aggregated demand ($900 - 800 = 100$), is not filled within the current call. Since order B5 is the last in the list of buyers involved in this fixing, it is filled only partially.

TABLE 1.1   An Example of the Pre-Auction Order Book

Buyers			Sellers	
Order	Size	Order Price	Order	Size
		9.95	S1	700
B1	100	9.90	S2	300
B2	200	9.85	S3	400
		9.85	S4	200
		9.85	S5	100
B3	600	9.80	S6	300
B4	500	9.75	S7	500
B5	600	9.70		

TABLE 1.2 Price Discovery in the Order Book Listed in Table 1.1

Price	Aggregate Demand	Aggregate Supply	Trading Volume	Excess Demand
9.95 and higher	0	2500	0	−2500
9.90	100	1800	100	−1700
9.85	300	1500	300	−1200
9.80	900	800	800	100
9.75	1400	500	500	900
9.70 and lower	2000	0	0	2000

If the rule of maximum aggregated size of matched orders does not yield a unique price, the auction price is chosen to satisfy the rule of minimum order imbalance (i.e., the minimum number of unmatched orders). If even the latter rule does not define a single price, the auction price is chosen to be the closest to the previous auction price.

The advantage of call auctions is that the entire interest in a particular instrument is concentrated at the same time, and is visible to all traders. On the other hand, continuous markets offer a flexibility of trading at traders' convenience.

Quote-Driven Markets and Hybrid Markets

In the quote-driven markets, only dealers submit maker orders. All other traders can submit only market orders. Price discovery in these markets means that market makers must choose such bid and ask prices that will cover their expenses (let alone generate profits) and balance buy and sell order flows. The theoretical models of dealers' strategies are discussed in Chapters 3 and 4.

Some markets combine quote-driven and order-driven systems in their structures. NYSE and NASDAQ are examples of such *hybrid markets*.

SUMMARY

- Two major trader types are profit-motivated traders and liquidity traders. Profit-motivated traders trade only if they expect to receive gains from trading. Liquidity traders may have other reasons, such as maintaining cash flow and hedging.
- Profit-motivated traders can be partitioned into informed traders, technical traders, and dealers. Informed traders base their trading

decisions on information on the asset fundamental value. Technical traders make their decisions using patterns in historical market data. Dealers provide liquidity on both sides of the market and profit from the bid/ask spread.

- Market liquidity is a measure of market breadth, depth, and resiliency.

- There are two major order types: market orders and limit orders. Price is not specified for market orders and these orders are executed at the best price available at the order arrival time. Limit orders are filled only at their (or a better) price.

- There are two major execution systems: order-driven markets and quote-driven markets. Order-driven markets can be partitioned into continuous markets and call markets (auctions).

- In the continuous order-driven markets, all traders can submit limit orders. Unfilled limit orders are placed in the limit order book according to the price-time precedence.

- In call auctions, orders submitted for a given call are batched and executed simultaneously at a price that yields maximum trading volume.

- In the quote-driven markets, dealers submit maker orders while other traders can submit only market orders.

Modern Financial Markets

In this chapter, the major U.S. and European equity exchanges and alternative trading systems are described. I also introduce the global FX market and the U.S. institutional fixed income markets. Finally, I discuss the specifics of high-frequency trading, which has received somewhat controversial coverage in 2009 and 2010.

THE U.S. EQUITY MARKETS

When a business issues a new security via *initial public offering* (IPO) at some exchange, it is said that the security is *listed* on this exchange. After IPO, the issuer sells this security to investors in *a primary market*. Subsequent trading of securities among investors other than the issuer is conducted in the *secondary market* (or *aftermarket*). Trading of exchange-listed securities in an OTC market is referred to as the *third market*. *Alternative trading systems* (ATS), which will be discussed later, are the typical examples of the third market.

The main U.S. primary markets are the New York Stock Exchange (NYSE) and NASDAQ. These markets are described in more detail in the two following sub-sections. There are also several U.S. regional exchanges and two new exchanges, BATS and Direct Edge. Regional exchanges were created primarily to list local companies that could not afford to become listed in the national exchanges. Current regional exchanges include Boston, Chicago, Pacific, and Philadelphia exchanges.[1]

The NYSE

The NYSE has been the major U.S. equity market. A brief history of the NYSE trading system, including recent changes, is offered by de Jong & Rindi (2009) and Hendershott & Moulton (2009). In 2007, the NYSE was merged with the pan-European electronic market Euronext (hence, the name of the new corporation is *NYSE Euronext*). The NYSE was founded as an open-outcry auction back in the end of the eighteenth century and has evolved since then into a complex hybrid market combining an open outcry with a quote-driven (dealer) market, and an electronic LOB. For every stock traded on the floor, there is a designated dealer (*specialist*) who maintains the LOB and makes the market using his own account when there is lack of liquidity from other traders. Another specialist's duty is conducting the opening and closing auctions.[2] However, specialists are not allowed to trade ahead of their customers at the same price on the same side of the market. In fact, trading by brokers and dealers for their own account using the knowledge of their customers' pending orders (so-called *front running*) is illegal.

In early 2007, the NYSE introduced the Hybrid Market architecture based on the merger of the NYSE with the *electronic communication network* (ECN) Archipelago.[3] The new system significantly expanded automatic execution and limited the role of specialists. Traders now can directly submit their orders to the electronic LOB bypassing brokers and specialists unless their order size exceeds one million shares. The NYSE Group (2006) indicates three reasons for launching the Hybrid Market. First, it satisfies the customers' desire to have a choice of using the existing auction mechanism for the possibility of better prices and accessing the LOB electronically to achieve faster execution. Second, the NYSE expects that trading volume will grow, which can be handled more efficiently with an automated system. Finally, the SEC has issued the new rule (so-called SEC Regulation NMS Order Protection Rule), which requires the market to honor better-priced quotes available in other fast markets before filling orders at the market's own prices. Sub-second order execution is required for the status of *fast market*, which is accomplished by the NYSE with introduction of the Hybrid Market.

Market orders and marketable limit orders in the Hybrid Market are by default executed automatically. There are, however, stock-specific price ranges (so-called *liquidity replenishment points*) that determine the limits for (erroneous) price jumps and volatility. If these limits are reached, trading is converted from automatic to *auction only* execution.

Recent analysis has shown that introducing the Hybrid Market has reduced an average execution time from 10 seconds to less than one second. This, however, increased the bid/ask spread (i.e., cost of immediacy) by about 10 percent (Hendershott & Moulton 2009).

NASDAQ

NASDAQ was founded by National Association of Securities Dealers (NASD) in 1971. In 2007, NASD was consolidated with the member regulation, enforcement, and arbitration functions of the NYSE into the Financial Industry Regulatory Authority (FINRA), which is the largest independent regulator for all securities firms doing business in the United States.

NASDAQ is a purely electronic market: It does not have a physical floor, and its dealers and brokers are connected via electronic network. The unique feature of NASDAQ is that several competing dealers can trade stocks of the same company (rather than one specialist in the NYSE). In the past, the NASDAQ computer system was used only for quoting prices and trading was conducted over the phone. During the market crash of 1987, the inefficiency of telephone-based trading became clear. As a result, the computer order matching system was implemented. In our days, the dealers' orders in the NASDAQ are consolidated into the integrated entry and execution system with LOB (called SuperMontage).

Alternative Trading Systems

ATS are designed for direct matching buyers and sellers. They are regulated by the SEC but are not registered as exchanges. As a result, ATS cannot list new securities. ATS serve as alternative sources of liquidity and compete with exchanges for customers using lower execution latency and fees. Advanced technology that facilitates high-frequency trading is what gives ATS an edge (Aite Group (2009a)). There are two main types of ATS: (1) ECN, and (2) crossing networks, which were introduced in Chapter 1.

ECNs allow their customers to submit their orders via an electronic network. Those orders that are not immediately matched form a LOB according to the rules typical for order-driven markets. The ECN LOB is visible to all ECN customers (orders usually are anonymous, though). Hence, price discovery is a distinctive feature of ECNs. One immediate advantage that ECNs offer to their customers is the possibility to trade before and after regular trading hours when the main exchanges are closed.

In recent years, the line between exchanges and ECNs have become blurred due to mergers and acquisitions. For example, as indicated above, the ECN Archipelago was merged with the NYSE in 2006. Also, one of the first ECNs, Instinet, was bought by NASDAQ in 2006.[4] The BATS Exchange was founded as ECN in 2005, but it became an exchange in early 2009. Another ECN, Direct Edge, became an exchange in 2010.

There is no price discovery in crossing networks. Instead, orders are matched upon prices quoted in the primary markets. Important feature of crossing networks is that trading in these systems has no explicit market impact. Another advantage of crossing networks (often called *dark pools*) is their anonymous nature, which conceals the intentions of block traders. Dark pools have significantly proliferated in recent years. Their share of the total U.S. equity trading in Q2 of 2009 reached 12 percent (here and further in this section, we follow taxonomy and estimates given by Aito Group 2009b). There have been more than three dozen dark pools with various business models. Historically, the first dark pools (ITG POSIT, Liquidnet, and Pipeline) offered anonymous block trading. Average trade sizes in these venues reach tens of thousands of shares.

Other dark pools serve increasingly important high-frequency trading where large orders are sliced into small pieces (see Chapter 13). Typical order size in these dark pools is in the range of 300 to 500 shares. Depending on ownership type, this venue can be partitioned into agency-, consortium-, or exchange-owned dark pools. Agency-based dark pools are usually owned by independent brokers who simply cross their clients orders and do not have principal interest in transactions.

Consortium dark pools (e.g., BIDS) are owned by groups of broker/dealers. They operate as a utility service for their owners rather than a purely profit-oriented business. Therefore, consortium pools may charge relatively low fees.

Another type of crossing network has been implemented by several large brokers for *internalization* of their customers' orders. In these dark pools, brokers can trade for their own account against their customers, too. The latter type of dark pools, including Credit Suisse Crossfinder, Goldman Saks Sigma X, GETCO Execution Services, and Knight Link are responsible for the major share of dark pool trading.

Some dark pools striving to increase their fill ratios have recently introduced so-called *indication-of-interest* (IOI) functionality. IOI allows external liquidity sources to submit information about their orders and request information about the dark pool liquidity. One can argue that IOI functionality somewhat compromises the anonymity of dark pools (Aito Group 2009b).

European Equity Markets

In the past, equity trading in Europe was concentrated in national exchanges, such as the London Stock Exchange and Deutsche Burse. These exchanges may have a hybrid structure, and generally, they operate automated order-driven systems (de Jong & Rindi 2009). Until recently, trading across geographic borders was expensive and slow due to the absence of common clearing and settlement facilities. The European equity trading landscape has dramatically changed since the end of 2007, when the European Union implemented a new law, *Markets in Financial Instruments Directive (MiFID)*. MiFID established new requirements for pre- and post-trade transparency (such as publishing aggregated order book, transaction volumes, etc.). Another important requirement was to implement *best execution* practices, which in particular means leveling off transaction fees regardless of the market location. This has led to the creation of several pan-European ATS (called the *Multilateral Trading Facilities* (*MTF*)) and clearing facilities in Europe. The traditional exchanges, particularly London Stock Exchange, Deutsche Burse, and NYSE Euronext still have the major market share in European equity trading but the MTF share has been growing: It reached about 15 percent in the first half of 2009 (Aite Group 2009c). Arguably, the most active MTF is Chi-X, whose market share in 2009 exceeded that of the Madrid and Swiss stock exchanges. Chi-X was launched by Instinet and is currently owned by a consortium of several financial institutions (Instinet still has a major share). Other MTF include (but are not limited to) BATS Europe and Turquoise (owned by several sell-side institutions). Several U.S. ATS (ITG, Liquidnet, NASDAQ/OMX, and NYSE Arca) have got a footstep in Europe, as well.

At the time of the writing of this section (December 2010), the equity markets in the United States and Europe are still evolving. Some of ATS/ MTF may merge or go out of business; others may become exchanges. But the general trend of moving equity trading to automated trading systems is expected to continue. One may also expect that specifics of the Frank-Dodd financial reform bill that became a law in summer of 2010 will increase the regulation of ATS.

Spot FX Market

Global foreign exchange is the largest and the most liquid market in the world that keeps growing with further globalization of the world economy. Between 2007 and 2010, the *average daily volume* (ADV) has grown from $3.3 trillion to $4.0 trillion.[5] London, New York, and Tokyo (listed in descending order of their ADV) are the major global FX centers. In recent years, Singapore, Australia, and Canada have also become important players in FX. Most of exchange (52 percent) is done with the following three currency pairs (listed in the descending ADV order): (1) EUR/USD, (2) USD/JPY, (3) GBP/USD. Other currency pairs that notably contribute into ADV include USD/AUD, USD/CAD, USD/CHF, EUR/JPY, EUR/GBP, and EUR/CHF.

Besides its sheer trading volume, the global FX market differs from equity markets in other important aspects. Its primary function is facilitating international trade and investment. FX is also frequently used for hedging and speculation. Yet it is difficult to use FX for long-term value investment. Indeed, despite the rich literature on the theory of exchange rates (Sarno & Taylor 2006), there is less certainty about fair values of exchange rates than about fair values of equities (Frydman & Goldberg 2007). This is one possible reason for notably higher shares of short-term trading in FX than in equity markets (Lyons 2001).

Here I focus on *spot FX*, which means trading one currency for another with delivery usually taking place within two days after the dealing date.[6] The share of spot FX in the ADV in 2010 is estimated between 37 percent worldwide and 55 percent in the United States. Other important FX instruments are *FX swaps*[7] (44 percent worldwide and 31 percent in the United States), *outright forwards*[8] (12 percent worldwide and 14 percent in the United States). The list of the FX instruments includes also *FX options,*[9] *non-deliverable forwards* (NDF),[10] and *currency swaps.*[11]

The very nature of foreign exchange complicates its national regulation. Indeed, major banks have offices worldwide and any government tightening of exchange regulation would probably move the FX business elsewhere. Hence, currencies are traded in the OTC markets rather than in exchanges.

Back in the 1980s, institutional FX was primarily done via voice brokers and in direct bank-to-customer transactions. In our time, electronic FX markets are responsible for about 65 percent of entire FX trading (Aite Group 2010). The FX spot markets, depending on their customer base, can be partitioned into two types: inter-dealer platforms and dealer-to-client platforms. The specifics are outlined in the following sections.

Inter-Dealer Platforms   The major *inter-dealer platforms* are EBS (acquired by ICAP plc in 2006) and Reuters (merged into Thomson Reuters in 2008). One specific of the inter-dealer platforms (among all others that differentiate OTC markets from exchanges) is that they do not have clearing facilities. Instead, credit risk is managed using trading limits that each customer provides to all others. Hence, two counterparts can trade only if they have bilateral credit. In the EBS system, trading credit limits are routinely updated on weekends, but they can be modified and cancelled at any time. It is not surprising that in the past only large banks were trading electronically. Banks use the inter-dealer platforms for managing their inventory, for executing customer orders, and for speculation. In recent years, the prime-bank business model was introduced, which significantly expanded the customer base of the inter-dealer platforms. Using this model, smaller banks, and even hedge funds and proprietary trading firms can use credit being assigned to them by their prime bank.

Inter-dealer platforms are essentially limit-order markets. In the EBS system, there are two types of orders: regular limit orders (*quotes*) and buy/sell orders (*hits*). The latter are automatically assigned current best offer/bid prices. If buy/sell orders cannot be matched at the time of their arrival in the market due to the latency, they are automatically cancelled. Due to credit constraints, the price-time execution precedence that is typical for order-driven markets may be violated. Namely, a taker order is matched with an order on top of the subset of the order book that has bilateral credit with the taker. The unique feature of the EBS system is that it has three interconnected regional matching facilities in London, New York, and Tokyo. The regional order books have the same aggregated order sizes at a given price. However, regional order positions at a given price may differ due to the latency effect.

Dealer-to-Client Platforms Another type of the electronic FX markets is *dealer-to-client platforms*. These platforms, in turn, can be partitioned into single-dealer platforms and multi-dealer platforms. The single-dealer platforms (portals) are provided by several major banks (Deutsche Bank, Barclays, Citi) and independent brokerages (FXCM, Gain Capital, Oanda) to buy-side firms, corporations, and even retail investors. These institutions attempt to maximally internalize their customers' order flows, which reduces their execution cost.[12] However, in case of demand/supply imbalance, single-dealer systems become less efficient as they must themselves reach external liquidity sources. Multi-dealer platforms (Currenex, FXAll, and FXConnect) offer the benefits of liquidity aggregators. They attract not only buy-side firms and corporations but also hedge funds and proprietary trading firms.

THE U.S. FIXED INCOME MARKETS

The U.S. fixed income market includes multiple instruments (Fabozzi 2005). *Mortgage-based securities* (MBS), corporate bonds, *U.S. Treasures* (UST), and money market have the major share of the market: 24 percent, 19 percent, 16 percent, and 10 percent, respectively (Aite Group 2008). Other instruments include *agencies* (U.S. agency bonds, such as Fannie Mae), *asset-backed securities* (ABS), and municipal bonds.

While the voice brokerage remains important, particularly in the inter-dealer markets, the market share of electronic trading in fixed income has been growing (it reached 65 percent in 2008). Brokertec (owned by ICAP), eSpeed (owned by the BGC Partners), and Tradeweb (owned by several financial institutions with Reuters Thompson having a majority stake) are the major players in this niche.

Electronic fixed income inter-dealer trading platforms have LOB. Yet, they are not truly continuous markets. Their interesting feature is so-called *workup* (called also *expandable limit order*, Boni & Leach 2004). Workup is reminiscent of the way the voice brokers handle their customers. Namely, a trader who just executed his order has the right-of-refusal to trade an additional amount at the same price. Hence, a maker of best price may display only a minimal trading amount. Once a taker willing to trade enters the transaction, both counterparts can reveal and trade their mutually desirable amount. Other traders can join trading at the current trading price (sometimes with some delay that depends on the trading platform and instrument). Workups last a predetermined time interval (several seconds). Since price is fixed during the workup, orders submitted during the workup at better prices become tradable only when the workup ends. Hence, price discovery in the electronic fixed income markets has a delay. Specifics of the fixed income market microstructure are discussed by Mizrach & Neely (2009) and Fleming & Mizrach (2009).

Another feature of the fixed income markets is that the fractional part of price is quoted in units of $\frac{1}{32}$ (or in its fractions), rather than in decimals. For example, a price of 90.27 in the Brokertec market means $90\frac{27}{32}$. In some markets, a dash is used to separate the fractional price part, for example: 90-27. Some fixed income instruments may have price increments as small as $\frac{1}{256}$. In the Brokertec market, the sign "+" denotes $\frac{1}{64}$, that is, "98.27+" equals $98 + \frac{27}{32} + \frac{1}{64}$. The third digit in the non-integer part denotes a number of $\frac{1}{256}$. For example, 98.273 equal $98 + \frac{27}{32} + \frac{3}{256}$. Note that the U.S. equity markets switched from quoting prices in eighths to decimal pricing in 2001.

HIGH-FREQUENCY TRADING

High-frequency trading (HFT) is characterized by very short time periods of holding assets, or in other words, by extremely high turnover of portfolio. While some HFT strategies imply holding portfolio for hours, sub-minute intervals have become common. The basic HFT strategies include execution of large orders sliced into smaller pieces (see Chapter 13), statistical and event arbitrage strategies (see Chapter 11), and market making. The latter strategy is stimulated in some markets by offering rebates for providing liquidity. These rebates, while being very small (fraction of a penny per share), may reportedly provide sufficient incentive for market making even in the case of frequent losses from adverse selection.

In any case, the idea behind HFT is to be the first—either in making price or in scalping price inefficiencies. Needless to say, advanced computer systems are required for implementing the HFT strategies. In fact, the HFT strategies (often called *algos*) are completely automated. Moreover, in order to minimize the data transfer latency, many HFT firms use *co-location*. Namely, they deploy computer servers in the immediate proximity of trading floors.

By some estimates, HFT in 2010 accounted for more than 50 percent of equity trading in the United States and more than 20 percent in Europe. The proponents of HFT emphasize increased liquidity and stability among the benefits that HFT brings to financial markets (Aldridge 2010). However, HFT is not free from controversies. Indeed, the danger of "algos gone wild," as Donefer (2010) puts it, is real: automated trading of extremely large asset volumes at the speed of light may lead to unforeseeable consequences. It is true that automated market making constitutes a significant share of liquidity of modern equity and FX markets (Aite Group 2009a; 2010). However, the high-frequency traders are not regulated in the same way as true market makers and can therefore leave the market any time if they find that the profit opportunities have evaporated. This can potentially lead to significant disruption in markets.

A recent example of serious market disturbance was the *flash crash* on May 6, 2010, when the Dow Jones index fell about 600 points within five minutes and then recovered within the next 10 minutes. A joint CFTC-SEC (2010) report issued almost five months later identified a single large order (~$4 billion) to sell Standard & Poor's (S&P) futures that provoked a chain of events leading to the crash. This order was placed by a mutual fund using an algorithm programmed to sell the entire order within 20 minutes without regard to price. Usually, trading of such a large order may take a few hours. Several HFT firms noticed unusually intense selling and attempted to profit from it. Hoping that the sell-off would end soon, they were buying S&P futures and hedging long positions by selling stocks that constitute S&P (see more about hedging in Chapter 11).

However, after accumulating futures above some threshold, HFT firms started selling futures back. While many market participants withdrew due to high volatility, other HFT firms kept trading among themselves, creating a so-called hot-potato effect. At some point, futures changed hands 27,000 times in 14 seconds, but only 200 contracts were actually being bought or sold. The selling algorithm that handled the original large order reacted at intense trading with an increasing selling rate. At some point, the selling pressure could not be absorbed by buyers anymore, and the price of futures fell dramatically. This led to the sell-off in the stock market. Further damage was prevented only when automatic functionality in the futures market paused trading for several seconds. After trading resumed, increased buying interest recovered the equity markets. The flash crash was not triggered by HFT, but it certainly highlighted the liquidity risk posed by possible withdrawal of HFT firms from trading. Indeed, the hot-potato effect implies that high trading volume is not necessarily an indicator of high liquidity. In order to mitigate similar crashes in the future, SEC introduced circuit breakers that halt trading of a stock for five minutes if the price moves 10 percent within a five-minute period.

Another controversy that surfaced in 2009 was that some brokers offered to the HFT firms a service that puts other market participants at a disadvantage and/or additional risk. This service is called direct sponsored (or *naked*) market access. It allows customers to access the market without the latency of time required for compliance monitoring. Trading done through the sponsored access was not controlled by brokers and regulators and therefore might potentially increase market risk. The SEC prohibited brokers and dealers from providing naked access to their customers in November 2010.

One more controversial practice implemented by some exchanges involves *flash orders*. These orders can be perceived as a sophisticated form of front running. Flash orders allow HFT firms to view order flow information prior to when it becomes available to other market participants. HFT firms may then post matching orders with prices better than those available at the moment. For example, an exchange that receives an order must route it to another (rival) exchange if the latter has a better price. According to the current regulation, this should be done within one second. Instead of immediate routing, the exchange creates a flash that is displayed just for a few dozen milliseconds. This flash can attract an HFT firm, which fills the order at a price better than the one available in a rival exchange. At the time of the writing of this section (December 2010), SEC reportedly was considering a ban on flash orders (Patterson et al 2009).

Then, there is *quote stuffing*, in which large numbers of orders are placed and cancelled almost immediately. HFT firms might engage in this practice to provoke other market participants to trade at a new price, which in fact is never available due to quick cancellations. One cause of future flash crashes might be some combination of quote stuffing with so-called *stub quotes*. The latter practice was sometimes used by market makers who are obligated by exchanges to provide liquidity on both sides of the market. If market makers were not willing to trade at the moment, they might set unreasonably low bids and high offers. In November 2010, the SEC banned stub quotes and mandated that market makers' quotes be within 8 percent of the *national best bid or offer* (NBBO).

Further growth of HFT fueled by technological progress is inevitable. However, one may also expect increased regulation of HFT for preventing possible disruptions of financial markets.

SUMMARY

- Exchanges are the major equity markets where securities are listed. Markets other than exchanges are called over-the-counter (OTC) markets.

- Electronic continuous order-driven markets have become the main market structures in exchanges.
- NYSE Euronext and NASDAQ are the main U.S. equity exchanges.
- London Stock Exchange, Deutsche Burse, and NYSE Euronext are the major European exchanges.[13]
- Institutional FX and fixed income trading is conducted in the OTC markets. While voice brokerage is still important for these instruments, they have been increasingly traded on electronic platforms.
- The inter-dealer FX and fixed income markets do not have centralized clearing and trading is conducted only between counterparts having bilateral credit.
- Multiple alternative trading systems have fragmented liquidity of equity and FX markets worldwide.
- High-frequency automated trading has become a new reality that will shape institutional trading for years to come.

CHAPTER 3

Inventory Models

It was indicated in Chapter 1 that market makers in dealers' markets provide liquidity for takers and make money from the bid/ask spread. This seems easy, particularly in the case of a single-dealer platform. However, there is always a danger that the buy order flows and the sell order flows are not balanced. For example, if there is selling pressure, the price decreases. Then the dealer (who has an obligation to maintain inventory) may have to sell an asset at a price lower than the price at which he bought the asset some time ago. In the long run, the price may revert, but the problem is that the dealer with limited cash resources can become broke before restoring his inventory.

In this chapter, I discuss the models that address the market maker's risk of maintaining inventory as well as show how the size of the bid/ask spread can compensate this risk. Various inventory models differ in whether they account for risk aversion explicitly. I start with the implicit (risk-neutral) models offered by Garman (1976), and Amihud & Mendelson (1980). Then I introduce a formalized notion of risk aversion and describe the explicit Stoll's model (1978).

RISK-NEUTRAL MODELS

The Garman's Model

The problem of dealer's inventory imbalance was first addressed by Garman (1976). In his model, a monopolistic dealer assigns ask (p_a) and bid (p_b) prices, and fills all orders. Each order size is assumed to be one unit. The dealer's goal is, as a minimum, to avoid bankruptcy (running out of cash) and failure (running out of inventory). Also, the dealer attempts to maximize his profits. Arrivals of buy and sell orders are assumed to follow independent continuous Poisson processes with price-dependent rates $\lambda_a(p_a)$ and $\lambda_b(p_b)$, respectively.[1] This implies a high number of takers who submit multiple (albeit small) independent orders. The Garman's model employs the classic *Walrasian equilibrium*, in which lower prices drive demand and suppress supply while higher prices decrease demand and increase supply. As a result, the price settles at a value that equates supply and demand.[2] Hence, it is expected that $\lambda_a(p_a)$ is a monotonically decreasing function, while $\lambda_b(p_b)$ monotonically increases.

The probability of a buy (sell) order to arrive within the time interval $[t, t+dt]$ equals $\lambda_a dt$ ($\lambda_b dt$). Let units of cash and stocks that are held by the dealer at time t be $I_c(t)$ and $I_s(t)$, respectively. If $N_a(t)$ and $N_b(t)$ are the total numbers of stocks sold and bought by the dealer since the beginning of trading ($t = 0$), then inventory dynamics are described as

$$I_c(t) = I_c(0) + p_a N_a(t) - p_b N_b(t) \tag{3.1}$$

$$I_s(t) = I_s(0) + N_b(t) - N_a(t) \tag{3.2}$$

Now, let's introduce the probability $Q_k(t)$ that $I_c(t) = k$. Since each order size is one, there may be three events at time $t - dt$ that yield the cash position of k units: the dealer had $k - 1$ units of cash and sold one stock; the dealer had $k + 1$ units of cash and bought one stock; the dealer did not trade. Then $Q_k(t)$ satisfies the following relation:

$$\begin{aligned}
Q_k(t) = {} & \lambda_a p_a dt \, [1 - \lambda_b p_b dt] \, Q_{k-1}(t - dt) \\
& + \lambda_b p_b dt \, [1 - \lambda_a p_a dt] \, Q_{k+1}(t - dt) \\
& + [1 - \lambda_a p_a dt] \, [1 - \lambda_b p_b dt] \, Q_k(t - dt)
\end{aligned} \tag{3.3}$$

This allows one to calculate the derivative

$$\begin{aligned}
\frac{\partial Q_k}{\partial t} &\approx [Q_k(t) - Q_k(t - dt)]/dt \\
&= \lambda_a p_a Q_{k-1} + \lambda_b p_b Q_{k+1} - (\lambda_a p_a + \lambda_b p_b) Q_k
\end{aligned} \tag{3.4}$$

A similar equation can be derived for the probability $R_k(t)$ that $I_s(t) = k$. In the Garman's model, the dealer cannot borrow cash or stocks. Therefore, the trader must ensure that both $Q_0(t)$ and $R_0(t)$ are always less than unity. Indeed, $Q_0(t) = 1$ and $P_0(t) = 1$ imply that the trader definitely runs out of cash and stocks, respectively. This goal can be formulated in terms of the *gambler's ruin problem*.[3] The latter considers a gambler with initial capital of size N_0 who has the probability q to win one unit and probability $1 - q$ to lose one unit. The gambler has a goal to end up with amount $N > N_0$. The solution to this problem defines the probability that the gambler reaches his goal before losing his initial capital (i.e., failure). The dealer's problem is not identical to the gambler's ruin problem in that the former does not have a defined target amount N. In fact, the dealer just attempts to maximize N. In this case, probability of failure equals one when $q < 0.5$. However, if $q \geq 0.5$, the probability of failure can be expressed as

$$Pr_{\text{failure}} = \left(\frac{(1-q)^{*}Loss}{q^{*}\,Gain}\right)^{N_0} \tag{3.5}$$

Using the approximate solution of (3.4), along with the relation (3.5) for $Gain = Loss = 1$, Garman has shown that the probability of running out of cash is determined from

$$\lim_{t \to \infty} Q_0(t) \approx \left(\frac{\lambda_b p_b}{\lambda_a p_a}\right)^{I_c(0)/\bar{p}} \quad \text{if } \lambda_a p_a > \lambda_b p_b \tag{3.6}$$

$$\lim_{t \to \infty} Q_0(t) = 1 \quad \text{otherwise}$$

In (3.6), $\bar{p}$ is the mean of ask and bid prices. Similarly, the probability of running out of stocks yields

$$\lim_{t \to \infty} R_0(t) \approx \left(\frac{\lambda_a}{\lambda_b}\right)^{I_c(0)} \quad \text{if } \lambda_b > \lambda_a \tag{3.7}$$

$$\lim_{t \to \infty} R_0(t) = 1 \quad \text{otherwise}$$

Hence, to avoid failure, the dealer must maintain the bid/ask spread that satisfies the following conditions:

$$\lambda_a p_a > \lambda_b p_b \tag{3.8}$$

$$\lambda_b > \lambda_a \tag{3.9}$$

These conditions still do not guarantee protection from failure since the probabilities in (3.6) and (3.7) always differ from zero.

While the current result points at the necessity for the maker to set the bid/ask spread, it does not specify the spread size and positioning of mid-price. Garman (1976) offers more specifics for the case when dealer implements zero-drift inventory. This implies relaxing the condition (3.9) to

$$\lambda_b = \lambda_a. \tag{3.10}$$

Then bid and ask prices can be defined by choosing such a bid/ask spread that maximizes the shaded field in Figure 3.1.

The relation (3.10) still implies imminent failure at some point in time. Hasbrouck (2007) indicates that " . . . with realistic parameter values, the expected ruin time is a matter of days." Hence, while the Garman's model offers important insights into the dealer's strategy, it cannot serve as practical advice for market making.

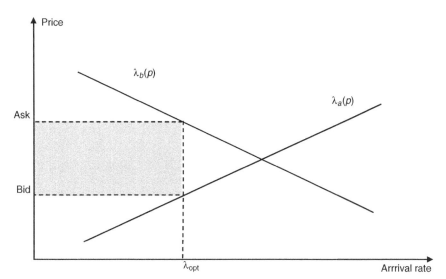

FIGURE 3.1   Dealers' profits in the Garman's model for the case (3.10).

Amihud-Mendelson Model

One significant simplification of the Garman's model is that the dealer establishes pricing in the beginning of trading and does not adjust it to ever-changing market conditions. This problem was addressed by Amihud & Mendelson (1980) by reformulating the Garman's model so that bid and ask prices depend on the dealer's stock inventory. More specifically, the dealer has an acceptable range and a preferred size of the inventory. The dealer maximizes trading profits by manipulating the bid/ask prices when inventory deviates from preferred. Amihud & Mendelson obtain their main results for linear demand and supply functions. Within their model, optimal bid and ask prices decrease (increase) monotonically when inventory is growing (falling) beyond the preferred size. The bid/ask spread increases as inventory increasingly deviates from the preferred size (see Figure 3.2). The practical conclusion from the Amihud-Mendelson model is that dealers should manipulate the bid/ask spread and mid-price for maintaining preferred inventory.

MODELS WITH RISK AVERSION

What Is Risk Aversion?

The concept of *risk aversion* is widely used in psychology, economics, and finance. It denotes an individual's reluctance to choose a bargain

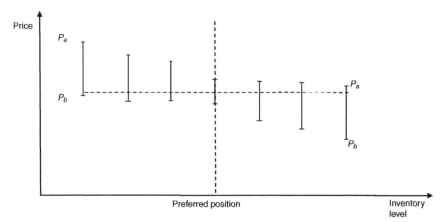

FIGURE 3.2　The dependence of bid and ask prices in the Amihud-Mendelson model.

with uncertain payoff over a bargain with certain but possibly lower payoff. Risk aversion is routinely observed in everyday life: Just recall that we put much of our savings in a bank, money market, or CDs rather than invest them in the ever volatile yet potentially rewarding equity market.

The concept of risk aversion was empirically tested and theoretically advanced in studies of *behavioral finance,* the field that focuses on psychological and cognitive factors that affect people's financial decisions (see Kahneman & Tversky, 2000, for a review). In widely popularized experiments with volunteers, Kahneman and Tversky suggested making choices in two different situations. First, participants assumed to have $1,000 and were given a choice between (1) gambling with 50 percent chances to gain $1,000 and 50 percent to gain nothing, or (2) sure gain of $500. In the second situation, participants assumed to have $2,000 and were given a choice between (1) 50 percent chance to lose $1,000 and 50 percent to lose nothing and (2) sure loss of $500. In both situations, option 2 guaranteed a gain of $1,500. Hence, *risk-neutral* participants would split equally between these two situations. And yet, the majority of participants chose option 2 in the first situation and option 1 in the second situation. Such an outcome implies that the majority of participants were risk-averse.

In classical economics, utility functions $U(W)$ of wealth W are used for quantifying risk aversion. The notion of utility function is rooted in the efficient market hypothesis, according to which investors are rational and act exclusively for maximizing their wealth (see Chapter 7). Findings in behavioral finance indicate that the utility function generally is not linear upon wealth. One of the widely used utility functions is the *constant absolute risk aversion* (CARA):

$$U(W) = \exp(-aW) \qquad (3.11)$$

The parameter a is called the *coefficient of absolute risk aversion*. The important property of CARA is that its curvature is constant:

$$z_{CARA}(W) = -U''(W)/U'(W) = a \qquad (3.12)$$

While it is relatively easy to use CARA in theoretical analysis, absolute aversion may not always be an accurate assumption. Indeed, the loss of $1,000 may be perceived quite differently by a millionaire and a college student. Then the *constant relative aversion function (CRRA)* can be used:

$$U(W) = \text{when} \qquad a \neq 1 \qquad (3.13)$$

$$= ln W \text{ when} \quad a = 1$$

In this case, the coefficient of relative risk aversion is constant:

$$z_{CARA}(W) = -WU''(W)/U'(W) = a \qquad (3.14)$$

The Stoll's Model

The Amihud–Mendelson model implies dealer's risk aversion in that he focuses on reducing deviations from preferred inventory. Stoll (1978) was the first to explicitly introduce the concept of risk aversion in the inventory models. In the Stoll's model, the dealer modifies his original portfolio (which is efficient in terms of CAPM[4]) to satisfy demand from liquidity traders in asset i and compensates his risk by introducing the bid/ask spread. Stoll considered a two-period model in which the dealer makes a transaction at time $t = 1$ and liquidates this position at $t = 2$. The price may change between (but not within) the trading periods. The main idea behind Stoll's approach is that the dealer sets such prices that his expected CARA utility function of the entire trader's portfolio does not change due to trading of the asset i

$$E[U(W)] = E[U(W_T)] \qquad (3.15)$$

In (3.15), W and W_T are the terminal wealth of the initial portfolio W_0 and the terminal wealth of the portfolio after transaction, respectively:

$$W = W_0(1 + r) \qquad (3.16)$$

$$W_T = W_0(1 + r) + (1 + r_i)Q_i - (1 + r_f)(Q_i - C_i) \qquad (3.17)$$

Here, r, r_i, and r_f are rates of return for the entire portfolio, for the risky
asset i, and for the risk-free asset, respectively[5]; Q_i is the true value of the
transaction in asset i; C_i is the present value of the asset i. Hence, Stoll
assumes that the dealer knows the true value of the asset i. Note that $Q_i > 0$
when the dealer buys and $Q_i < 0$ when the dealer sells.

For the analytical solution, Stoll sets $r_f = 0$ and expands both sides of
(3.15) into the Taylor series around the mean wealth $\overline{W}$ and drops the terms
of order higher than two:

$$E[U(W)] \approx E[U(\overline{W})] + U'(W - \overline{W}) + 0.5U''(W - \overline{W})^2 \qquad (3.18)$$

The asset return is assumed to have the normal distribution

$$W = N(W_0, \sigma_p) \qquad (3.19)$$

Ultimately, this yields the relation

$$c_i(Q_i) = C_i/Q_i = z\sigma_{ip}Q_p/W_0 + 0.5z\sigma_i^2 Q_i/W_0 \qquad (3.20)$$

where z is the coefficient of relative risk aversion (3.14), σ_{ip} is the covariance
between the asset i and the initial portfolio, Q_p is the true value of the original
portfolio, and σ_i^2 is variance of the asset i. If the true price of the asset i is P_i^*,
then the prices of the immediacy to sell Q_i^b to (to buy Q_i^a from) the dealer P_i^b
(P_i^a) satisfy the relations

$$(P_i^* - P_i^b)/P_i^* = c_i(Q_i^b) \qquad (3.21)$$

$$(P_i^* - P_i^a)/P_i^* = c_i(Q_i^a) \qquad (3.22)$$

Then the bid/ask spread is defined from the round-trip transaction for
$|Q_i^a| = |Q_i^b| = |Q|$

$$(P_i^a - P_i^b)/P_i^* = c_i(Q_i^b) - c_i(Q_i^a) = z\sigma_i^2|Q|/W_0 \qquad (3.23)$$

This spread depends linearly on the dealer's risk aversion, trading size,
and asset volatility, but is independent of the initial inventory of the asset i.
However, bid and ask prices are affected with the initial asset inventory: the
higher the inventory is, the lower the bid and ask prices are.

An obvious shortcoming of the Stoll's model is that it assumes complete
liquidation of the asset position at $t = 2$. Stoll's original work was expanded
by Ho and Stoll (1981) into a multi-period framework. In this work, the true
trading asset value is fixed while both order flow and portfolio returns are
stochastic. Namely, order flow follows the Poisson process and return is a
Brownian motion with drift. The dealer's goal is to maximize utility of his
wealth at time T. This problem can be solved using the methods of dynamic
programming.[6] The intertemporal model shows that the optimal bid/ask

spread depends on the dealer's time horizon. Namely, the closer to the end of trading, the smaller is the bid/ask spread. Indeed, as duration of exposure to risk of carrying inventory decreases, so does the spread being the compensation for taking risk. In general, the spread has two components. The first one is determined by specifics of supply and demand curves (assumed to be linear by Ho & Stoll, and the second one is an adjustment due to the risk the dealer accepts by keeping inventory. This adjustment depends on the same factors as the spread in the Stoll's one-period model (3.23): risk aversion, price variance, and the size of transaction. Also, similar to the two-period model, the spread is independent of the asset's inventory size.

Ho & Stoll (1983) offered another generalization of the Stoll's model that describes the case with competing dealers. Namely, dealers in this work can trade among themselves and with liquidity traders. It is assumed that dealers can have varying endowments but they have the same risk aversion. Liquidity traders trade with the dealer(s) that offer the best price. When several dealers offer the best price, the matching dealer is chosen randomly. The bid/ask spread in this model, too, depends on the product $z\sigma_i^2|Q|$ [see (3.23)] and it decreases with the growing number of dealers.

An interesting point indicated by Ho & Stoll (1983) is that trading fees are reflected by the second best prices rather than by the prices on top of the order book. Indeed, say the best bid price is B1 and the second best price is B2 < B1. Then the first dealer can decrease his price to B2 + ε < B1 (where ε is an infinitesimal increment) and still remain on top of the book. The importance of the second best price has some parallel with the *Vickrey's auction*, in which bidders submit sealed bids and a bidder with the highest bid wins; yet, the winner pays the second high bid rather than his own price.

O'Hara (1995) and de Jong & Rindi (2009) provide detailed reviews of inventory market models.

SUMMARY

- Inventory models address the dealer's problem of maintaining inventory on both sides of the market. Since order flows are not synchronized, dealers face the possibility of running out of cash (bankruptcy) or out of inventory (failure).

- Risk-neutral models (Garman 1976; Amihud & Mendelson 1980) are based on the Walrasian framework according to which lower (higher) price drives (depresses) demand. These models demonstrate that rational dealers attempting to maximize their profits must establish a certain bid/ask spread and manipulate its size for maintaining preferred inventory.

- Risk aversion is a concept that refers to an individual's reluctance to choose a bargain with uncertain payoff over a bargain with certain but possibly a lower payoff.

- In mathematical terms, risk aversion is usually described with some utility function that is non-linear upon wealth. Inventory models with risk aversion are based on optimizing this utility function.

- The basic two-period inventory model offered by Stoll (1978) considers a single dealer who optimizes the CARA utility function (3.11) and assumes that the return of a risky asset has the normal distribution. This model yields the bid/ask spread that depends linearly on the dealer's risk aversion, trading size, and the asset volatility.

- Extensions of the Stoll's model for multi-period framework and for competing dealers (Ho & Stoll 1981, 1983) retain linear dependence of the bid/ask spread on risk aversion and volatility. In the multi-period model, the optimal spread narrows since the risk for maintaining inventory diminishes as trading comes to the end. The spread also decreases with the growing number of competing dealers as the risk is spread among them.

CHAPTER 4

Market Microstructure: Information-Based Models

The idea behind the information-based models of market microstructure is that price is a source of information that investors can use for their trading decisions (see O'Hara 1995 and de Jong & Rindi 2009, for a detailed review). For example, if security price falls, investors may suggest that price will further deteriorate and refrain from buying this security. Note that such a behavior contradicts the Walrasian paradigm of market equilibrium, according to which demand grows (falls) when price decreases (increases).

The information-based models are rooted in the rational expectations theory. Namely, informed traders and market makers make conjectures on rational behavior of their counterparts, and they do behave rationally in the sense that all their actions are focused on maximizing their wealth (or some utility function in the case of risk-averse agents). Market in these models reaches an equilibrium state that satisfies participants' expectations. Obviously, informed investors trade only on one side of the market at any given time. The problem that market makers face while trading with informed investors is called *adverse selection*.

In this chapter, I consider two information-based models that were introduced for describing two different markets. The first is the Kyle's (1985) model, which was developed for batch auction markets. Another model is offered by Glosten & Milgrom (1985) to address the adverse selection problem in sequential trading.

KYLE'S MODEL

One-Period Model

Kyle (1985) considers a one-period model with a single risk-neutral informed trader (insider) and several liquidity traders who trade a single risky security with a risk-neutral market maker (dealer). The batched auction setup implies that the market clears at a single price. Hence, the bid/ask spread is irrelevant. The informed trader (insider) knows that the security value in the end of the period has the normal distribution

$$v = N(p_0, \sigma_0^2) \tag{4.1}$$

The insider trades strategically, that is, submits an order of size $x(v)$ to optimize her profits in the end of the period. Liquidity traders submit their orders randomly and their total demand y is described with the normal distribution

$$y = N(0, \sigma_y^2) \tag{4.2}$$

Both random variables v and y are independently distributed. The dealer observes the aggregate demand, $z = x + y$, but is not aware what part of it comes from the informed trader. The dealer sets the clearing price $p(z)$ that is expected to optimize his profits. Naturally, $p(z)$ increases with growing aggregate demand. The insider's profit equals

$$\pi_I = x(v - p) \tag{4.3}$$

Kyle obtains the equilibrium price (i.e., the price that yields the optimal profits for both dealer and insider) analytically for the case when the clearing price depends linearly on demand:

$$p(z) = \lambda z + \mu \tag{4.4}$$

In (4.4), λ characterizes inverse liquidity. Indeed, lower λ (higher liquidity) leads to lower impact of demand on price. Sometimes, inverse liquidity is called illiquidity (see Eq. (1)). It follows from (4.3) and (4.4) that

$$E[\pi_I] = x(v - \lambda x - \mu) \tag{4.5}$$

As a result, the optimal insider's demand equals

$$x = (v - \mu)/2\lambda \tag{4.6}$$

Another form of (4.6) is

$$x = a + \beta v, \ a = -\mu/2\lambda, \ \beta = 1/2\lambda \tag{4.7}$$

Then, all variables of interest can be expressed in terms of the model parameters (p_0, σ_0, and σ_y). Indeed, since v and z have normal distributions, it can be shown that $E[v|z]$ has the following form[1]

$$E[v|z] = p_0 + \frac{\beta(z - \alpha - \beta p_0)\sigma_0^2}{\sigma_y^2 + \beta^2 \sigma_0^2} \tag{4.8}$$

In equilibrium, the right-hand sides of (4.4) and (4.8) must be equal for all z. Then

$$a^* = p_0\sigma_y/\sigma_0, \beta^* = \sigma_y/\sigma_0, \tag{4.9}$$

$$\mu^* = p_0, \tag{4.10}$$

$$\lambda^* = \sigma_0/2\sigma_y \tag{4.11}$$

The equality (4.10) $\mu^* = p_0 = E[v|z = 0]$ implies that the dealer sets price at its mean (true) value in case of zero demand. Note also that the inverse liquidity in equilibrium (4.11) is determined with variances of price and demand.

An interesting property of the Kyle's model is that price variance conditional on the aggregate demand equals

$$\text{Var}(v|z) = \sigma_0^2/2, \tag{4.12}$$

which is only one half of the unconditional price variance. The result (4.12) implies that the order flow provided by liquidity traders distorts the information available to informed traders. Indeed, even if an insider knows that the traded security is overpriced and hence is not interested in buying it, a large idiosyncratic buy order from a liquidity trader will motivate the dealer to increase the price.

Now, consider profits and losses of all market participants. It follows from (4.5) that the expected insider's profit equals

$$E[\pi_I] = 0.5\sigma_y\sigma_0 \tag{4.13}$$

Note that only the expected insider's profit is positive. In fact, insiders may experience a loss according to (4.3), when the idiosyncratic rise of demand from liquidity traders leads to the condition $v - \lambda z - \mu < 0$. The trading cost of liquidity traders turns out to be equal to the insider's profit (de Jong & Rindi 2009)

$$E[\pi_L] = E[y(p - v)] = \lambda\sigma_y^2 = 0.5\sigma_y\sigma_0 \tag{4.14}$$

Hence, the expected insider profits are funded with losses incurred by liquidity traders. The total dealer's profits in the Kyle's model are zero. The (sufficiently) good news is that the dealer has no losses. There is a general rationale for expecting the dealer's zero profits (unless he is monopolistic). The so-called *Bertrand competition model* demonstrates that competing businesses inevitably lower the price on their product until the price reaches the product marginal cost. Why then does anyone bother to run batch auctions? Firstly, auction owners receive transaction fees. And secondly, a constantly informed trader is just an abstraction.

Multi-Period and Multi-Insider Models

Kyle (1985) considers also a model with K auctions that are held at times $t_k = k\Delta t = k/K$; $k = 1, 2, \ldots, K$. Note that the discrete model approaches a continuous auction when $\Delta t = 1/K$ decreases. It is assumed that the order flow from liquidity traders follows the Brownian motion: $\Delta y_k = N(0, \sigma_y{}^2 \Delta t)$. The insider's demand is

$$\Delta x_k = \beta_k(v - p_k)\Delta t \tag{4.15}$$

The dealer sets a price that depends linearly on total demand:

$$p_k = p_{k-1} + \lambda_k(\Delta x_k + \Delta y_k) \tag{4.16}$$

In the end of the auction k, the dealer's expected profits have the form

$$E(\pi_k | p_1, \ldots, p_{k-1}, v) = \alpha_{k-1}(v - p_{k-1})^2 + \delta_{k-1} \tag{4.17}$$

In equilibrium, the coefficients in (4.15)–(4.17) satisfy the relations

$$\lambda_k = \beta_k \sigma_k^2 / \sigma_y^2 \tag{4.18}$$

$$\beta_k \Delta t = \frac{1 - 2\alpha_k \lambda_k}{2\lambda_k(1 - \alpha_k \lambda_k)} \tag{4.19}$$

$$\alpha_{k-1} = 1 / [4\lambda_k(1 - \alpha_k \lambda_k)] \tag{4.20}$$

$$\delta_{k-1} = \delta_k + \alpha_k \lambda_k^2 \sigma_y^2 \Delta t \tag{4.21}$$

In contrast to the single-period model, the variance is now time-dependent:

$$\sigma_k^2 = (1 - \beta_k \lambda_k \Delta t)\sigma_{k-1}{}^2 \tag{4.22}$$

Since the system of equations (4.18)–(4.22) is non-linear, an iterative procedure is needed for solving it.

In the multiple-period model, the insider splits her orders into small pieces with sizes varying with time. Such a strategy has become a standard practice in executing large orders (see Chapter 13). In the real world, this leads to positive autocorrelations in order flows, which implies some predictability of an insider's actions. However, this is not the case in the Kyle's model, which allows the insider to hide her orders behind uncorrelated orders submitted by liquidity traders. Ultimately, however, the price reflects the entire insider's information and her profits are limited.

GLOSTEN-MILGROM MODEL

In the sequential trading model derived by Glosten & Milgrom (1985), a risk-neutral dealer sets the bid and ask prices for trading one unit of security with informed traders (insiders) and uninformed (liquidity) traders, one trade at a time. The type of trader who trades at a given time is chosen randomly.[2] Another assumption is that each trader can trade only one unit of security (or none). To obtain analytical results, Glosten & Milgrom consider a simple case when the security value V can have either high value $V = V_H$ with probability $1 - \theta$ (that reflects good news) or low value $V = V_L$ (bad news) with probability θ. Insiders and liquidity traders trade with probabilities μ and $1 - \mu$, respectively. In this framework, insiders buy on good news and sell on bad news, while liquidity traders buy and sell with equal probability (equal 0.5). The trading process for this model is shown in Figure 4.1.

As in the Kyle's model, the dealer in the Glosten-Milgrom model is not expected to make profits due to the Bernard competition and insider profits are equal to the liquidity trader's loss. The dealer sets prices that are *regret-free* in the sense that these prices are the dealer's expectations of the security's value based on the trading signals that he receives. Let us denote buy and sell events as B and S, respectively. Then, the dealer sets the following bid b and ask a

$$a = E[V|B] = V_L \Pr(V = V_L|B) + V_H \Pr(V = V_H|B) \qquad (4.23)$$

$$b = E[V|S] = V_L \Pr(V = V_L|S) + V_H \Pr(V = V_H|S) \qquad (4.24)$$

The conditional probabilities in (4.23) and (4.24) can be calculated using the *Bayes' rule*[3]:

$$\Pr(A|B) = \frac{\Pr(B|A)\Pr(A)}{\Pr(B)} \qquad (4.25)$$

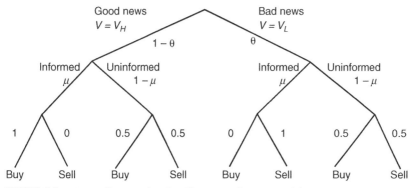

FIGURE 4.1   Event diagram for the Glosten-Milgrom model.

For example, $\Pr(V = V_L | B) = \Pr(V = V_L)\dfrac{\Pr(B | V = V_L)}{\Pr(B)}$ (4.26)

Note that

$$\begin{aligned}\Pr(B) &= \Pr(V = V_L)\Pr(B | V = V_L) + \Pr(V = V_H)\Pr(B | V = V_H) \\ &= 0.5(1 + \mu(1 - 2\theta))\end{aligned}$$ (4.27)

Hence,

$$\Pr(V = V_L | B) = \frac{(1 - \theta)(1 - \mu)}{1 - \mu(1 - 2\theta)}$$ (4.28)

As a result,

$$a = \frac{\theta(1 - \mu)V_L + (1 - \theta)(1 + \mu)V_H}{1 + \mu(1 - 2\theta)}$$ (4.29)

$$b = \frac{\theta(1 + \mu)V_L + (1 - \theta)(1 - \mu)V_H}{1 - \mu(1 - 2\theta)}$$ (4.30)

Then, the bid/ask spread equals

$$s = a - b = \frac{4\theta(1 - \theta)\mu(V_H - V_L)}{1 - (1 - 2\theta)^2\mu^2}$$ (4.31)

According to (4.31), the spread increases with the growing number of insiders (i.e., higher μ), which illustrates the effect of adverse selection. The spread has a particularly simple form when the good and bad news arrive with equal probability (i.e., $\theta = 0.5$):

$$s = \mu(V_H - V_L)$$ (4.32)

Therefore, in this case, the spread grows linearly with the number of informed traders.

The bid and ask prices in (4.29) and (4.30) are their expected values before the first trade. This trade itself is a signal with which the dealer updates his expectations. For example, if the first trade is a buy, it causes the trader to revise the probability of lower security value:

$$\theta_1 = \Pr(V = V_L | B) = \frac{\theta(1 - \mu)}{1 + \mu(1 - 2\theta)}$$ (4.33)

Note that θ_1 is always lower than θ. Hence, a buy signal increases the probability of a higher security value. New buy orders modify this probability according to the recurrence relation (see also Hasbrouck 2007)

$$\theta_k(B) = \frac{\theta_{k-1}(1 - \mu)}{1 + \mu(1 - 2\theta_{k-1})} \tag{4.34}$$

where $\theta_0 = \theta$. Similarly, a sell signal decreases the probability of a higher security value:

$$\theta_k(S) = \frac{\theta_{k-1}(1 + \mu)}{1 - \mu(1 + 2\theta_{k-1})} \tag{4.35}$$

The relations (4.34) and (4.35) can be used for simulations of price dynamics.

The Glosten-Milgrom model offers a relatively simple description of adverse selection costs that the dealer must incorporate into the spread in order to avoid losses. The model also has other implications. In particular, price dynamics follow a *martingale*; that is, the expectation of price p_{t+1} at time $t + 1$ based on all information I_t available at time t is p_t:

$$E[p_{t+1}|I_t] = p_t \tag{4.36}$$

This, in turn, implies that price is semi-strongly efficient; that is, it incorporates all information available to the dealer.[4] As a result, returns in the Glosten-Milgrom model are uncorrelated. This certainly contradicts empirical observations (see Chapter 7).

FURTHER DEVELOPMENTS

The Kyle's and Glosten-Milgrom models have been expanded in several ways. In particular, Easley & O'Hara (1987) considered an extension to the latter model in which traders may submit orders of small and large sizes. In general, informed traders are motivated to trade large amounts to benefit from their knowledge as much as possible. However, large orders reveal private information to the entire market and therefore cut the insider's advantage. In one model, both informed and uninformed traders may trade small and large orders. In other words, all traders are *pooled* together. This helps to hide some private information with small orders and improve the price for large orders. Another option for informed traders is to *separate* themselves from liquidity traders so that informed traders trade only large orders. Note that adverse selection grows with order size. On the other hand, there is no adverse selection in trading small orders, and therefore, the dealer can establish zero bid/ask spread for small orders. Since informed traders maximize their profits, they will trade in the separated mode only if trading at the worse price is compensated with sufficiently large amounts. If this does not happen due to the particular choice of the model parameters, trading will be conducted in the pooling mode.

In another model offered by Easley & O'Hara (1992), the bad/good news bifurcation in the root of the trading event diagram (see Figure 4.1) is complemented with the *no-news* case, in which only uninformed traders may want to trade. Also, uninformed traders have an option of *no trade* besides the buy/sell choice. The no-news case increases the probability of uninformed trading, thereby decreasing the bid/ask spread.

Subrahmanyam (1991) discusses the effects of multiple informed traders on liquidity. As private information is now shared by several insiders, so are the profits. Subrahmanyam shows that while the liquidity in equilibrium increases with the number of risk-neutral insiders, a growing number of risk-averse insiders can, in fact, decrease liquidity. Namely, liquidity decreases with a small but growing number of insiders as risk aversion causes them to trade more cautiously. However, after the number of insiders reaches some threshold, their sheer number yields increasing liquidity.

Back & Baruch (2004) considered two models that explore the relationships between the Kyle's and Glosten-Milgrom frameworks. In the first model, orders from liquidity traders arrive as a Brownian motion and dealers see only total demand (as in the Kyle's model). In another model, these orders arrive as a Poisson process, and the dealer sees them. The Back-Baruch model differs from the Glosten-Milgrom model in that the insider can optimize her times of trading. Back & Baruch have found that there is equilibrium in which the insider employs a mixed strategy randomizing at each instant between trading and waiting. They have shown also that the distinction between this modified Glosten-Milgrom model and the Kyle's model is unimportant when orders are small and arrive frequently.

SUMMARY

- Price in information-based market models is a source of information that investors can use for their trading decisions. For example, if security price falls, investors may suggest that price will further deteriorate and refrain from buying this security.

- Market makers face an adverse selection problem while trading with informed investors who trade only on one side of the market at any given time.

- In information-based models, dealers and informed investors behave rationally; that is, they make trading decisions to maximize their wealth (or utility function depending on wealth in case of risk-averse agents). As a result, price converges to some equilibrium value that satisfies rational expectations.

- In the batch auctions, dealers compensate potential losses from adverse selection by setting asset price as increasing with demand.

- The Kyle's model (1985) describes a one-period batched auction among a risk-neutral dealer, a risk-neutral insider, and several liquidity traders. It is assumed that price/demand dependence is linear, which allows one to derive the equilibrium price analytically. The slope of this dependence has the sense of inverse liquidity (illiquidity). The security value and liquidity trader demand are assumed to have independent, normal distributions and their variances determine the equilibrium price.

- In the sequential trade models, dealers compensate potential losses from adverse selection by setting the bid/ask spread that grows with the number of informed traders and with order size.

- In the Glosten-Milgrom model (1985), insiders and liquidity traders arrive randomly and the dealer sets regret-free prices, which reflect the dealer's expectations based on the trading events. Specifically, it is assumed that bad/good news arrives in the market randomly and security can assume either low value (bad news) or high value (good news). Insiders sell in the former case and buy in the latter case, while liquidity traders buy and sell with equal probability, regardless of news. This yields an analytic solution for the bid/ask spread in terms of asset values, probabilities of arrival of different trader types, and probabilities of arrival of different news.

- In the Easley-O'Hara model (1987), traders may submit orders of small and large sizes. Large orders yield higher gains to informed traders but reveal their private information to the market. On the other hand, small orders help to hide some private information and improve price for large orders. Hence, informed traders face a choice between trading exclusively large orders and mixing them with small ones.

CHAPTER 5

Models of the Limit-Order Markets

Two former chapters were devoted to the models for dealer markets. With proliferation of order-driven continuous trading platforms, theoretical research has also focused on the markets where each trader can become a maker or a taker. The critical question for a trader in an order-driven market is whether to submit a market order for immediacy and for minimizing an opportunity cost,[1] or to submit a limit order, which saves the spread but has uncertainty of execution. A compromise in this strategy is placing a limit order inside the market, which narrows the bid/ask spread and increases probability of execution. Ambiguity of this choice remains a challenge for both theoreticians and practitioners.[2] In this chapter, several noted models of limit-order markets are described. I start with introducing one of the first contributions to analysis of this problem by Cohen, Maier, Schwartz, and Whitcomb (1981, called further CMSW). Then, I proceed with the models offered by Parlour (1998) and Foucault (1999). I conclude with an overview of recent developments in this field (see Parlour & Seppi 2008, for details).

THE CMSW MODEL

In the CMSW model, all traders are assumed to maximize their wealth, which consists of cash and a risky asset. Traders trade only at a set of fixed points of time. Trading costs include a fee for submitting a limit order and another fee paid in case an order is filled. It is assumed that trading is symmetric on both sides of the market, and hence, one-sided trading is considered. Namely, the ask price is defined exogenously as the random walk with price shocks summed up between the trading times according to the compound Poisson process:

$$ln\, S_t(\Delta) = ln\, S_t + \sum_{i=1}^{N(\Delta)} Z_i \qquad (5.1)$$

In (5.1), Δ is the time between trading points, price shocks Z_i are an independent and identically distributed variable with zero mean and $N(\Delta)$ is a Poisson process with arrival rate ν.

At each time, the trader can choose not to trade or obtain a long position with either a market buy order or a limit bid order with a price below the current ask price. CMSW formulate a dynamic programming problem of maximizing trader's wealth.

One conclusion that CMSW make is that the probability to fill a limit order is always less than unity. It should be noted that this probability can be further estimated using the notion of the *first passage time* (FPT). Say the ask price at $t = 0$ is $S = S_0$ and the price of the bid order is $S_0 - s$. We assume that the order is matched when $S(t) = S_0 - s$. By definition, FPT for given shock s equals the time of the first instance when $S <= S_0 - s$. The probability distribution for FPT, in the case of the Brownian motion without drift, equals (Feller 1968)

$$f_{\mathrm{FPT}}(s, t) = \frac{s}{\sqrt{2\pi\sigma^2}} t^{-3/2} \exp\left(-\frac{s^2}{2\sigma^2 t}\right) \qquad (5.2)$$

For any fixed s, t has the following asymptote at long times:

$$f_{\mathrm{FPT}}(s, t) \sim t^{-3/2} \qquad (5.3)$$

$$\Pr(s, t) = \int_0^t f_{\mathrm{FPT}}(s, \tau)d\tau \qquad (5.4)$$

As a result, the expected value of FPT is infinite. However, the probability for the first passage at time t is finite.[3] Since filling of a market order is certain, there is a jump in probability when the order type is changed. CMSW show that if a bid price approaches the ask price (i.e., $s \to 0$), the jump in probability disappears when trading costs are neglected. In the CMSW model, the bid/ask spread is determined with transaction costs. If the spread is wide, traders submit new limit orders that have lower spread but still have lower loss than market orders. When the spread narrows to the extent that fees for submitting limit orders negate their gain, traders may want to submit market orders. CMSW call this effect *gravitational pull*. Order matching widens the spread as market orders *wipe out* the top of the book. Ultimately, the spread attains some equilibrium value. CMSW characterize growth of market thickness with the increasing arrival rate of the Poisson process and show that the spread increases as the market becomes thinner.

THE PARLOUR MODEL

In the Parlour model (1998), risk-neutral traders trade a risky asset with the fundamental value of v. Each trader perceives the asset value as $v\beta(t)$ where $\beta(t)$ is randomly distributed over the interval $(\underline{\beta}, \overline{\beta})$. Bid (B) and ask (A) prices are defined exogenously and remain fixed; $A < v < B$. Since order execution does not affect the values of A and B, this implies that market depth is infinite. Trading time is divided into $t = 0, 1, \ldots, T$ periods. Only one trader can trade at a given time. Hence, time t is also the trader's index. Traders buy or sell one asset unit with a probability of 0.5. The active LOB accounts only for limit orders that were submitted by traders, that is, exogenous liquidity that maintains prices A and B is neglected. If the active LOB is empty, the exogenous liquidity provider matches market orders. Orders are matched using the FIFO rule (see Chapter 1). Namely, if the active bid LOB at time t has n_t^B orders and a trader submits a bid order, it is placed in the end of the order book and $n_{t+1}^B = n_t^B + 1$. If the trader submits a sell order, it matches with the first bid order in the active LOB and $n_{t+1}^B = n_t^B - 1$. Whether a trader t submits a market or limit order depends on his evaluation of the asset value. If the buyer's asset value estimate satisfies the condition $v\beta(t) > A$, he submits a market order; otherwise, a buyer submits a bid order at price B. Similarly, a seller submits a market order if $v\beta(t) < B$; otherwise, he submits an ask order at price A.

The traders' optimal strategies cannot be defined in advance, since the probability to fill a limit order depends on the actions of those traders who enter the market later. For example, a bid order that has the kth position in the active LOB is filled only if there will be at least k market sell orders submitted in future. However, the problem can be solved with backward recursion. Namely, for trader T, submitting a limit order does not make sense since he is the last one in the sample. Say trader T happens to be a buyer. If $v\beta(T) > A$, he submits a market buy order; otherwise, he does nothing. Similar logic applies to trader T being a seller. Now that we know whether trader T changed the active LOB, we can consider trader $T - 1$. If he is a seller and $n_{T-1}^S = 0$, then he can submit a sell limit order, which will be executed if trader T submits a buy market order. However, this order cannot be executed within the remaining trading time if $n_{T-1}^S > 0$. This protocol can be continued from trader $T - 1$ to trader $T - 2$, and so on.

The Parlour model in equilibrium has some properties that coincide with empirical findings in equity markets (Biais et al. 1995). In particular, market orders are more likely submitted after market orders on the same side of the market. Indeed, one may expect that a buy order diminishes liquidity on the ask side, which motivates a seller to submit a limit ask order. Another interesting result is that a buyer (seller) is more likely to submit a market order in case of a thick LOB on the bid (ask) side. On the other hand, a thick LOB on the offer (bid) side motivates a buyer (seller) to submit a limit order.

A variation of the Parlour model in which the direction of trade is determined by the value of $\beta(t)$ (rather than by the independent parameter) is offered by de Jong & Rindi (2009).

THE FOUCAULT MODEL

Foucault (1999) addresses the so-called *winner's curse* problem. In the context of the limit-order market, this problem implies that the highest bid (lowest offer) is executed (*picked-off*) by a sell (buy) market order first. Yet, it may be mispriced, that is, the asset price may become lower (higher) after this transaction. Foucault offers a model that describes a mix of market and limit orders in equilibrium. In this model, a single asset is traded at discrete moments of time $t = 0, 1, \ldots, T$, where T is random, that is, there is a probability of $1 - \rho$ that trading ends at any time. It is assumed that the asset value follows the random walk

$$v(t) = v(t-1) + \varepsilon(t) \tag{5.5}$$

where $\varepsilon(t)$ are innovations caused by public news that are assumed independent and identically distributed. Innovations can have only values $\pm\sigma$ with probability 0.5. Note that σ is a measure of price volatility.[4] Then, the payoff of the asset at time T is

$$V(T) = v(0) + \sum_{t=1}^{T} \varepsilon(t) \tag{5.6}$$

At each time t, a new risk-neutral trader submits an order for one unit with a reservation price that has the trader's individual estimate $y(t)$

$$R(t) = v(t) + y(t) \tag{5.7}$$

It is assumed that $y(t)$ is independently and identically distributed, and can take values $y_h = L$ and $y_l = -L$ with the probability 0.5. Furthermore, the values y_h and y_l are used to denote the trader type. In the end of trading, the utility function of a trader who traded the asset at price P is

$$U(y) = q(V(T) + y - P) \tag{5.8}$$

where $q = 1$ and $q = -1$ correspond to buyers and sellers, respectively. Traders choose between the buy orders and sell orders, and may submit market or limit orders. If there is no difference in the outcome of submitting market or limit orders, it is assumed that traders submit limit orders. For certainty, limit orders live only one period and cannot be revised. If a limit order submitted at time t is not filled at time $t + 1$, it is cancelled. If the order book is empty, the arriving trader submits ask and bid limit orders. The state of the book is defined with the bid, $B(t)$, and ask, $A(t)$, prices. If the bid side is empty, $B(t) = -\infty$; if the ask side is empty, $A(t) = \infty$.

Equilibrium at Zero Volatility

In a simpler case with $\sigma = 0$, the asset value v is constant and there is no winner's curse problem. It is assumed that traders with type y_h (y_l) submit only long (short) orders. Consider first a trader with type y_h who submits at time t a limit order with the bid price $B^*(v, + L, t)$. This order will be executed only if

- Trading does not stop before the arrival of the next trader (with probability ρ).
- The next trader has type y_l (with probability 0.5).
- The next trader submits a market sell order.

The probability of the last event depends on the market state. Namely, if the current bid price is too low, the trader with type y_h submits a limit sell order. Let us denote $C^{s*}(v, -L, t + 1)$ as such a bid price that the trader with type y_l is indifferent between a market order and a limit order. If the trader with type y_h submits an order with a price slightly above $C^{s*}(v, -L, t + 1)$, then its execution probability is 0.5ρ, and expected gain equals $0.5\rho[v + L - C^{s*}(v, -L, t + 1)]$. The bid price $C^{s*}(v, -L, t + 1)$ is optimal since a higher bid price has the same probability of execution (but a lower gain) while a lower bid price has zero probability of execution.

Now, consider the optimal order placement decision of trader with type y_h. Let's denote $C^{b*}(v, +L, t)$ as such an ask price that the trader is indifferent between a buy market order and a buy limit order. At this price, gain from market order equals the expected gain from the limit order for any t within the trading time T:

$$v + L - C^{b*}(v, L, t) = 0.5\rho[v + L - C^{s*}(v, -L, t + 1)] \qquad (5.9)$$

If the best ask price in the market, A, is greater than $C^{b*}(v, +L, t)$, the (rational) trader with type y_h submits a buy limit order with price $B^*(v, +L, t) = C^{s*}(v, -L, t + 1)$ rather than a market order. A similar consideration for a trader with type y_l yields

$$L - v + C^{s*}(v, -L, t) = 0.5\rho[L - v + C^{b*}(v, L, t + 1)] \qquad (5.10)$$

If the best bid price, B, is lower than $C^{s*}(v, -L, t)$, the trader with type y_l submits a sell limit order with price $A^*(v, -L, t) = C^{b*}(v, L, t + 1)$ rather than a sell market order.

If the trading time, T, was deterministic, the functions $C^{b*}(v, +L, t)$ and $C^{s*}(v, -L, t)$ could be calculated using the backward induction. However, the trading process in the Foucault model has a non-zero probability to continue at any time. Hence, there is no terminal point in time from which one can start recursive calculations. Foucault (1998) offers a stationary solution for the system of equations (5.9) and (5.10), in which the functions $C^{b*}(v, +L, t)$ and $C^{s*}(v, -L, t)$ do not depend on time. Namely,

$$B^*(v, +L) = C^{s*}(v, -L) = v + L - 2L/(1 + 0.5\rho) \qquad (5.11)$$

$$A^*(v, -L) = C^{b*}(v, +L) = v - L + 2L/(1 + 0.5\rho) \qquad (5.12)$$

These relations yield the following stationary spread:

$$s^* = A^*(v, -L) - B^*(v, +L) = 2L(1 - 0.5\rho)/(1 + 0.5\rho) \qquad (5.13)$$

Volatility Effect

In the generic case with non-zero volatility σ, the assumption made in the former section that traders with type y_h (y_l) submit only long (short) orders is dropped. The attention is now focused on the order placement strategy when arriving traders face an empty order book and submit both bid and ask limit orders. Foucault shows that in equilibrium only traders with type y_h purchase the asset and only traders with type y_l sell the asset. The bid/ask spread in equilibrium equals

$$S^* = \sigma + 2(2L - \sigma)/(2 + \rho) \quad \text{when} \quad \sigma < 4L/(4 + \rho) \qquad (5.14)$$

$$S^* = 2\sigma + 8L/(4 + \rho) \quad \text{when} \quad \sigma \geq 4L/(4 + \rho) \qquad (5.15)$$

Hence, the spread increases with volatility. The first terms in the right-hand sides of (5.14) and (5.15) being proportional to σ account for the winner's curse. Namely, these costs relate to the case when a trader submits a bid (offer) with the price higher (lower) than the asset future value—and this order is filled (unfortunately for the trader). As a result, the spread and hence the cost of market orders increases, which motivates traders to submit limit orders rather than market orders. This, in turn, decreases the probability of execution at higher volatility. The second terms in the right-hand sides of (5.14) and (5.15) reflect the execution costs. Obviously, increasing ρ leads to a smaller spread and to a higher probability of execution.

NEW DEVELOPMENTS

The Parlour (1998) and Foucault (1999) models are attractive in that they are simple enough to have analytic solutions; yet, they offer rich and testable implications. Therefore, these models serve as the starting points for further analysis of the limit-order markets.

Foucault, Kadan, and Kandel (2005, called further FKK) study how traders' patience affects order placement strategy, bid/ask spread, and market resiliency. The latter is measured with the probability that the spread after liquidity shock returns to its initial value before the next transaction. FKK made several assumptions to obtain a tractable equilibrium solution. In particular, there is an infinite liquidity source for buying (selling) an asset at price A (B); $A > B$. This liquidity source defines the outside spread, $K = A - B$. All prices here and further are given in units of ticks. Buyers and sellers arrive sequentially according to a Poisson process and trade one unit of the asset. Each trader can place one market order or limit order, which depends on the state of the order book and trader's impatience level. The latter is a measure of trader's perceived opportunity cost[5] and can have two values: low δ_P and high δ_I; $\delta_I > \delta_P$. The proportion of patient traders, $0 < \theta < 1$, remains constant. Limit orders can be submitted j ticks away from the current best price ($j = 0$ for market orders) and cannot be changed or cancelled. Namely, the order bid price and order ask price equal $b - j\Delta$ and $a + j\Delta$, respectively, where $b \geq B$ and $a \leq A$ are the best bid and best ask prices; Δ is the tick size. The *inside spread* is therefore equal $s = a - b$. It is expected that limit orders must improve price, that is, narrow the spread. The trader's utility function contains a penalty proportional to the execution waiting time and impatience level. Namely, the expected profits of trader i ($i = I, P$) with filled order j are equal:

$$\Pi(i,j) = V_b - a\Delta + j\Delta - \delta_i T(j) \text{ for buyers} \qquad (5.16)$$

$$\Pi(i,j) = b\Delta - V_s + j\Delta - \delta_i T(j) \text{ for sellers} \qquad (5.17)$$

where $V_b > A\Delta$ and $V_a < B\Delta$ are the buyers' and sellers' asset valuations, respectively. Hence, for a given spread s, traders place orders to maximize the value:

$$\max \pi(i,j) = j\Delta - \delta_i T(j) \qquad (5.18)$$

$$j \in \{0, 1, \ldots, s - 1\}$$

The FKK model benefits from its strong constraints in that it has a tractable solution for the equilibrium placement of limit orders and expected execution times. It shows, in particular, that expected execution times are higher in markets with a high proportion of patient traders. This motivates liquidity providers to submit more aggressive orders and to lower the inside spreads. Market orders are less frequent when the portion of patient traders is high, as it is impatient traders who use market orders. New limit orders may top current best prices by more than one tick, which creates holes in the order book—an effect found in real markets (Biais et al. 1995). Another finding is that the tick size may increase the average inside spread if the portion of patient traders is small, since they can place even less aggressive limit orders. Also, a lower order arrival rate leads to smaller spreads as liquidity providers strive to shorten the execution times.

Rosu (2008) has expanded the FKK model in that traders can dynamically modify their limit orders. This implies multi-unit orders and a variable (random) number of traders at any time. The model is still analytically tractable. In particular, it describes the distribution of orders in the order book and market impact from orders of different size. Rosu discerns temporary (or instantaneous) and permanent (or subsequent) market impacts. The former is the result of executing a market order; the latter results from the regrouping of remaining limit orders that are submitted by strategic makers.

The Rosu model (2008) has a number of interesting predictions. First, higher activity of impatient traders causes smaller spreads and lower price impact. Market orders lead to a temporary price impact that is larger than the permanent price impact (so-called *price overshooting*). Limit orders can cluster outside the market, generating a hump-shaped LOB. In other words, there is a price level inside the order book where aggregated order size has a maximum. Rosu shows also how trading may widen the bid-ask spread. For example, when a sell market order moves the bid price down, the ask price also falls but by a smaller amount. Another observation is related to the *full* order book, that is, when the total cost of limit orders—including the waiting cost—is higher than that of market orders. When the order book is full, patient traders may submit quick (or *fleeting*) limit orders with the price inside the spread. These orders illustrate traders' attempts to simultaneously gain some cost savings and immediacy.

Goettler et al. (2005) have offered a more generic model in which traders can submit market orders and multiple limit orders at different prices. This model has no analytic solution and search of the market equilibrium represents a computational challenge. Traders in this model are characterized by their private estimate of the asset value and by their maximum trading size. The order book is assumed to be open, which allows traders to make rational decisions. Traders arrive sequentially and submit several market orders and limit orders to maximize their expected trading gains. Unexecuted limit orders are subject to stochastic cancellation over time when the asset value moves in adverse direction. The Goettler et al. model offers a rich set of conditional order dynamics. In particular, it shows that traders with low private values often submit ask orders below the consensus value of the asset. On the other hand, overly optimistic traders submit bid orders above the consensus value. As a result, many market orders yield negative transaction costs, that is, these buy (sell) orders matched below (above) the consensus value. Another finding is that the transaction price is closer to the true value of the asset rather than the midpoint of the bid-ask spread. Hence, the former is a better proxy to the true asset value.

SUMMARY

Solutions of several stylized models of order-driven markets that are reviewed in this chapter have properties that coincide with empirical findings in continuous order-driven markets. In particular,

- A thinner LOB has a wider bid/ask spread.
- Market orders are more likely submitted after market orders on the same side of LOB.
- Buyer (seller) is more likely to submit market order in case of thick LOB on the bid (ask) side.
- Buyer (seller) is more likely to submit limit order in case of thick LOB on the ask (bid) side.
- The bid/ask spread increases with volatility.
- Winner's curse occurs when a limit order filled due to price volatility turns out to be mispriced.
- Patient traders submit less aggressive limit orders. As a result, the bid/ask spread increases.
- Limit orders may cluster outside the market, generating a hump-shaped LOB.

CHAPTER **6**

Empirical Market Microstructure

Empirical analysis of market microstructure focuses on specifics of order flows, the bid/ask spread, and structure of the limit-order book. Significant amount of empirical market data has been accumulated in the literature (see Hasbrouck 2007 and de Jong & Rindi 2009, for a review). However, since financial markets continue to evolve with ever changing macroeconomic conditions, new technology, and regulation, much of the information relevant to empirical market microstructure may need regular updating.

Several theoretical models have been used in empirical market microstructure research. In the next section, I describe the classical Roll's model (1984) of the bid/ask spread. Then, I turn to the Glosten-Harris model (1998), which quantifies the contribution of the adverse selection into the bid/ask spread. In contrast to these and other models discussed in Chapters 3 through 5, some models used for analysis of empirical microstructure are not derived using some assumptions on the trader behavior, market structure, and price dynamics; rather, they are based on the regression analysis of the variables of interest. These structural models pioneered by Hasbrouck (1991) have become a popular tool in empirical analysis. I describe one such model in this chapter. Finally, I provide an overview of some recent empirical findings in the equity and FX markets.

ROLL'S MODEL

The Roll's model (1984) relates the bid/ask spread to transaction prices. Hence, it can be particularly helpful when ask and bid prices are not available. This model is derived using several assumptions. First, the transactional (observable) price P_t bounces between bid and ask values:

$$P_t = P_t^* + 0.5Sq_t \qquad (6.1)$$

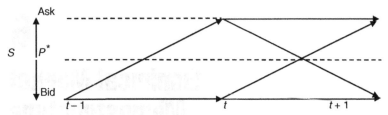

FIGURE 6.1 Possible transaction price paths in the Roll's model.

In (6.1), S is the bid/ask spread assumed to be constant; q_t is the directional factor that equals 1 for buy orders and -1 for sell orders; P_t^* is the fundamental price that is assumed to follow the random walk and is not affected by trading. Therefore,

$$\Delta P_t^* = P_t^* - P_{t-1}^* = \varepsilon_t \qquad (6.2)$$

where $\varepsilon_t = N(0, \sigma^2)$. Another assumption is that probabilities for buying and selling are equal and independent of past transactions:

$$\Pr(q_t = 1) = \Pr(q_t = -1) = \Pr(q_t = q_{t-1}) = 0.5 \quad \text{for all } t \qquad (6.3)$$

Roll focuses on estimating the covariance $\text{Cov}(\Delta P_t, \Delta P_{t-1})$. Note that if $S = 0$, then $\Delta P_t = \Delta P_t^*$ and $\text{Cov}(\Delta P_t, \Delta P_{t-1}) = \text{Cov}(\varepsilon_t, \varepsilon_{t-1}) = 0$. Consider now $\text{Cov}(\Delta P_t, \Delta P_{t-1})$ for the case with non-zero spread. Possible transactional price paths between two consecutive time periods are depicted in Figure 6.1.

Note that P^* within the Roll's model is fixed (unless new information is available). Hence, if P_{t-1} is at the bid, ΔP_t can be either 0 or $+S$; if P_{t-1} is at the ask, ΔP_t can be either 0 or $-S$. The corresponding probabilities are listed in Table 6.1. Since transaction at $t-1$ can be bid or ask with the same probability, the joint probability has the following form (see Table 6.2).

TABLE 6.1 Probability Distribution for Successive Price Changes ΔP_t and ΔP_{t+1} in the Roll's Model

		P_{t-1} at the Bid ΔP_t		P_{t-1} at the Ask ΔP_t	
		0	S	$-S$	0
ΔP_{t+1}	$-S$	0	0.25	0	0.25
	0	0.25	0.25	0.25	0.25
	S	0.25	0	0.25	0

TABLE 6.2 Joint Probability Distribution for Successive Price Changes ΔP_t and ΔP_{t+1} in the Roll's Model

		ΔP_t		
		$-S$	0	S
ΔP_{t+1}	$-S$	0	0.125	0.125
	0	0.125	0.25	0.125
	S	0.125	0.125	0

As a result,

$$\text{Cov}(\Delta P_t, \Delta P_{t-1}) = 0.125(-S^2 - S^2) = -0.25S^2 \tag{6.4}$$

This is equivalent to

$$S = 2\sqrt{-\text{Cov}(\Delta P_t, \Delta P_{t-1})} \tag{6.5}$$

Obviously, the relation (6.5) makes sense only if the empirical co-variance is negative. While this is generally the case, several assumptions made in the Roll's model may look simplistic. In particular, empirical data in both equity (Hasbrouck 2007) and FX (Hashimoto et al. 2008) markets show that q_t can be correlated (so-called *runs*), that is, buys (sells) follow buys (sells). Fortunately, if

$$\Pr(q_t = q_{t-1}) = q \neq 0.5 \tag{6.6}$$

then the Roll's formula for the spread can be easily modified (de Jong & Rindi 2009):

$$S = q^{-1}\sqrt{-\text{Cov}(\Delta P_t, \Delta P_{t-1})} \tag{6.7}$$

Trading within the Roll's model does not affect bid and ask prices. Hence, within this model, the realized spread (1.4) equals the effective spread (1.3): $S^R = S^E$.

THE GLOSTEN-HARRIS MODEL

The Glosten-Harris model (1998) expands the Roll's model in that it treats the bid/ask spread as a dynamic variable and splits it into the transitory, C_t, and the adverse selection, Z_t, components

$$S_t = 2(C_t + Z_t) \tag{6.8}$$

Hence the observable transactional price equals[1]

$$P_t = P_t^* + (C_t + Z_t)q_t \tag{6.9}$$

This implies that the fundamental price is now affected by the adverse selection component

$$P_t^* = P_{t-1}^* + Z_t q_t + \varepsilon_t \qquad (6.10)$$

Glosten & Harris (1998) assume in the spirit of Kyle's model (see Chapter 4) that both spread components are linear upon the trading size V_t:

$$C_t = c_0 + c_1 V_t, \quad Z_t = z_0 + z_1 V_t \qquad (6.11)$$

It follows from (6.8)–(6.11) that the price change equals

$$\Delta P_t = c_0(q_t - q_{t-1}) + c_1(q_t V_t - q_{t-1} V_{t-1}) + z_0 q_t + z_1 q_t V_t + \varepsilon_t \qquad (6.12)$$

Let's calculate the price change for the round-trip transaction of a sale immediately following a purchase of the same asset size. Namely, let's put $q_t = 1$ and then $q_{t-1} = -1$ into (6.12). Then (neglecting ε_t),

$$\Delta P_t = 2C_t + Z_t \qquad (6.13)$$

In fact, ΔP_t is a measure of the effective spread that is conditioned on the round-trip transaction. It differs from the unconditional quoted spread $2C_t + 2Z_t$ that is observable to uninformed traders.

The model coefficients c_0, c_1, z_0, and z_1 can be estimated using empirical market data. Glosten & Harris (1991) made such estimates with transactional data for 20 NYSE stocks traded in 1981. Their results confirm the prediction made using the information-based microstructure models (see Chapter 4) that the adverse-selection spread component grows with increasing trade size.[2]

STRUCTURAL MODELS

Both Roll's and Glosten-Harris models depart from the efficient market canon in that the observable (transactional) prices are not treated as martingales anymore. One can argue that bid/ask bounces described in the Roll's model are small short-lived frictions in otherwise efficient market, and the mid-price equated with the asset fundamental value still follows the random walk. Glosten and Harris go further by offering a price discovery equation (6.10) in which trading volume of informed investors can result in a (possibly long-lived) market impact.

The information-based market impact may have lagged components related to quote revisions and past trades. Hasbrouck (1991) suggests that information-based price impact can be separated from the inventory-based price impact since the former remains persistent at intermediate time intervals while the latter is transient.[3] Hasbrouck (1991) offers a structural model in which it is assumed that the expectation of the quoted mid-price conditioned on public information I_t available at time t approaches the true asset value P_T at some future time T:

$$E\left[\left(p_t^a + p_t^b\right)/2 - P_T | I_t\right] \to 0 \quad \text{as} \quad t \to T \qquad (6.14)$$

In (6.14), p_t^a and p_t^b are ask and bid prices at time t, respectively. Let's introduce the revision of the mid-price:

$$r_t = 0.5\left[\left(p_t^a + p_t^b\right)/2 - \left(p_{t-1}^a + p_{t-1}^b\right)/2\right] \qquad (6.15)$$

In the general case, r_t can be represented in the following form:

$$r_t = a_1 r_{t-1} + a_2 r_{t-2} + \ldots + b_0 x_t + b_1 x_{t-1} + \ldots + \varepsilon_{1,t} \qquad (6.16)$$

In (6.16), a_i and b_i are the coefficients; $\varepsilon_{1,t}$ is a disturbance caused by new public information; x_t is the signed order flow (positive for buy orders and negative for sell orders) that, in turn, has the general form

$$x_t = c_1 r_{t-1} + c_2 r_{t-2} + \ldots + d_1 x_{t-1} + d_2 x_{t-2} + \ldots + \varepsilon_{2,t} \qquad (6.17)$$

It should be noted that the term *order flow* employed in empirical market microstructure research generally refers to trading (transactional) volumes. However, equating trading volumes and order flows neglects the limit orders that are not filled. This distinction is particularly important in limit-order markets where market orders are not permitted. Empirical data available for academic research often do not specify what side of the market initiated transactions. It is usually assumed that a buy (sell) order initiated a transaction if its price is higher (lower) than the bid/ask mid-price.

The specific of the Hasbrouck's model (1991) is that the equation for r_t(6.16) has the contemporaneous term, $b_0 x_t$, while (6.17) has only lagging terms. This implies that the quote revision follows trade impact immediately but the latter cannot instantly reflect the former. Hasbrouck assumes also that disturbances have zero means and are not serially correlated:

$$\begin{aligned} E\left(\varepsilon_{1,t}\right) = E\left(\varepsilon_{2,t}\right) = 0; \\ E\left(\varepsilon_{1,t}\,\varepsilon_{1,s}\right) = E\left(\varepsilon_{1,t}\,\varepsilon_{2,s}\right) = E\left(\varepsilon_{2,t}\,\varepsilon_{2,s}\right) = 0 \quad \text{for} \quad t \neq s \end{aligned} \qquad (6.18)$$

The system (6.16)–(6.18) represents a bivariate *vector auto-regression* (VAR).[4] Assuming that $x_0 = \varepsilon_{2,0}$ and $\varepsilon_{1,t} = 0$, the long-term price impact can be estimated using the *cumulative impulse response*:

$$\alpha_m(\varepsilon_{2t}) = \sum_{t=0}^{m} E\left[r_t | \varepsilon_{2,0}\right] \qquad (6.19)$$

It follows from (6.14) that as m approaches T, $\alpha_m(\varepsilon_{2t})$ converges to the revision of the efficient price. Hence, $\alpha_m(\varepsilon_{2t})$ can serve as a measure of the market impact due to the new information.

Hasbrouck (1991) offers a structural model that is formulated in terms of the efficient price M_t, bid/ask mid-price p_t, and signed trading size x_t:

$$M_t = M_{t-1} + \varepsilon_{1,t} + z\varepsilon_{2,t} \tag{6.20}$$

$$p_t = M_t + a(p_t - M_t) + bx_t \tag{6.21}$$

$$x_t = -c(p_{t-1} - M_{t-1}) + \varepsilon_{2,t} \tag{6.22}$$

The value x_t is positive (negative) if a trade is initiated by a buyer (seller).

The random shocks $\varepsilon_{1,t}$ and $\varepsilon_{2,t}$ satisfy (6.18) and are related to non-trading and trading information, z is intensity of the latter, and a, b, and c are the model coefficients that satisfy the following conditions:

$$0 < a \leq 1, \, b > 0, \, c > 0 \tag{6.23}$$

The coefficient a is responsible for inventory control (which is *imperfect* when $a < 1$). Indeed, say $p_t = p_0$ at $t = 0$ and $x_1 > 0$. Then the market maker encourages traders to sell by raising p_t. On the other hand, demand is controlled by the negative sign in the first term in (6.22). While the efficient price is unobservable, the system (6.20)–(6.22) can be expressed in terms of observable variables x_t and $r_t = p_t - p_{t-1}$. The case with $a < 1$ yields an infinite VAR[5]:

$$\begin{aligned} r_t = (z + b)x_t + [zbc - (1 - a)b]x_{t-1} \\ + a[zbc - (1 - a)b]x_{t-2} + \ldots + \varepsilon_{1,t} \end{aligned} \tag{6.24}$$

$$x_t = -bcx_{t-1} - abcx_{t-2} - a^2 bcx_{t-3} + \ldots + \varepsilon_{2,t} \tag{6.25}$$

While $a < 1$, the coefficients of higher terms decrease and regressions can be truncated at some lag with acceptable accuracy. Then the cumulative impulse response (6.19) has a rather fast convergence.

RECENT EMPIRICAL FINDINGS

Equity Markets

Intraday Patterns   The intraday patterns of trading volumes and bid/ask spreads are well documented (see, e.g., recent reviews by Emrich 2009 and

Malinova & Park 2009). In the past, intraday U.S. equity trading volumes were U-shaped. Since 2008, the end-of-day turnover[6] of S&P constituents has significantly increased and the intraday volume pattern has become closer to J- (or even reverse-L-) shaped. London stock exchange and some Asian markets, too, have reverse-L intraday trading volume patterns.

Several theoretical models have been offered to explain the intraday trading volume patterns. Admati & Pfleiderer (1988) have shown that if some liquidity traders have discretion with regard to trading timing (i.e., trade strategically), they concentrate their trading at times when the market is thick and this concentration grows with the increasing number of informed traders. Hong & Wang (2000) explain the U-shaped pattern by assuming that increasing trading in the morning is caused by risk-averse investors willing to hedge their assets while the high-volume trading in the end of the day is dominated by informed speculators. The latter approach is corroborated by Schiereck & Voigt (2008). On the other hand, according to Hora (2006), the intraday trading pattern can be caused by risk-averse execution strategies with time constraints widely used in algorithmic trading (see Chapter 13). Proliferation of algorithmic trading has also significantly affected an average trade size: for S&P 500 constituents, it has fallen between 2004 and 2009 from about 1,000 shares to below 300 shares (Emrich 2009).

The intraday bid/ask spreads in equity markets usually have an L-shaped pattern. However, this pattern flattens for illiquid stocks with wide average spreads.

Order Flows and Market Impact Hasbrouck & Seppi (1999) analyzed market data for 30 Dow stocks and demonstrated that signed order flows and returns are characterized by common factors.[7] Commonality in the order flows explains roughly half of the commonality of returns. On the other hand, commonality in bid/ask spreads is small.

Long-range autocorrelations in signed order flows in equity markets have been reported in several studies (see Farmer et al. 2006, Bouchaud et al. 2006, and references therein). These autocorrelations with values of approximately 0.05 or higher may last up to 100 five-minute intervals. Mimetic contagion of chartists (see Chapter 9) and slicing large orders into small pieces (see Chapter 13) can be the source of such autocorrelations. An interesting attempt to reconcile these autocorrelations with the random-walk behavior of returns was undertaken by Bouchaud et al. (2006). Namely, it was suggested that the random walk, being a simple diffusional process (i.e., the Brownian motion; see Chapter 7), results from two opposite but compensating processes. The first one is super-diffusion, which manifests with long autocorrelations in order flows (caused by takers).

Another process is sub-diffusion, which manifests with a power-law decay of the orders' market impact (facilitated by market makers).

The impact of market orders on price (or simply, *market impact*) is the key notion in execution strategies (Kissell & Glantz 2003). It is often estimated as a combination of permanent and transitory components with the latter pertinent only to the order that caused it (Almgren et al. 2005). On the other hand, Weber & Rosenow (2005) reported that market impact in equities grows with trading volume as a power law with the exponent lower than one. Also, Bouchaud et al. (2004) indicated that market impact in equities has power-law decay. It should be noted that market impact is generally estimated as a function of trading volume—that is, realized market impact. However, the expected market impact (estimated by parsing the order book) is much higher than the realized one (Weber & Rosenow 2005). This may be explained with the traders' attempt to avoid placing their orders at times of low liquidity when potential market impact may be high.

Global FX Spot Market

The FX market microstructure before and around the introduction of the Euro in 1999 is addressed by Lyons (2001) and Dacorogna et al. (2001). A recent detailed overview of this field is offered by Osler (2010).

Intraday Patterns The global spot FX is a 24-hour market for which GMT time is generally used in discussions of intraday effects. FX trading is usually available from Sunday nights when the Pacific markets open (around 21:00 GMT) to Friday nights when the U.S. market closes (around 21:00 GMT). However, only the most liquid currency pairs, EUR/USD and USD/JPY, are persistently traded around the clock. Still, these currency pairs have different intraday patterns (see Chaboud et al. 2004 and Ito et al. 2006). Namely, the EUR/USD trading volume has two pronounced maxima, one around 9:00 GMT when trading in London becomes intense and another, even a higher one, at around 15:00 GMT when active trading in London and New York overlap. Note that in New York, there is no maximum in the trading volume at the end of day (typical in equity markets). This is due to the fact that the New York FX traders start trading early in order to use liquidity coming from London, and therefore, they end trading relatively early. The USD/JPY trading volume has an additional maximum at around 2:00 GMT, after the opening of the Pacific markets. The EUR/USD and USD/JPY spreads are roughly U-shaped and J-shaped, respectively. Other currency pairs are mostly traded during typical working hours in the countries where the relevant currencies are used.

The effects of macroeconomic data releases on price and order dynamics in the United States and Japan are discussed by Berger et al. (2005) and Hashi & Ito (2009), respectively. Some announcements, particularly GDP and payrolls releases, have a significant effect on the order flows in the minute immediately after the announcement. Others, such as CPI and PPI releases, have little effect (if any). Usually, shocks from surprising announcements do not last more than several minutes, though, which implies high resilience of the global FX market.

Order Flows, Trading Volumes, and Market Impact As was indicated above, order flows and trading volumes in the limit-order markets must be discerned. Estimates made for EUR/USD in the EBS market in 2006 show that less than one-third of all orders are fully filled (Schmidt 2010b). One reason is that the majority of orders is placed at the best price or outside the market; that is, bid (offer) orders are placed at or below (above) the best bid (offer). With proliferation of high-frequency trading, the share of filled orders has become even lower as multiple market makers compete for occupying the top of the order book.

Schmidt (2010b) reports a significant difference between autocorrelations in the hit flows and the quote flows in the EBS market.[8] Namely, autocorrelations in the signed hit flows are practically non-existent. Autocorrelations in the signed quote flows are much stronger than autocorrelations in the signed trading volumes: the former remain above 0.1 for at least 10 five-minute intervals. This decay is still much faster than in equity markets (see above). Relatively small autocorrelations in trading volume flows in the institutional FX market may be explained with rather large minimal order size (one million units of the base currency), which constrains the slicing of large orders.

Important characteristics of the order book are the distributions of the aggregated order size at best price and its depletion rate. For liquid currency pairs, such as EUR/USD and USD/JPY, these distributions can be described rather accurately with the gamma distribution. These distributions can be used for simulation of the order execution costs (Schmidt 2009a).

The market impact of signed trading volumes for EUR/USD and USD/JPY at various frequencies, ranging from one minute to one month, was studied by Berger et al. (2005). It was found that the signed trading volumes do not have forecasting ability with the exception of the next time increment on the one-minute grid.

While market impact at one-minute and lower frequencies has an academic interest, there is a need for estimates of instant market impact for implementing optimal execution strategies. Analysis of instant market impact caused by trades (i.e., *realized* market impact) is complicated in limit-order markets where market impact depends not only on the order size but also on the order price. For estimating market impact in the case of execution time constraints, Schmidt (2010a) suggests using *expected* market impact rather than the realized one. His estimates show that the former is notably higher than the latter one. Another finding in Schmidt (2010a) is that market impact in FX has power-law decay similar to that shown in equity markets.

SUMMARY

- Empirical analysis of market microstructure focuses on order flows, the bid/ask spread, and structure of the limit-order book.

- The classical Roll's model (1984) relates the bid/ask spread to return covariance. This relation makes sense only if return covariance is negative.

- The Glosten-Harris model (1998) splits the bid/ask spread into the transitory and the adverse selection components that depend linearly on trading volume. The model calibrated with empirical market data confirms that the adverse selection component grows with trading volume.

- The structural models for the market microstructure variables in the spirit of Hasbrouck (1991) are formulated in terms of vector autoregressive models for returns and trading volumes.

- Intraday trading volume patterns in modern equity markets are close to J- or reverse-L shape.

- Intraday bid/ask spreads in equity markets usually have an L-shaped pattern. However, this pattern flattens for illiquid stocks with wide average spreads.

- Market impact in equities grows with trading volume as a power law with the exponent lower than one and has power-law decay.

- In general, intraday trading volume in FX varies for different currency pairs. In particular, EUR/USD has two maxima related to active trading in London: the first at around 9:00 GMT, and the second one at around 15:00 GMT, when trading is active in both London and New York.

- Autocorrelations in trading volumes in FX are significantly smaller than those in equities.

- Market impact in FX has power-law decay, similar to that observed in equities.

PART

Two

Market Dynamics

CHAPTER 7

Statistical Distributions and Dynamics of Returns

This chapter starts with introducing the notion of return. Then, I describe the efficient market hypothesis and its relationship with the random walk. In particular, I define three types of the random walk and address the problem of predictability of returns. I also offer an overview of recent empirical findings and models describing distributions of returns. Finally, I introduce the concept of fractals and its applications in finance.

PRICES AND RETURNS

Let's start with the basic definitions. The logarithm of price P denoted further as $p = log(P)$ is widely used in quantitative finance. One practical reason for this is that simulation of random price variations can move price into the negative region, which does not make sense. On the other hand, the negative logarithm of price is perfectly acceptable. Log price is closely related to *return*, which is a measure of investment efficiency. Its advantage is that some statistical properties, such as *stationarity* and *ergodicity*[1] are better applicable to returns than to prices (Campbell et al. 1997). The single-period return (or *simple return*) $R(t)$ between two subsequent moments t and $t-1$ is defined as[2]

$$R(t) = P(t)/P(t-1) - 1 \qquad (7.1)$$

Note that return is sometimes defined as the absolute difference $[P(t) - P(t-1)]$. Then, $R(t)$ in (7.1) is named *rate of return*. We, however, use (7.1) as the definition of return.

Multi-period returns, or *compounded returns,* define returns between the times t and $t-k$:

$$R(t, k) = P(t)/P(t-k) - 1 \qquad (7.2)$$

The continuously compounded returns (or log returns) are defined as

$$r(t) = \log[R(t) + 1] = p(t) - p(t - 1) \qquad (7.3)$$

Calculation of the compounded log returns is reduced to simple summation:

$$r(t, k) = r(t) + r(t - 1) + \ldots + r(t - k) \qquad (7.4)$$

Prices and returns being time-ordered sequences of random variables (time series) are described with the theory of stochastic processes (see, e.g., Hamilton 1994, Taylor 2005, or Tsay 2005). Major concepts of time series analysis, such as the statistical distributions and their moments, and autoregressive and moving-average models are listed in Appendix B.

THE EFFICIENT MARKET HYPOTHESIS

The efficient market hypothesis (EMH) states that markets instantly incorporate all new information in the asset prices. Since news generally comes unexpectedly, prices change unpredictably.[3] In other words, markets are informationally efficient; that is, any attempt to forecast future price using some information does not produce better results than a forecast that neglects this information. The very notion of *hypothesis* implies explanation of some empirical facts. The empirical background of EMH is multiple observations of asset price dynamics that follow the random walk. These observations have led to the random walk hypothesis (RWH). The latter implies that the asset prices are unpredictable. The EMH, however, is more than the trivial consequence of RWH. EMH is also based on the concept of rational investors who immediately incorporate new information into fair prices. The evolution of the EMH paradigm, starting with the Bachelier's pioneering work on random price behavior back in 1900 to the formal definition of EMH by Fama in 1965 and its expansion by multiple followers is well publicized (see, e.g., Lo & MacKinlay 1999 and Malkiel 2003).

The EMH implies two unfortunate for investors consequences. First, arbitrage, or risk-free profiteering based on difference in prices of the same asset in different markets, is all but impossible. And second, investors should not expect earnings exceeding the total market return. Three forms of EMH are discerned in the modern economic literature:

1. In the *weak* form of EMH, current price reflects all information on past prices. Then, the technical analysis that is often used for forecasting future price direction (see Chapter 10) must be helpless. The weak EMH form still allows for possibility that the fundamental analysis (in the spirit of Graham & Dodd 2008) may yield some excess returns.

2. The *semi-strong* form of EMH states that prices reflect *all* publicly available information. If this is true, the fundamental analysis is not helpful either.
3. The *strong* EMH form requires that prices instantly reflect not only public but also private (insider) information.

While EMH remains a powerful concept in classical finance, its criticism has been offered on several fronts. First, human actions cannot be reduced to the rational optimizing of some universal utility function. Even if investors are always rational, they may have heterogeneous beliefs in terms of both expected returns and perceived risk.[4] In fact, traders are often driven by human emotions, such as greed and fear, rather than by rational expectations (see a popular account on the Keynesian concept of *animal spirits* by Akerlof & Shiller, 2010). The Internet bubble in 1999 to 2000 and the global financial crisis in 2008 to 2009 have dealt serious blows to the ideal world of the EMH.

EMH has also several other methodological difficulties. In particular, the famous Grossman-Stiglitz paradox states that if market is informationally efficient, investors have no rationale for collecting economic information (let alone paying for it). Also, it has been shown that the random walk hypothesis is, in fact, neither a necessary nor sufficient condition for rationally functioning efficient markets. Finally, careful statistical analysis of price dynamics demonstrates that RWH does not always hold (Lo & MacKinlay 1999).

To address the conflict between the EMH and empirical findings, Lo (2004) has proposed the *Adaptive Market Hypothesis* (AMH), according to which the modern market represents an ecological system in which its agents (mutual funds, hedge funds, and individual investors) compete for scarce resources (profits). Prices in such a market reach their new efficient values not instantly but over some time, during which agents adapt to new information by trial and error. In a highly liquid and competitive market (e.g., the U.S. Treasury market), price quickly attains its efficient value. On the other hand, a market with abundant resources and few competitors may be less efficient (e.g., antiques). Since many agents have limited resources for optimizing their decisions, they exhibit *bounded rationality* and therefore leave profit opportunities for more capable (or fortunate) competitors. These profit opportunities are limited but when they are exhausted, new information may stimulate novel trading ideas.

The AMH is an attractive concept that encourages everlasting learning and offers a hope for *beating the market*. However, it does not address an important pragmatic argument of unabated defenders of EMH: No individual or institution has yet demonstrated the capacity to *consistently* produce excess returns (Malkiel 2003). Therefore, the practical problem for ambitious investors is whether returns are (at least partially) predictable. This problem is further explored in the following section.

RANDOM WALK AND PREDICTABILITY OF RETURNS

Three models of the random walk are discussed in the modern economic literature (Campbell et al. 1997; Fabozzi et al. 2006). In the first one (called RW1), the dynamics of log prices are described using the following equation:

$$p_t = p_{t-1} + \mu + \varepsilon_t, \varepsilon_t = \text{IID}(0, \sigma^2) \qquad (7.5)$$

where μ is the expected drift and $\text{IID}(0, \sigma^2)$ implies that random innovations are independently and identically distributed with zero mean and variance σ^2. In other words,

$$E[\varepsilon_t] = 0; \quad E[\varepsilon_t^2] = \sigma^2; \quad E[\varepsilon_t \varepsilon_s] = 0, \quad \text{if} \quad t \neq s \qquad (7.6)$$

This form of innovations is called *strict white noise*. When ε_t has the normal distribution (denoted by $N(0, \sigma^2)$), RW1 (7.5) coincides with the *Brownian motion* that is usually represented in the differential form

$$dp_t = \mu_t dt + \sigma_t dW_t \qquad (7.7)$$

In (7.7), W_t is the *standard Brownian motion* with random innovations being $\text{IID}(0, 1)$. When σ_t is not constant, it is called *instantaneous volatility*. RW1 with non-zero drift has non-stationary conditional mean

$$E[p_t|p_0] = p_0 + \mu t \qquad (7.8)$$

where p_0 is return at $t = 0$. RW1 has non-stationary conditional variance

$$\text{Var}[p_t|p_0] = \sigma^2 t \qquad (7.9)$$

in the case of RW1, expectations and higher moments are unpredictable.

In a more generic form of the random walk (RW2), ε_t has independent but not identical innovations. In other words, innovations can be drawn from different distributions. RW2 is based on the martingale model, which, in turn, is rooted in the gambling theory. Note that a stochastic process X_t is a martingale if

$$E[X_t|X_{t-1}, X_{t-2}, \ldots] = X_{t-1} \qquad (7.10)$$

The martingale difference process,

$$E[X_t - X_{t-1}|X_{t-1}, X_{t-2}, \ldots] = 0 \qquad (7.11)$$

represents the outcome of *fair game*. Namely, *martingale* implies that the expected future value equals the current value. This martingale property has a close connection with the weak form of the efficient market. While forecasting of expected values is impossible for RW2, its higher moments may be predictable (Fabozzi et al. 2006).

RW2 can be relaxed further, so that innovations remain uncorrelated (i.e., $Cov(\varepsilon_t, \varepsilon_{t-k}) = 0$) yet higher moments—for example, variance—can be dependent, and hence forecastable: $Cov(\varepsilon_t^2, \varepsilon_{t-k}^2) \neq 0$. This model (RW3) is also called *white noise* (but not the strict one). Such a model exhibits *conditional heteroskedasticity*, which is well supported with empirical data on volatility and will be discussed in Chapter 8. RW3 does not permit linear forecasting of expectations, but non-linear forecasting, for example, with neural nets (Gencay et al. 2001), may be possible.

Comprehensive analysis of various financial time series has shown that the RWH may often be rejected. In particular, Lo & MacKinlay (1999) have found that daily returns may exhibit slight serial correlations. This implies that RW3 can be technically rejected. Since RW3 is the weakest form of the random walk, its rejecting implies also the rejecting of RW1 and RW2. Hence, financial markets are predictable to some degree. Alas, this does not guarantee noticeable (let alone persistent) excess returns. Such market imperfections as the bid/ask spread, trading expenses, and limited liquidity can completely absorb potential profits expected from predictive models. In the following chapters, I describe some of these models as well as approaches to testing their efficiency.

RECENT EMPIRICAL FINDINGS

As was indicated above, RWH is based on early empirical research and still enjoys great popularity in classical finance. Another (practical) reason for the vitality of the RWH is that it often significantly simplifies tractability of statistical models. In fact, RWH remains what it is: a hypothesis. This implies that RWH must be tested for each asset, and for every new time period and timescale. Here, I describe the main stylized facts for daily returns that have been accumulated in recent years.

Statistical properties of daily equity and FX returns demonstrate notable deviations from the normal distribution (see, e.g., the recent review by Taylor, 2005). Generally, daily returns have low (if any) serial correlations. It is known also that conditional expected daily returns are close to zero. This makes forecasting of returns very difficult and leads to the martingale hypothesis. Therefore, a description of return dynamics can be based on the random walk model that is less restrictive than the strict white noise.

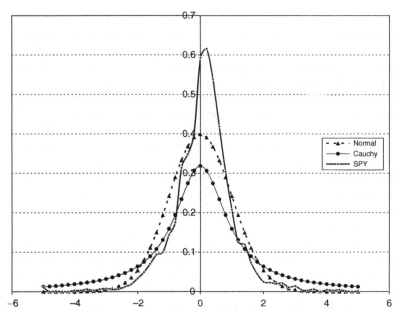

FIGURE 7.1   Distribution of returns for SPY (ETF that mimics S&P 500) for the period 1997 to 2009 in comparison with normal distribution and Cauchy distribution.

Another important finding is that squared (or absolute) returns are clearly correlated. This implies that while returns are practically uncorrelated, they are not independent. Volatility of returns may vary over time. Volatility can also be clustered, that is, large returns (of any sign) follow large returns. These facts lead to even greater relaxation of the strict random walk model.

In fact, distributions of returns may differ significantly from the Gaussians. In particular, these distributions may have high kurtosis, *fat* distribution tails (which implies a decay slower than the exponential one), and asymmetrical shape (see the distribution of S&P 500 returns in Figure 7.1).

Importance of long-range dependencies in the financial time series was greatly emphasized by Mandelbrot (1997). Early research of long-range behavior in the financial time series was based on the *stable distributions* called *Levy flights* (see Appendix A). This approach, however, has an important drawback: Levi flights have infinite variance. Such uncertainty of the volatility measure is generally unacceptable for financial applications. The truncated Levy flights that satisfy the requirement for finite volatility are sometimes used as a way around (Mantegna & Stanley 2000; Bouchaud & Potters 2000).

Recent findings by Gabaix et al. (2003) indicate that the asymptotic distributions of returns in equity markets for the period 1984 to 1996, at the timescales varying from one minute to several days, follow the power law with an index close to three. At longer timescales, distributions of returns slowly approach the Gaussian form. Power-law distributions were also found in the FX market (Ohnishi et al. 2008). The presence of fat tails means that financial crises are less improbable than one might expect from the normal distribution. This certainly has important implications for risk management.

In general, power-law distributions describe *scale-free processes*. Scale invariance implies that the distribution has similar shape on different scales of the independent variable. Namely, function $f(x)$ is scale-invariant to the transformation $x \rightarrow \alpha x$ if there is such a parameter L that

$$f(x) = Lf(\alpha x) \qquad (7.12)$$

Equation (7.12) has the power-law solution

$$f(x) = x^n \qquad (7.13)$$

where $n = -\ln(L)/\ln(\alpha)$. The function $f(x)$ is scale-free since the ratio $f(\alpha x)/f(x) = L$ does not depend on x.

Several theoretical models offered in explanation of the power-law distributions in finance are reviewed by Schmidt (2004) and Gabaix (2009). In particular, Gabaix et al. (2003) have derived a model that is based on two observations:

1. Distribution of the trading volumes obeys the power law with an index of about 1.5.
2. Distribution of the number of trades is a power law with an index of about 3 (in fact, it is close to 3.4).

Two other assumptions were made in this model:

1. Price movements are caused primarily by activity of large mutual funds whose size distribution is the power law with an index of 1 (so-called *Zipf's law*).
2. Mutual fund managers trade in an optimal way.

The mathematical transformations based on these rules yield a power-law return distribution with an index of 3.

In another approach, LeBaron (2001) has shown that power-law distributions can be generated by a mix of normal distributions with different timescales. Namely, fitting a combination of Gaussians with a half-life of about 2.7 years, 2.5 weeks, and 1 day to the Dow returns for 100 years (from 1900 to 2000), yields the power-law index in the range between 2.98

and 3.33 for the timescales in the range between 1 and 20 days. The rationale for three different Gaussians reflects various time horizons for investors: from buy-and-hold strategy to daily trading.

While studying the power-law distributions, it is important to remember the comments on spurious scaling laws made by Lux (2001a). There may be a problem with extracting the scaling index from finite (and not sufficiently long) financial data samples if the true distribution has the form

$$f(x) = x^{-\alpha}L(x) \tag{7.14}$$

where $L(x)$ is a slowly varying function that determines the behavior of the distribution in the short-range region. In other words, the power law may be valid only asymptotically. Obviously, the universal scaling exponent $\alpha = -\log[f(x)]/\log(x)$ is as accurate as $L(x)$ is close to a constant.

FRACTALS IN FINANCE

Now, let's examine the basic notions of the fractal theory, as it has become popular in analysis of financial market data.[5] In natural sciences, fractals denote the geometric objects whose defining property is *self-similarity*; that is, they can be constructed by repeating some geometric pattern at a smaller and smaller scale. The original fractal theory and its applications in finance were developed by Mandelbrot (1997). Self-similarity of an object implies its isotropic properties. This is not applicable for time series in which dependent variables (price, return) and independent variable (time) are measured with different units. In this case, the notion of *self-affinity* is used instead.

A self-affine random process $X(t)$ satisfies the following scaling rule:

$$X(ct) = c^H X(t) \tag{7.15}$$

where the parameter H is called the *Hurst exponent*.

Now, let's take a look at the *fractional Brownian motion* $B_H(t)$. This random process satisfies the following condition for all t and T:

$$E[B_H(t + T) - B_H(t)] = 0 \tag{7.16}$$

$$E[B_H(t + T) - B_H(t)]^2 = T^{2H} \tag{7.17}$$

The fractional Brownian motion is reduced to the regular Brownian motion when $H = 1/2$. It can be shown that the correlation between the past average $E[B_H(t) - B_H(t - T)]/T$ and the future average $E[B_H(t + T) - B_H(t)]/T$ equals

$$C = 2^{2H-1} - 1 \tag{7.18}$$

Note that this correlation does not depend on T. If $1/2 < H < 1$, then $C > 0$ and it is said that $B_H(t)$ is a *persistent process*. Namely, if $B_H(t)$ grew (fell) in the past, most probably it will grow (fall) in the immediate future. In other words, persistent processes maintain trend. In the opposite case $(0 < H < 1/2, C < 0)$, the process is named *anti-persistent*. It is also said that anti-persistent processes are mean reverting; that is, if the current process innovation is positive, then the next one will most probably be negative, and vice versa.

The Hurst exponent of a time series sample can be estimated using the *rescaled range (R/S) analysis*. Consider a data set x_i $(i = 1, \ldots N)$ with mean m_N and the standard deviation σ_N. First, the partial sums S_k must be calculated:

$$S_k = \sum_{i=1}^{k} (x_i - m_N), \quad 1 \le k \le N \tag{7.19}$$

The rescaled range equals

$$R/S = [\max(S_k) - \min(S_k)]/\sigma_N, \quad 1 \le k \le N \tag{7.20}$$

The value of R/S is always greater than zero since $\max(S_k) > 0$ and $\min(S_k) < 0$. For a given R/S, the Hurst exponent can be estimated using the relation

$$R/S = (aN)^H \tag{7.21}$$

where a is a constant. Namely, when $\log(R/S)$ and $\log(N)$ are plotted against each other, the slope of the line determines H.

The R/S analysis is superior to many other methods of determining the long-range dependencies and hence can be useful in trading. Obviously, confirming current trend is important for choosing trend-based trading strategies (see Chapter 10). Still, it should be noted that the R/S analysis has a shortcoming: high sensitivity to the short-range memory (Campbell et al. 1997).

A more complex *multifractal theory* has recently drawn the attention of economists. In a nutshell, the multifractal theory describes the objects defined with a generic relationship

$$X(ct) = M(c)X(t) \tag{7.22}$$

A general multifractal process (7.22) is reduced to the fractional Browning motion when

$$M(c) = c^H, \quad H = \text{const} \tag{7.23}$$

Application of the multifractal theory in finance can be found in Lux (2001b) and Calvet and Fisher (2002).

SUMMARY

- EMH states that markets instantly incorporate all new information in the asset prices. EMH is based on the RWH and on the concept of rational investors. Both RWH and rational investor behavior have been questioned in recent empirical research.

- Predictability of returns is determined by the properties of innovations in the time series. The random walk with strict white noise (RW1) is completely unpredictable.

- When innovations have independent but not identical increments, the process (RW2) is a martingale. While the process expectations are not forecastable, higher moments of RW2 may be predictable.

- In RW3 (white noise), innovations are uncorrelated yet higher moments, for example variance, can be dependent and hence forecastable. RW3 exhibits conditional heteroskedasticity, which is well supported with empirical data on volatility. RW3 does not permit linear forecasting of expectations, but non-linear forecasting may be possible.

- Empirical distributions of returns may differ significantly from the Gaussians. Namely, they may have high kurtosis, power-law asymptotes, and asymmetrical shape.

- Fractal theory has proven to be a promising framework for describing empirical properties of returns.

CHAPTER 8

Volatility

This chapter starts with the basic definitions of volatility and practical methods of its forecasting. I go on to provide an overview of the heteroskedastic volatility models, which allow for modeling well-documented volatility clustering. Then, I turn to the realized volatility that has been drawing strong attention in current econometric research. Finally, I outline the application of volatility measures in market risk management.

BASIC NOTIONS

Volatility is a generic notion for measuring price variability. This concept is very important in risk measurement and is widely used in defining trading strategies. Standard deviation of returns is usually used for quantifying volatility. For a data sample with N returns r_i at $i = 1, 2, \ldots, N$ and the average value $\bar{r}$, or *realized volatility* (called also *historical volatility*), is defined as

$$\sigma = \left[\frac{1}{N} \sum_{i=1}^{N} (r_i - \bar{r})^2 \right]^{1/2}$$

Usually, returns are calculated on a homogeneous time grid with spacing Δt. For financial reporting, volatility is often calculated as the annualized percentage, that is, $\sigma(T/\Delta t)^{1/2} 100$ percent, where T is the annual period in units of Δt. For example, in the case of daily returns, $\Delta t = 1$, and $T = 252$ (which is the yearly number of working days). More complicated expressions for calculating volatility on inhomogeneous time grids are offered by Dacorogna et al. (2001).

Usage of all available data points for calculating the historic volatility may turn out to be not such a good idea: In general, volatility may be nonstationary, so that the recent returns reflect current volatility better than the older data. Then, only the last n data points are used for calculating current volatility:

$$\sigma_t = \left(\frac{1}{n} \sum_{i=t-n+1}^{t} r_i - \bar{r} \right)^{1/2} \tag{8.1}$$

Poon & Granger (2003) describe several practical approaches used for forecasting volatility. The simplest forecast in the spirit of the martingale hypothesis is referred to as the *random walk forecast*: $\hat{\sigma}_t = \sigma_{t-1}$. Other popular linear forecasting methods are:

- *Simple moving average* (SMA):

$$\hat{\sigma}_t = (\sigma_t + \sigma_{t-1} + \ldots + \sigma_{t-T})/T \tag{8.2}$$

- *Exponential smoothing average* (often called exponential moving average or EMA):

$$\hat{\sigma}_t = (1 - \beta)\sigma_{t-1} + \beta\hat{\sigma}_{t-1}, 0 < \beta < 1 \tag{8.3}$$

Note that the value of $\hat{\sigma}_1$ in (8.3) is not defined. Often it is assumed that $\hat{\sigma}_t = \sigma_1$; sometimes SMA for a few initial values of σ_t is used instead.

- *Exponentially weighed moving average* (EWMA), which is a truncated version of EMA:

$$\hat{\sigma}_t = \sum_{i=1}^{n} \beta^i \sigma_{t-i} \Big/ \sum_{i=1}^{n} \beta^i \tag{8.4}$$

It can be shown by comparing EMA and EWMA in the limit of high n that the smoothing parameter equals

$$\beta = 2/(n+1) \tag{8.5}$$

EMA with relation (8.5) is widely used in technical analysis (see Chapter 10).

As indicated previously, the concept of *conditional volatility* appears in the random walk RW3, in which variance is uncorrelated but not independent. Forecasting volatility with conditional heteroskedasticity models is widely used in financial research. This topic is addressed in the following section.

Traditionally, estimates of volatility are made using daily returns. However, with the proliferation of publicly available high-frequency market data, there has been a growing interest in the analysis of high-frequency effects on realized volatility (see details below).

The notion of *implied volatility* is based on the Black-Scholes theory of option pricing (see, e.g., Hull 2006). In this theory, volatility is one of parameters that determines the price of an option. Hence, reverse calculation of volatility is possible when the option price is available. There are several volatility indices that are used to gauge market uncertainty. Arguably the most famous index, VIX (the so-called *fear index*) represents an estimate of expected volatility for the next 30 days using prices of several S&P 500 index options.

Finally, there is the notion of *stochastic volatility*. This implies that price dynamics is not a weakly stationary process, and that volatility follows its own stochastic process. The current state of art in this field can be found in Shephard (2005) and Taylor (2005).

CONDITIONAL HETEROSKEDASTICITY

As was indicated in Chapter 7, there may be noticeable autocorrelations in squared asset returns. This means that large returns (either positive or negative) follow large returns. In this case, it is said that the volatility of returns is clustered.[1] The effect of volatility clustering is named also *autoregressive conditional heteroskedasticity* (ARCH). Several models in which past shocks contribute to the current volatility have been developed. Generally, these models are rooted in the ARCH(m) model, where the conditional variance is a weighed sum of m squared lagged returns:

$$\sigma^2(t) = \omega + a_1\varepsilon^2(t-1) + a_2\varepsilon^2(t-2) + \ldots + a_m\varepsilon^2(t-m) \qquad (8.6)$$

In (8.6), $\varepsilon(t) = N(0, \sigma^2(t)), \omega > 0, a_1, \ldots, \geq 0$. Unfortunately, application of the ARCH(m) process to modeling the financial time series often requires polynomials with high order m.

A more efficient model is the *generalized ARCH* (GARCH) process. The GARCH(m, n) process combines the ARCH(m) process with the AR(n) process[2] for lagged variance:

$$\sigma^2(t) = \omega + a_1\varepsilon^2(t-1) + a_2\varepsilon^2(t-2) + \ldots + a_m\varepsilon^2(t-m) + b_1\sigma^2(t-1) \\ + b_2\sigma^2(t-2) + \ldots + b_n\sigma^2(t-n)$$

The simple GARCH(1, 1) model is widely used in financial applications:

$$\sigma^2(t) = \omega + a\varepsilon^2(t-1) + b\sigma^2(t-1) \qquad (8.7)$$

Equation (8.7) can be transformed into

$$\sigma^2(t) = \omega + (a+b)\sigma^2(t-1) + a[\varepsilon^2(t) - \sigma^2(t-1)] \qquad (8.8)$$

The last term in (8.8) being conditioned on information available at time $(t-1)$ has zero mean and can be treated as a shock to volatility. Therefore, the unconditional expectation of volatility for the GARCH(1, 1) model equals

$$E[\sigma^2(t)] = \omega/(1-a-b) \qquad (8.9)$$

This implies that the GARCH(1, 1) process is weakly stationary when $a+b < 1$. The advantage of the stationary GARCH(1, 1) model is that it can be easily used for forecasting. Namely, the conditional expectation of volatility at time $(t+k)$ equals

$$E[\sigma^2(t+k)] = (a+b)^k[\sigma^2(t) - \omega/(1-a-b)] + \omega/(1-a-b) \qquad (8.10)$$

The GARCH(1, 1) model (8.8) can be rewritten as

$$\sigma^2(t) = \omega/(1-b) + a(\varepsilon^2(t-1) + b\varepsilon^2(t-2) + b^2\varepsilon^2(t-3) + \ldots) \qquad (8.11)$$

Equation (8.11) implies that the GARCH(1, 1) model is equivalent to the infinite ARCH model with exponentially weighed coefficients. This explains why the GARCH models are more efficient than the ARCH models.

Several other GARCH models have been derived for addressing specifics of various economic and financial time series. One popular GARCH(1, 1) model, in which $a+b = 1$, is named *integrated* GARCH (IGARCH). This model has the autoregressive unit root; that is, volatility in this case follows the random walk. For IGARCH, the expectation (8.10) is reduced to

$$E[\sigma^2(t+k)] = \sigma^2(t) + k\omega \qquad (8.12)$$

Then, IGARCH can be presented in the form

$$\sigma^2(t) = \omega + (1-\lambda)\varepsilon^2(t-1) + \lambda\sigma^2(t-1) \qquad (8.13)$$

where $0 < \lambda = 1 - b < 1$. It can be shown that in the case with $\omega = 0$, IGARCH has the EWMA form (8.4)

$$\sigma^2(t) = (1 - \lambda) \sum_{i=1}^{n} \lambda^{i-1} \varepsilon^2(t - i) \tag{8.14}$$

The GARCH models discussed so far are symmetric in that the sign of price innovations does not affect the resulting volatility. In practice, however, negative price shocks often influence volatility more than the positive shocks. An example of the GARCH model that describes such an asymmetric effect is the *exponential GARCH* (EGARCH). It has the form

$$\log[\sigma^2(t)] = \omega + \beta \log[\sigma^2(t - 1)] + \lambda z(t - 1) \\ + \gamma(|z(t - 1)| - \sqrt{2/\pi}) \tag{8.15}$$

In (8.15), $z(t) = \varepsilon(t)/\sigma(t)$. Note that $E[z(t)] = \sqrt{2/\pi}$. Therefore, the last term in (8.15) is the mean deviation of $z(t)$. When the EGARCH parameters satisfy the conditions $\gamma > 0$ and $\lambda < 0$, the negative price shocks lead to higher volatility than the positive shocks.

REALIZED VOLATILITY

As was indicated previously, volatility is usually calculated using historical data for daily returns. Such a measure, however, does not reflect intraday price dynamics. Indeed, if opening and closing prices are the same, all possible wild intraday price fluctuations remain unaccounted. Therefore, there has been growing interest in realized volatility (RV), which is calculated using intraday returns.

Consider the Brownian motion $X(t)$ with trend $\mu(t)$ and instantaneous variance $\sigma(t)$

$$dX = \mu(t)dt + \sigma(t)dW \tag{8.16}$$

In (8.16), dW is a standard Brownian process that can be independent from $\sigma(t)$.

The integrated volatility (IV),

$$IV = \int_0^T \sigma^2(t)dt \tag{8.17}$$

is a natural measure for variance of the process (8.16) within the interval $[0, T]$. IV equals the *quadratic variation* (QV) (see Anderson et al. 2000)[3]:

$$QV = \plim_{N \to \infty} \sum_{i=1}^{N-1} (X(t_i) - X(t_{i-1}))^2 \qquad (8.18)$$

for any sequence of partitions $t_0 = 0 < t_1 < \ldots < t_{N-1} = T$ with $\sup(t_i - t_{i-1}) -> 0$ as $N \to \infty$. In practice, empirical data are available on a finite grid with spacing $\tau = T/N$ and RV is estimated as

$$RV = \sum_{i=1}^{N-1} (X(t_i) - X(t_{i-1}))^2 \qquad (8.19)$$

It can be shown that $RV \to QV$ as $N \to \infty$ (see Barndorff-Nielsen & Shephard 2002). Hence, RV can be used as a practical measure of intraday volatility. Obviously, if the process $X(t)$ within the period $[0, T]$ follows random walk with zero trend and stationary σ, RV should not depend on N or τ

$$RV = \sigma^2 T \qquad (8.20)$$

The dependence $RV(\tau)$ is often called the *volatility signature* (Anderson et al. 2000). In the general case with variable instantaneous volatility, one might expect that RV calculated at the smallest time interval available is the most accurate estimate for the integrated volatility. However, the market microstructure effects (such as ask-bid bounce, liquidity gaps, etc.) add additional noise $\varepsilon(t)$, so that the observable variable is $Y(t) = X(t) + \varepsilon(t)$ rather than the process $X(t)$. It is known that the microstructure noise induces autocorrelations in returns. As a result, the observable sum has the following form (Chang et al. 2005):

$$\sum_{i=1}^{N-1} (Y(t_i) - Y(t_{i-1}))^2 = 2NE[\varepsilon^2] + O(N^{0.5}) \qquad (8.21)$$

This implies that RV may not approach integrated volatility at the highest sample frequency. Indeed, typical $RV(\tau)$ have a maximum at the smallest τ available, which decays growing τ to some plateau expected from (8.20). It is reasonable to estimate RV at the highest frequencies where the microstructure effects are not important. Several methods have been offered for reducing the microstructure effects. In a nutshell, they can be partitioned into such smoothing techniques as combining calculations on different timescales (Ait-Sahalia et al. 2005) and moving averages (Hansen et al. 2008). Another promising approach for filtering out high-frequency noise is designing realized kernel estimators (Barndorff-Nielsen et al. 2008).[4]

Recently, it was found that volatility signatures for very busy days in the global FX market do not follow the typical RV pattern (Schmidt 2009b). In particular, RV(τ) may have maxima higher than the values at the lowest sample timescale available. As smoothing techniques did not remedy this problem, Schmidt (2009b) suggested that price micro-trends caused by automated trading might yield unconventional RV patterns. Indeed, detrending of the original time series recovered volatility signatures with a pronounced plateau at higher timescales.

MARKET RISK MEASUREMENT

Several possible causes of financial losses are described in the literature (Jorion 2000). First, there is *market risk* resulting from unexpected changes in the market prices, interest rates, or foreign exchange rates. Other types of financial risk include *liquidity risk*, *credit risk*, and *operational risk*. The liquidity risk being closely related to the market risk is determined by a finite number of assets available at given price. Another form of the liquidity risk (so-called *cash-flow risk*) refers to the inability to pay off debt on time. Credit risk arises when one of the counterparts involved in a financial transaction does not fulfill its obligation. Finally, operational risk is a generic notion for unforeseen human and technical problems, such as fraud, accidents, and so on. Here, I focus exclusively on measurement of market risk.

Historical volatility σ calculated using the daily returns is the most straightforward measure of market risk. In equities, the parameter beta

$$\beta_i = \mathrm{Cov}(R_i, R_p)/\mathrm{Var}(R_p) \qquad (8.22)$$

is also used for measuring risk. In (8.22), $R_i = r_i - r_f$ and $R_p = r_p - r_f$ are the excess returns of a stock i and entire market portfolio, respectively; r_f is a risk-free asset return. The definition of beta stems from the classical *Capital Asset Pricing Model* (CAPM), according to which (e.g., Bodie & Merton 1998)

$$E[r_i] = r_f + \beta_i(E[r_p] - r_f) \qquad (8.23)$$

Usually, the S&P 500 index and three-month U.S. Treasury bills are used as proxies to the market portfolio and the risk-free asset, respectively. Beta defines sensitivity of the risky asset i to the market dynamics. Namely, $\beta_i > 1$ means that the asset is more volatile than the entire market, while $\beta_i < 1$ implies that the asset has lower sensitivity to the market movements. Note that CAPM is valid only if $\beta_i \geq 0$; otherwise, investment in a risky asset does not make sense. Hence, CAPM is not applicable in a bear market.

The classical performance measure that combines excess return with risk into a single parameter is the *Sharpe ratio*

$$SR = (E[r_i] - r_f)/\sigma_i \qquad (8.24)$$

Arguably, the most widely used risk measure is *value at risk* (VaR) (Jorion 2000). VaR refers to the maximum amount of an asset that is likely to be lost over a given period at a specific confidence level α. This implies that the probability density function for *profits and losses* (P/L)[5] is known. It is often assumed that this distribution is normal and hence is determined with mean μ and standard deviation σ. Then,

$$\text{VaR}(\alpha) = -\sigma z_\alpha - \mu \qquad (8.25)$$

The value of z_α can be determined from the cumulative distribution function for the standard normal distribution

$$Pr(Z \leq z_\alpha) = \int_{-\infty}^{z_\alpha} \frac{1}{\sqrt{2\pi}} \exp\left[-z^2/2\right] dz = 1 - \alpha \qquad (8.26)$$

Since $z_\alpha < 0$ at $\alpha > 50\%$, the relation (8.25) implies that positive values of VaR point to losses. In general, VaR(α) grows with the confidence level α. Sufficiently high values of mean (that satisfy the condition $\mu > -\sigma z_\alpha$) move VaR(α) into the negative region, which implies profits for a given α rather than losses. Examples of z_α for frequently used values of $\alpha = 95$ percent and $\alpha = 99$ percent are given in Figure 8.1.

The advantage of VaR is that it is a simple and universal measure that can be used for determining the risks of different financial assets and entire portfolios. Yet, VaR has some drawbacks (Dowd 2002). First, the accuracy of VaR is completely determined by the model assumptions. Also, VaR provides an estimate for losses within a given confidence interval α but says nothing about possible outcome outside this interval. A somewhat paradoxical feature of VaR is that it can discourage investment diversification. Indeed, adding volatile assets to a portfolio may move VaR above the chosen

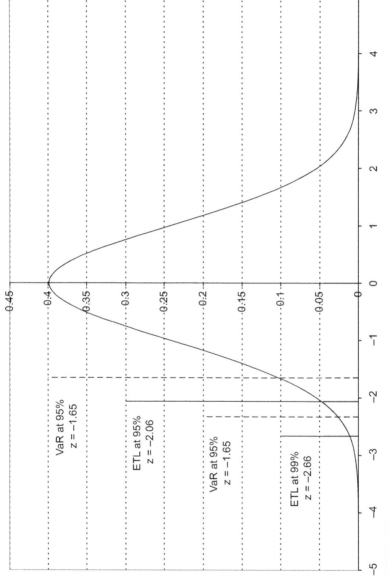

FIGURE 8.1 VaR and ETL for the standard normal probability distribution of P&L.

risk threshold. Another problem with VaR is that it can violate the sub-additivity rule for portfolio risk. According to this rule, the risk measure ρ must satisfy the condition

$$\rho(A + B) \leq \rho(A) + \rho(B) \tag{8.27}$$

Basically, the risk of owning the sum of two assets must not be higher than the sum of the individual risks of these assets. The condition (8.27) yields an upper estimate of combined risk. Violation of the sub-additivity rule may lead to several problems. In particular, it may provoke investors to establish separate accounts for every asset they have. Unfortunately, VaR satisfies (8.27) only if the probability density function for P/L is normal (or, more generally, elliptical) (Dowd 2002).

The generic criterions for the risk measures that satisfy the requirements of the modern risk management include the following conditions:

$$\rho(\lambda A) = \lambda\rho(A), \lambda > 0 \text{ (homogeneity)} \tag{8.28}$$

$$\rho(A) \leq \rho(B), \text{ if } A \leq B \text{ (monotonicity)} \tag{8.29}$$

$$\rho(A + C) = \rho(A) - C \text{ (translation invariance)} \tag{8.30}$$

In (8.30), C represents a risk-free amount. Adding this amount to a risky portfolio should decrease the total risk, since this amount is not subject to potential losses. The risk measures that satisfy the conditions (8.27) to (8.30) are named the *coherent risk measures*. It can be shown that any coherent risk measure represents the maximum of the expected loss on a set of *generalized scenarios*, where every such scenario is determined with its value of loss and probability of occurrence (Artzner 1999). This result yields the coherent risk measure named *the expected tail loss* (ETL):[6]

$$ETL = E[L|L > VaR] \tag{8.31}$$

While VaR is an estimate of loss within a given confidence level, ETL is an estimate of loss within the remaining tail (i.e., an average worst-case scenario). For a given probability distribution of P/L and a given α, ETL is always higher than VaR (see Figure 8.1). As a simple example of calculating VaR and ETL, consider a sample of 100 P/L values. Say the chosen confidence level is 95 percent. Then, VaR is the sixth smallest number in the sample, while ETL is the average of the five smallest numbers within the sample.

SUMMARY

■ Volatility is a measure of price variability. Historical volatility being the standard deviation of past returns is widely used in applications.

■ Implied volatility that is based on the Black-Scholes theory of option pricing is another popular risk measure.

■ Various smoothing techniques (SMA, EMA) are used for volatility forecasts.

■ Autocorrelations in squared returns lead to volatility clustering (autoregressive conditional heteroskedasticity (ARCH)). Several extended ARCH models (GARCH, IGARCH, EGARCH) are used for describing this effect.

■ The concept of realized volatility is used in accounting for intraday price dynamics.

■ Market microstructure effects can notably affect the intraday volatility pattern.

■ Value at risk (VaR) based on historical volatility is a widely used measure of market risk.

■ The expected tail loss (ETL) being a coherent risk measure is an attractive alternative to VaR.

CHAPTER 9

Agent-Based Modeling
of Financial Markets

The main idea behind the agent-based modeling is that agents' actions affect or even determine the environment in which they function. This framework is similar to the methodology of statistical physics where macroscopic properties of a continuum are calculated using averaging over interparticle interactions. Agent-based modeling has become very popular in economics and finance (see the reviews by Hommes 2006, LeBaron 2006, and Chiarella et al. 2009).

The notion of agents is used in many market microstructure models discussed in former chapters (see, e.g., a review by Parlour & Seppi 2008). However, the two fields differ in their assumptions and in the object of research. Namely, the current market microstructure theory is focused primarily on the properties of the order book in equilibrium. It is usually assumed that all investors are rational and returns follow the random walk in the spirit of the EMH (see Chapter 7).[1] On the other hand, the main goal of agent-based market modeling is to describe how the asset price dynamics are affected by trader behavior. The deterministic component in agent-based models implies that financial markets are at least partially predictable, which is difficult to reconcile with the classical financial theory.

The agent-based models are capable of describing several stylized facts observed in financial markets. One of the first agent-based models of financial markets was offered by Beja & Goldman (1980). In this paper, two major trading strategies, value investing and trend following, were considered. Beja & Goldman have shown, in particular, that the system equilibrium may become unstable as the number of trend followers grows. Since then, multiple agent-based models of financial markets have been offered. Some of these models describe, at least qualitatively, market cycles, booms, and crashes (Levy et al. 2000) and reproduce such important empirical properties of returns as power-law scaling in price distributions, and volatility clustering (Lux & Marchesi 2000).

Current agent-based models of financial markets differ in various ways. Schmidt (2004) discerns two major groups of models depending on how price discovery is formulated:

1. In the first group, *the adaptive equilibrium models*, agents adapt their heterogeneous beliefs using past returns. Price in these models is derived from the supply-demand equilibrium (see, e.g., Brock & Hommes 1998; Chiarella & He 2001).
2. In the second group, the assumption of the equilibrium price is not employed. Instead, price is a dynamic variable determined via its empirical relation to excess demand (Lux 1998; Farmer & Joshi 2002). Therefore, this group is called *the non-equilibrium price models*.

In the following two sections, I introduce the main concepts used in deriving both groups of the agent-based models. Then, I describe a parsimonious non-equilibrium price model that is derived exclusively in terms of observable variables (Schmidt 1999). Finally, I offer two examples of how the agent-based models can be used in describing market liquidity effects. Namely, I formulate a model of birth of a two-sided market (Schmidt 2000) and a model of the possible effects of technical trading (Schmidt 2002).

ADAPTIVE EQUILIBRIUM MODELS

To describe this group of models, I follow the work of Chiarella & He (2001). It is assumed in this model that agents can invest either in a risk-free asset (bond) or in a risky asset. The risk-free asset is assumed to have an infinite supply and a constant interest rate. Agents are rational and use some risk aversion criterion for maximizing their wealth. Agents may predict future returns using past returns. The solution to the wealth maximization problem yields the investor demand for the risky asset, which, in turn, determines the asset price in equilibrium. So far this approach remains within the framework of the classical asset pricing theory. The difference, as we shall see later, is in that agents may have heterogeneous beliefs.

Consider the return on a risky asset at time t:

$$\rho_t = (p_t - p_{t-1} + y_t)/p_{t-1} \tag{9.1}$$

where p_t and y_t are the (ex-dividend) price and dividend of one share of the risky asset, respectively. Wealth dynamics of agent i is given by

$$W_{i,t+1} = W_{i,t}[R + \pi_{i,t}(\rho_{t+1} - r)] \tag{9.2}$$

In (9.2), r is the interest rate of the risk-free asset, $R = 1 + r$, and $\pi_{i,t}$ is the proportion of wealth of agent i invested in the risky asset at time t. Every agent is assumed to be a taker of the risky asset at the price that is established in the demand-supply equilibrium. Let's denote $E_{i,t}$ and $V_{i,t}$ as the *beliefs* of trader i at time t regarding the conditional expectation of wealth and the conditional variance of wealth, respectively. It follows from (9.2) that

$$E_{i,t}[W_{i,t+1}] = W_{i,t}[R + \pi_{i,t}(E_{i,t}[\rho_{t+1}] - r)] \tag{9.3}$$

Also, every agent i believes that return of the risky asset is normally distributed with mean $E_{i,t}[\rho_{t+1}]$ and variance $V_{i,t}[\rho_{t+1}]$. The latter is usually assumed to be constant ($V_{i,t}[\rho_{t+1}] = \sigma^2$). Agents choose such a proportion $\pi_{i,t}$ of their wealth to invest in the risky asset that maximizes the utility function U:

$$\max_{\pi_{i,t}} \{E_{i,t}[U(W_{i,t+1})]\} \tag{9.4}$$

The CARA and CRRA functions are generally used in the adaptive equilibrium models (see Chapter 3). In the former case,

$$U(W_{i,t+1}) = E_{i,t}[W_{i,t+1}] - \frac{a}{2} V_{i,t}[W_{i,t+1}] \tag{9.5}$$

where a is the risk aversion constant. For the constant conditional variance $V_{i,t} = \sigma^2$, the CARA function yields the following demand:

$$\pi_{i,t} = \frac{E_{i,t}[\rho_{t+1}] - r}{a\sigma^2} \tag{9.6}$$

The number of shares of the risky asset that corresponds to demand $\pi_{i,t}$ equals

$$N_{i,t} = \pi_{i,t} W_{i,t}/p_t \tag{9.7}$$

Since the total number of shares is assumed to be fixed ($\sum_i N_{i,t} = N = $ const), the market-clearing price equals

$$p_t = \frac{1}{N} \sum_i \pi_{i,t} W_{i,t} \tag{9.8}$$

The concept of heterogeneous beliefs can be presented in the following generic form:

$$E_{i,t}[\rho_{t+1}] = f_i(\rho_t, \ldots, \rho_{t-Li}) \qquad (9.9)$$

The deterministic function f_i in (9.9) must be specified for describing various trading strategies. It depends on past returns with lags up to L_i and may vary for different agents. In many models, agent type is represented by a single trading strategy. First, there are *fundamentalists* who use analysis of the risky asset fundamentals for forecasting its risk premium. In simple models, the risk premium $\delta_F > 0$ is a constant:

$$E_{F,t}[\rho_{t+1}] = r + \delta_F \qquad (9.10)$$

In the general case, risk premium can be a function of time and/or variance.

Another major strategy is momentum trading (see Chapter 10). Traders who use it are often called *chartists*. Momentum traders use the history of past returns for making their forecasts. In the general (yet linear) case, their strategy can be described as

$$E_{M,t}[\rho_{t+1}] = r + \delta_M + \sum_{k=1}^{L} a_k \rho_{t-k} \qquad (9.11)$$

In (9.11), $\delta_M > 0$ is a constant (value) component of the momentum risk premium and $a_k > 0$ are the weights of past returns ρ_{t-k}.

Also, some agents may be *contrarians* who expect market reversal and hence act in the opposite way to chartists. The contrarian strategy is formally similar to the momentum strategy (9.11) but has negative weights a_k.

Agents in the adaptive equilibrium models are able to analyze the performance of different strategies and choose the most efficient one. Obviously, these strategies have limited accuracy due to the linear form of forecast and finite number of lags L. Sometimes, such a constrained adaptability is called *bounded rationality*.

NON-EQUILIBRIUM PRICE MODELS

The basic assumption of instant market clearing that is made in the adaptive equilibrium models is a serious simplification. In fact, the number of shares involved in trading varies with time, and asset prices may deviate from their equilibrium (fair) values for a long time. A reasonable alternative to instant market clearing is a model of price formation that is based on the empirical relation between price change and excess demand (Beja & Goldman 1980).

Here, I outline an elaborate model offered by Lux (1998). In this model, two groups of agents, chartists, and fundamentalists are considered. Agents can compare the efficiency of different trading strategies and switch from one strategy to another. Therefore, the numbers of chartists, $n_c(t)$, and fundamentalists, $n_f(t)$, vary with time while the total number of agents in the market N is assumed constant. The chartist group, in turn, is subdivided into optimistic (bullish) and pessimistic (bearish) traders with the numbers $n_+(t)$ and $n_-(t)$, respectively:

$$n_c(t) + n_f(t) = N, n_+(t) + n_-(t) = n_c(t) \qquad (9.12)$$

Lux (1998) considers several patterns of the trader behavior. First, chartists are influenced by the peer opinion (so-called *mimetic contagion*). Second, traders switch strategies while seeking optimal performance. Finally, traders may exit and reenter markets. For example, the bullish chartist dynamics is formalized in the following way:

$$\frac{dn_+}{dt} = (n_- p_{+-} - n_+ p_{-+})(1 - n_f/N) + \text{mimetic contagion}$$

$$n_f n_+ (p_{+f} - p_{f+})/N + \text{changes of strategy} \qquad (9.13)$$

$$(b - a)n_+ \text{ market entry and exit}$$

Here, p_α denotes the probability of transition from group β to group α, and the probabilities of market entry and exit satisfy the relation $bn_c = aN$. The bearish chartist dynamics, $\dfrac{dn_-}{dt}$, are described similarly to (9.13). Conversion of the bullish chartists into the bearish chartists is given by the following relation:

$$p_{+-} = 1/p_{-+} = \nu_1 \exp(-U_1), \ U_1 = \alpha_1(n_+ - n_-)/n_c + (\alpha_2/\nu_1)\frac{dP}{dt} \quad (9.14)$$

where ν_1, α_1, and α_2 are the model parameters, P is price. Conversion of fundamentalists into bullish chartists and back is described with the relations

$$p_{+f} = 1/p_{f+} = \nu_2 \exp(-U_{21}),$$

$$U_{21} = \alpha_3\left(\left(r + \nu_2^{-1}\frac{dP}{dt}\right)\Big/ P - R - s|(P_f - P)/P|\right) \qquad (9.15)$$

In (9.15), v_2 and α_3 are the model parameters, r is the stock dividend, R is the average revenue of economy, s is a discounting factor $0 < s < 1$, and P_f is the fundamental price of the risky asset assumed to be an input parameter. Similar relations are used to describe the conversion of fundamentalists into bearish chartists, p_{-f}.

As was pointed out earlier, price dynamics in the non-equilibrium price models are described with an empirical relation between the price change and the excess demand[2]

$$\frac{dP}{dt} = \beta D \qquad (9.16)$$

In the Lux's model, excess demand equals

$$D = t_c(n_+ - n_-) + \gamma n_f(P_f - P) \qquad (9.17)$$

The first and second terms in the right-hand side of (9.17) describe excess demands of chartists and fundamentalists, respectively; β, t_c, and γ are parameters.

The Lux model (1998) has rich dynamic properties. Depending on input parameters, its solutions may include stable equilibrium, periodic patterns, and chaotic attractors. Lux & Marchesi (2000) extended this model for describing the arrival of news, which affects the fundamental price. Namely, the news arrival process was modeled with the Gaussian random variable $\varepsilon(t)$ so that

$$\ln P_f(t) - \ln P_f(t-1) = \varepsilon(t) \qquad (9.18)$$

The resulting model exhibits such stylized market facts as power-law scaling in the price distribution and volatility clustering.

THE OBSERVABLE-VARIABLES MODEL

One may notice that there is a degree of arbitrariness in agent-based modeling as the number of different agent types and their behavior can vary upon the modeler's imagination. This is not that innocuous, as some interesting model properties (e.g., chaos) can be an artifact of the model's complexity and irrelevant to real market dynamics (see the discussion in Schmidt 2004).

Schmidt (1999) has offered a parsimonious approach to choosing variables in the agent-based modeling of financial markets. Namely, Schmidt suggested that only observable variables should be used in deriving the agent-based models. Schmidt defines observable variables in finance as those that can be retrieved or calculated from the records of market events (such as order submissions and cancellations, transactions, etc.). Numbers of agents of different types generally are not observable. Indeed, one cannot discern *chartists* and *fundamentalists* in such a typical situation when the price is growing being lower than the fundamental one. In this case, all traders (let alone contrarians) would rather buy than sell. Only price and the total numbers of buyers and sellers are always observable. Whether a trader becomes a buyer or seller can be defined by mixing different behavior patterns in the trader decision-making rules.

A simple non-equilibrium price model derived along these lines has a constant number of traders, N, including buyers $N_+(t)$ and sellers $N_-(t)$:

$$N_+(t) + N_-(t) = N \tag{9.19}$$

The scaled numbers of buyers, $n_+(t) = N_+(t)/N$, and sellers, $n_-(t) = N_-(t)/N$, are described with the dynamics equations:

$$\frac{dn_+}{dt} = v_{+-}n_- - v_{-+}n_+ \tag{9.20}$$

$$\frac{dn_-}{dt} = v_{-+}n_+ - v_{+-}n_- \tag{9.21}$$

The factors v_{+-} and v_{-+} characterize the probabilities for transfer from seller to buyer and back, respectively:

$$v_{+-} = 1/v_{-+} = v\exp(U), \quad U = \alpha p^{-1}\frac{dp}{dt} + \beta(1-p) \tag{9.22}$$

Price $p(t)$ is given in units of its fundamental value. The first term in the utility function U characterizes the *chartist* behavior, while the second term describes the *fundamentalist* pattern. The factor v has the sense of the frequency of transitions between the seller and buyer behavior. Since $n_+(t) = 1-n_-(t)$, the system (9.20)–(9.22) is reduced to the equation

$$\frac{dn_+}{dt} = v_{+-}(1 - n_+) - v_{-+}n_+ \tag{9.23}$$

The price formation equation is assumed to have the following form:

$$\frac{dp}{dt} = \gamma D \tag{9.24}$$

In (9.24), the excess demand, D, is proportional to the excess number of buyers.

$$D = \delta(n_+ - n_-) = \delta(2n_+ - 1) \qquad (9.25)$$

The model described above is defined with two observable variables: $n_+(t)$ and $p(t)$. In equilibrium, the number of buyers and sellers are equal, and price equals the fundamental values:

$$n_+ = n_- = 0.5, \quad p = 1 \qquad (9.26)$$

The necessary stability condition for this model is

$$\theta = \alpha\delta\gamma\nu \leq 1 + \varepsilon \qquad (9.27)$$

In the continuous limit, $\varepsilon = 0$. However, the numerical solution on a finite-difference grid leads to some computational noise accounted with a finite ε. Violation of the condition (9.27) leads to system instability, which can be interpreted as a market crash.

When the condition (9.27) is satisfied, weak perturbations to the equilibrium values quickly decay (see an example in Figure 9.1).

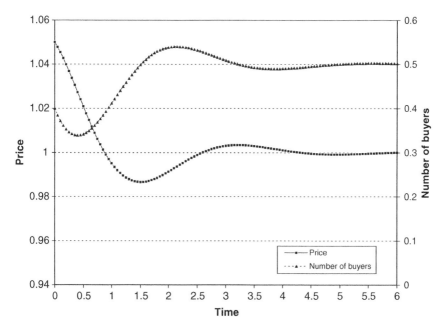

FIGURE 9.1 Decay of perturbations to equilibrium state in the observable-variables model with $\alpha = 1$, $\beta = 10$, $\gamma = 0.2$, and $\delta = 1$.

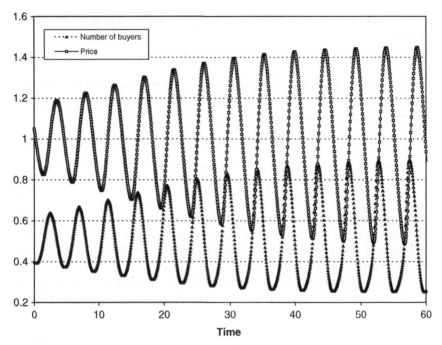

FIGURE 9.2   Limit cycle in the observable-variables model with $\alpha = 1.05$, $\beta = 1$, $\gamma = 1$, and $\delta = 1$.

Lower values of α and γ suppress oscillations of price and facilitate relaxation of the initial perturbations. On the other hand, raising α, which controls the strength of the chartist behavior, increases price volatility.

When the value of θ is close to violation of the condition (9.27), price oscillations do not decay; rather, they exhibit the so-called limit cycle (see details in Schmidt 2004). An example of such behavior is shown in Figure 9.2. Further growth of θ leads to ever-growing oscillation amplitudes, which may be interpreted as a market crash.

MODELING EFFICIENCY OF TECHNICAL TRADING

Various technical strategies and opinions on their efficiency will be reviewed in Chapter 10. Here, I offer a simple application of the observable-variables model that shows why technical trading may be sometimes successful (Schmidt 2002).

Consider a system with the number of traders N that consists of *regular* traders N_R and *technical* traders N_T. The regular traders are divided into buyers, $N_+(t)$, and sellers, $N_-(t)$:

$$N_T + N_R = N = \text{const}, N_+ + N_- = N_R = \text{const} \qquad (9.28)$$

The relative numbers of regular traders, $n_+(t) = N_+(t)/N$ and $n_-(t) = N_-(t)/N$, and price discovery are described with the equations (9.20) through (9.24). The excess demand in this model includes also the technical traders.

$$D = \delta(n_+ - n_- + Fn_T) \qquad (9.29)$$

Here, $n_T = N_T/N$, and the function F is defined by the technical trader strategy. Schmidt (2002) considers a simple technical rule: *buying on dips— selling on tops*. In other words, buying at the moment when the price starts rising and selling when the price starts falling.

$$
\begin{aligned}
F(k) &= 1, \quad \text{when} \quad p(k) > p(k-1) \quad \text{and} \quad p(k-1) < p(k-2) \\
&= -1, \quad \text{when} \quad p(k) < p(k-1) \quad \text{and} \quad p(k-1) > p(k-2) \qquad (9.30) \\
&= 0, \quad \text{otherwise}
\end{aligned}
$$

Schmidt (2002) shows that inclusion of the technical traders into the model strengthens price oscillations and increases return on their strategy. Indeed, if technical traders decide that price is going to fall, they sell and thus decrease the excess demand. Due to selling pressure, the price does fall, and the chartist component in regular traders' behavior motivates them to sell, too. This suppresses price further until the fundamentalist component in regular traders' behavior becomes overwhelming. The opposite effect occurs if technical traders decide that it is time to buy: They increase demand and the price starts to grow until it notably exceeds its fundamental value. Then, regular traders start selling. In other words, if the concerted actions of technical traders produce a noticeable market impact, they can provoke the regular traders to amplify this trend. This moves price in the direction favorable to the technical strategy.

MODELING THE BIRTH OF A TWO-SIDED MARKET

Founders of a new market face many challenges. In particular, they must attract buyers and sellers immediately after opening the market. For example, founders of a new electronic market must overcome inertia of their potential customers who are used to trade via voice brokers.

Right after opening a new market, the order book is empty. A casual buyer may submit an order. But if he does not see sellers for some time, he cancels his order and places it elsewhere. Then a seller may show up—and leave with the same outcome. In short, trading cannot start until a sufficient number of traders is present on both sides of the market. Schmidt (2000) offered a model describing the birth of a two-sided market:

$$\frac{dn_+}{dt} = v_{+-}n_- - v_{-+}n_+ + \sum R_{+i} + \rho_+ \qquad (9.31)$$

$$\frac{dn_-}{dt} = v_{-+}n_+ - v_{+-}n_- + \sum R_{-i} + \rho_- \qquad (9.32)$$

The functions $R_{\pm i}$ ($i = 1, 2, \ldots, M$) and $\rho_\pm$ are the deterministic and stochastic rates of entering and exiting the market, respectively. Three deterministic effects defining the total number of traders are considered.

First, some traders stop trading immediately after completing a trade since they have limited resources and/or need some time for making new decisions:

$$R_{+1} = R_{-1} = -bn_+n_-, \quad b > 0 \qquad (9.33)$$

Second, some traders currently present in the market will enter the market again and possibly will bring in some newcomers (mimetic contagion). Therefore, the inflow of traders is proportional to the number of traders present in the market:

$$R_{+2} = R_{-2} = a(n_+ + n_-), \quad a > 0 \qquad (9.34)$$

Third, some unsatisfied traders leave the market. Namely, it is assumed that those traders who are not able to find the trading counterparts within some time exit the market:

$$\begin{aligned} R_{+3} &= -c(n_+ - n_-) \quad \text{if} \quad n_+ > n_- \\ &= 0, \quad \text{if} \quad n_+ \leq n_- \end{aligned} \qquad (9.35)$$

$$\begin{aligned} R_{-3} &= -c(n_- - n_+) \quad \text{if} \quad n_- > n_+ \\ &= 0, \quad \text{if} \quad n_- \leq n_+ \end{aligned} \qquad (9.36)$$

The parameter $c > 0$ in (9.35) and (9.36) is the *impatience* factor. To simplify the model, Schmidt (2000) neglected stochastic rates $\rho_\pm$ and price variation. Hence, $v_{+-} = v_{-+} = 0$.

If the initial state is specified as

$$n_+(0) - n_-(0) = \delta > 0 \qquad (9.37)$$

then equations (9.31) and (9.32) can be transformed into the following:

$$\frac{dn_+}{dt} = a(n_+ + n_-) - bn_+n_- - c(n_+ - n_-) \qquad (9.38)$$

$$\frac{dn_-}{dt} = a(n_+ + n_-) - bn_+n_- \qquad (9.39)$$

It follows from (9.38) and (9.39) that the equation for the total number of traders $n = n_+ + n_-$ has the form

$$\frac{dn}{dt} = 2an - 0.5bn^2 + 0.5b\,\delta^2\exp(-2ct) - c\delta\exp(-ct) \qquad (9.40)$$

Equation (9.40) has the following asymptotic stationary solution at $t \to \infty$:

$$n_0 = 4a/b \qquad (9.41)$$

The continuous model considered here has a drawback in that the total number of traders, n, may fall very low at intermediate times. Yet, n still reaches the asymptotic value (9.41). However, $n < 1$ does not make sense. Therefore, the discrete analog of equations (9.31) and (9.32), along with a constraint on the minimal value of $n_\pm(t)$, may be preferable (see Schmidt 2000, for details).

$$n_\pm(t) = 0 \quad \text{if} \quad n_\pm(t) < n_{\min} \qquad (9.42)$$

In real life, the number of traders coming and leaving the market has a stochastic component. Hence, it is natural to assume that the terms ρ_+ and ρ_- in equations (9.31) and (9.32) are independent Gaussians with the zero mean and dispersion σ: $\rho_\pm = dN_\pm(0, \sigma)$. Examples of discrete simulations in Figure 9.3 demonstrate how a high level of trader impatience can delay the birth of a two-sided market.

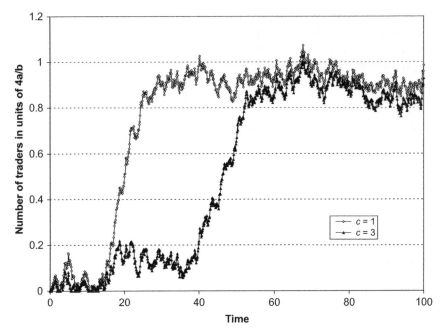

FIGURE 9.3 Simulations of the birth of a two-sided market for $a = 0.25$, $b = 1$, $d = 0.1$, $n_{min} = 0$, and $\sigma = 1$.

SUMMARY

■ Agent-based modeling in finance is a framework in which agents' trading decisions depend on price and their trading, in turn, affects price.

■ The two main agent types are fundamentalists and momentum traders (chartists). Fundamentalists buy (sell) when price is lower (higher) than the fundamental asset value. Chartists buy (sell) when price grows (falls).

■ Two types of agent-based models can be discerned depending on the formulation of price discovery: the adaptive equilibrium models and non-equilibrium price models.

■ In the adaptive equilibrium models, price is determined by supply-demand equilibrium. In these models, agents are rational and are focused on maximizing their wealth by choosing various strategies based on predictions of future price. Agents' heterogeneous beliefs are the major specific that discerns this framework from the classical asset pricing theory.

■ In the non-equilibrium price models, price dynamics is determined by an empirical dependence on excess demand. Agents in these models can compare the efficiency of different trading strategies and switch from one strategy to another.

■ Some ambiguities in formulating the agent-based models may be addressed by deriving the models exclusively in terms of observable variables.

■ Agent-based models are capable of reproducing such empirical findings as market crashes, power-law scaling in price distributions, and volatility clustering.

PART

Three

Trading Strategies

CHAPTER 10

Technical Trading Strategies

Technical analysis (TA) is a field comprising various methods for forecasting the future direction of price. These methods are generally based on analysis of past prices but may also rely on other market data, such as trading volume and volatility (see e.g., Kaufman 2005).[1] As was indicated in Chapter 7, the very premise of TA is in conflict even with the weakest form of the efficient market hypothesis. Therefore, TA is discarded by some influential economists. Yet, TA continues to enjoy popularity not only among practitioners but also within a distinctive part of the academic community (see Park & Irwin 2007 and Menkhoff & Taylor 2007, for recent reviews). What is the reason for "obstinate passion" to TA (as Menkhoff & Taylor put it)?[2] One explanation was offered by Lo et al. (2000): TA (sometimes referred as *charting*) fits very well into the visual mode of human cognition. As a result, TA became a very popular tool for pattern recognition prior to the pervasive electronic computing era. Obviously, TA would not have survived if there were no records of success. There have been a number of reports demonstrating that while some TA strategies could be profitable in the past, their performance has been deteriorated in recent years (see, e.g., Kerstner 2003, Aronson 2006, and Neely et al. 2009). In a nutshell, simple TA strategies were profitable in equities and in FX until the 1980s and 1990s, respectively. This conclusion per se does not imply the death sentence to TA. The very assumption that one particular trading strategy will be profitable for years seems to be overly optimistic. It is hard to imagine a practitioner who keeps putting money into a strategy that has become unprofitable after a certain (and not very long) period of time. Fortunately (for believers), TA offers uncountable opportunities for modifying trading strategies, and hence, there is always a chance for success. As we shall see, TA strategies are determined by several input parameters and there are no hard rules for determining them. These parameters may be non-stationary, which is rarely explored in the literature.[3] Another possible venue for increasing the profitability of TA is diversification across trading strategies and/or instruments. Timmerman (2006) concludes that simple forecasting schemes, such as equal-weighting of various strategies, are difficult to beat. For example, one popular approach is using multiple time frames (Kaufman 2005). Several trading strategies can be used simultaneously for the same asset. Hsu & Kuan (2005) have shown that trading strategies based on several simple technical rules can be profitable even if the standalone rules do not make money. Namely, Hsu & Kuan (2005) considered three strategies along with several technical rules including but not limited to moving averages and channel break-outs. One of these strategies, the learning strategy, is based on the periodic switching of investments to the best performing rule within a given class of rules. Another one, the voting strategy, assigns one vote to each rule within a given rule class. There are two choices: long positions and short positions. If most votes point at, say, a long position, this position is initiated. Finally, the position-changing strategy expands the voting strategy to fractional long/short allocation according to the ratio of long/short votes.

A promising approach has been offered by Okunev & White (2002). They tested three TA strategies for a portfolio consisting of up to seven currency pairs and found that this diversified portfolio outperformed returns for single currency pairs. Schulmeister (2009) performed simultaneous back-testing of 2,265 trading strategies for EUR/USD daily rates. This produced positive average yearly returns in 1999 through 2006.

Another option is to diversify portfolio assets rather than trading strategies. Wilcox and Crittenden (2005) applied long trend strategies to more than 24,000 securities for a period spanning 22 years, which significantly outperformed the buy-and-hold strategy for the S&P 500. Obviously, diversification has practical limits in partitioning a given investment capital among multiple strategies/instruments. Also, if transaction costs depend on the number of trades, maintaining a highly diversified dynamic portfolio may become prohibitively expensive. Still, these examples demonstrate that diversification may provide rich opportunities for implementing profitable TA strategies.

Recently, Neely et al. (2010) suggested mixing the trend strategies with an economic-variable model. This, too, may be a promising approach as the fundamental values improve in the end of recessions when prices are still depressed. On the other hand, the trend models are more sensitive to the beginning of recessions since the economic variables are generally updated quarterly. Hence, TA may be useful not only per se but also in combination with the fundamental value analysis.

The classical TA operates with daily market closing prices. Closing (and opening) of equity markets has an obvious meaning. However, it is less definitive in FX that operates around the clock five days a week. With pro-liferation of day trading in recent years, numerous attempts to apply classi-cal TA strategies to intraday price dynamics have been made.[4]

A generic notion of a *bar* is used in TA. Bar is usually defined with the time interval (e.g., daily bar or 10-minute bar). Sometimes equal-volume bars are used. Their size is determined with some trading volume typical for a given asset. Equal-volume bars have a shorter time duration within active trading hours (e.g., right after market opening) and a longer time duration during passive hours (e.g., around lunch time). Other major bar parameters include opening price, closing price, minimum price, and maximum price. In some strategies, such bar parameters as average price or volume-weighed average price may be used. Unless specified otherwise, we shall imply bar closing price while using the term price.

One common rule in the formulation of any trading strategies is to avoid *look-ahead bias*.[5] Namely, trading rules should be expressed only in terms of lagged values. Indeed, while back-testing of trading strategies can be expanded into models defined in terms of present values, it is impossible to implement. In the following sections, I provide an overview of the pri-mary strategies used in TA: trend strategies, momentum and oscillator strat-egies, as well as more complex patterns.

TREND STRATEGIES

Trend strategies can be defined with the famous slogan, *Buy low, sell high*. The question is how low is *low* and how high is *high*? In other words, defin-ing the market entry and market exit points remain a real challenge.

Filter Rules

According to the simple *filter rule* (sometimes dubbed as the *naive trading rule*), one should buy/sell at the next opening if the last closing price P_k is higher/lower than the former closing price P_{k-1} by a certain threshold $\delta > 0$ (usually chosen as higher than the asset daily volatility):

$$\text{Buy: } P_k/P_{k-1} > 1 + \delta$$
$$\text{Sell: } P_k/P_{k-1} < 1 - \delta \tag{10.1}$$

The naïve strategy is sometimes used as a benchmark for comparative testing of other trading strategies (Dunis et al. 2003). In a more generic approach, the highest/lowest closing prices for a given past period of length n are used for the trading decision (Taylor 2005). Namely,

$$\text{Buy}: P_k/M_k > 1 + \delta$$
$$\text{Sell}: P_k/m_k < 1 - \delta \tag{10.2}$$

where

$$M_k = \max(P_{k-1}, \ldots, P_{k-n}), \quad m_k = \min(P_{k-1}, \ldots, P_{k-n}) \tag{10.3}$$

Recent studies show that several filter rules (in terms of δ and s) might be profitable in FX (but not in equities) until the 1980s, but this is not the case anymore, particularly if realistic transaction costs are accounted for (Park & Irwin 2007; Menkhoff & Taylor 2007). Still, filter rules offer great flexibility in formulating new strategies that may be worthy of further exploration. For example, Cooper (1999) suggested using prices *and* trading volumes at two (weekly) lagged periods for deriving buy/sell signals and demonstrated that increasing-volume stocks have weaker reversals (i.e., more pronounced trends), which leads to returns higher than those obtained from the buy-and-hold strategy.

Moving-Average Rules

Adding lagged periods in determining trends brings us to the moving averages techniques, which were already used in forecasting volatility (see Chapter 7). In the moving-average strategy, two moving averages (the short one and the long one) are compared to make a trading decision.

Let's denote SMA over n lagged periods at time t with $\text{sma}(P_t, n)$:

$$\text{sma}(P_t, n) = (P_{t-1} + P_{t-2} + \ldots + P_{t-n})/n \tag{10.4}$$

and consider the relative difference between the short-term (fast) $\text{sma}(P_t, S)$ and the long-term (slow) $\text{sma}(P_t, L)$:

$$r_t = [\text{sma}(P_t, S) - \text{sma}(P_t, L)]/\text{sma}(P_t, L) \tag{10.5}$$

The moving-average strategy generates the following trading signals:

$$\text{Buy}: r_t > \delta$$
$$\text{Sell}: r_t < -\delta \tag{10.6}$$

Simple moving averages may be replaced with the exponential moving average (EMA)

$$\text{ema}(P_t, \beta) = \beta P_t + (1 - \beta)^* \text{ema}(P_{t-1}, \beta) \tag{10.7}$$

As was indicated in Chapter 7, the smoothing coefficient β has the following relation to the number of lagged periods:

$$\beta = 2/(n+1) \tag{10.8}$$

The value of P_0 is usually chosen to be equal to the $\text{sma}(P_t, n)$ for a short initial period. Typical ratios L/S in the known literature vary in the range 4 ÷ 20. An example of the moving-average strategy (and the challenges it faces) is given for SPY in Figure 10.1. While the buy signal in April 2009 can be noticed in a rather wide range of δ (i.e., there is a pronounced trend), low δ can generate a *Sell* signal in February 2010, which probably could be ignored.

Several adaptive moving-average strategies have been proposed by practitioners to account for the potentially non-stationary nature of price dynamics (Kaufman 2005). The idea here is to treat lags S and L as variables that depend on price variations. An example of such an approach is Chande's Variable Index Dynamic Average (VIDYA), in which exponential smoothing depends on price volatility:

$$\text{VIDYA}_t = \beta k P_t + (1 - \beta k)^* \text{VIDYA}_{t-1} \tag{10.9}$$

In (10.9), β is the smoothing coefficient and $k = stdev(P_t, S)/stdev(P_t, L)$ is the relative volatility calculated for S recent lags and a longer past period L.

Channel Breakouts

A channel (or band) is an area that surrounds a trend line within which price movement does not indicate formation of a new trend. The upper and bottom walls of channels have a sense of *resistance* and *support*. Trading strategies based on the channel breakouts are popular among practitioners and in academy (Park & Irwin 2007). One way to formulate the trading rules with channel breakouts is as follows (Taylor 2005). If a trader has long position at time t, the sell signal is generated when

$$P_t < (1 - B)m_{t-1} \tag{10.10}$$

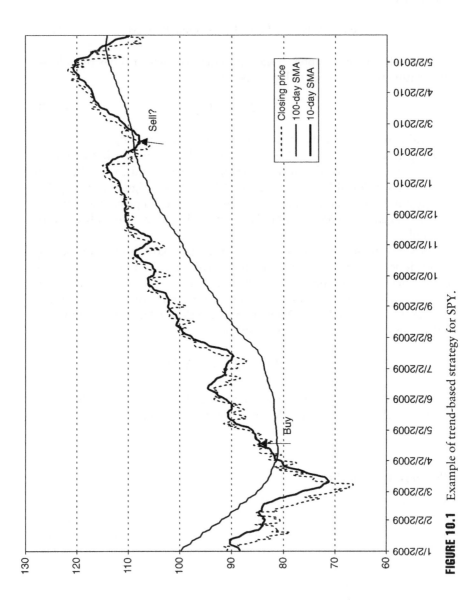

FIGURE 10.1 Example of trend-based strategy for SPY.

Here, B is the channel bandwidth and the values of m_t and M_t are defined in (10.3). If a trader has a short position at time t, a buy signal is generated when

$$P_t > (1 + B)M_{t-1} \qquad (10.11)$$

Finally, if a trader is neutral at time t, the conditions (10.10) and (10.11) are signals for acquiring short and long positions, respectively. A more risky strategy may use a buy signal when

$$P_t > (1 + B)m_{t-1} \qquad (10.12)$$

and a sell signal when

$$P_t < (1 - B)M_{t-1} \qquad (10.13)$$

In the *Bollinger bands*, which are popular among practitioners, the trend line is defined with the price SMA (or EMA), and the bandwidth is determined by the asset volatility

$$B_t = k^* \, stdev(P_t, L) \qquad (10.14)$$

The parameters k and L in (10.14) are often chosen to be equal to 2 and 20, respectively.

MOMENTUM AND OSCILLATOR STRATEGIES

In TA, the term *momentum* is used for describing the rate of price change. In particular, K-day momentum at day t equals

$$M_t = P_t - P_{t-K} \qquad (10.15)$$

Momentum smoothes price and can be used either for generating trading signals or as a trend indicator. For example, a simple momentum rule may be a buy/sell signal when momentum switches from a negative/positive value to a positive/negative one.

Sometimes, momentum is referred to as the difference between current price and its moving average (e.g., EMA).

$$m_t = P_t - ema(P_t, K), \qquad (10.16)$$

Momentum (10.16) leads to further price smoothing (see Figure 10.2).

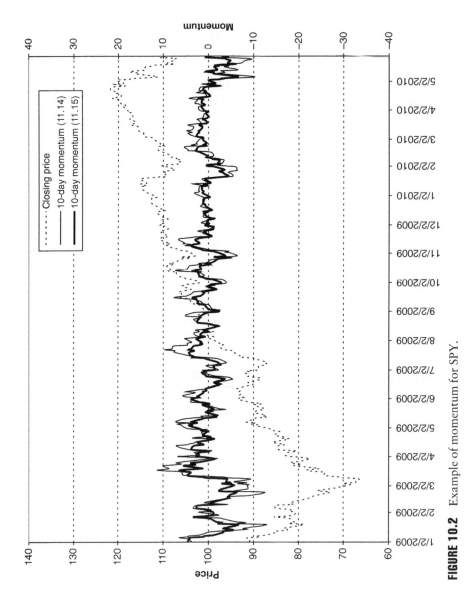

FIGURE 10.2 Example of momentum for SPY.

Momentum can also be used as an indicator of trend fading. Indeed, momentum approaching zero after a big price move may point toward possible market reversal.

Moving Average Convergence/Divergence (*MACD*) is a momentum indicator widely popular among practitioners. In MACD, momentum is calculated as the difference between a fast EMA and a slow EMA. Typical fast and slow periods are 12 and 26 days, respectively. This difference

$$\text{MACD}_t = \text{ema}(P_t, 12) - \text{ema}(P_t, 26) \qquad (10.17)$$

is called the MACD *line*. Its exponential smoothing (performed usually over nine days) is called the *signal line*:

$$signal\_line = \text{ema}(\text{MACD}_t, 9) \qquad (10.18)$$

Since the signal line evolves slower than the MACD line, their crossovers can be interpreted as trading signals. Namely, buying opportunity appears when the MACD line crosses from below to above the signal line. On the other hand, crossing the signal line by the MACD line from above can be interpreted as a selling signal.

The difference between the MACD and signal lines in the form of a histogram often accompanies the MACD charts (see Figure 10.3). This difference fluctuates around zero and may be perceived as an *oscillator*, another pattern widely used in TA.

One of the most popular oscillators used for indicating oversold and overbought positions is the *relative strength index* (*RSI*). This oscillator is determined with directional price moves during a given time period N (usually $N = 14$ days).

$$\text{RSI}_N = 100^*RS/(1 + RS), \quad RS = n_{\text{up}}/n_{\text{down}} \qquad (10.19)$$

In (10.19), n_{up} and n_{down} are the numbers of upward moves and downward moves of closing price, respectively. Usually, these numbers are exponentially smoothed[6]

$$n_{\text{up}}(t) = (1 - \beta)^* n_{\text{up}}(t - 1) + \beta U(t), \qquad (10.20)$$

$$n_{\text{down}}(t) = (1 - \beta)^* n_{\text{down}}(t - 1) + \beta D(t)$$

where

$$
\begin{aligned}
U(t) &= 1, P_t > P_{t-1}; \quad U(t) = 0, \quad P_t \le P_{t-1} \\
D(t) &= 1, P_t < P_{t-1}; \quad D(t) = 0, \quad P_t \ge P_{t-1}
\end{aligned}
\qquad (10.21)
$$

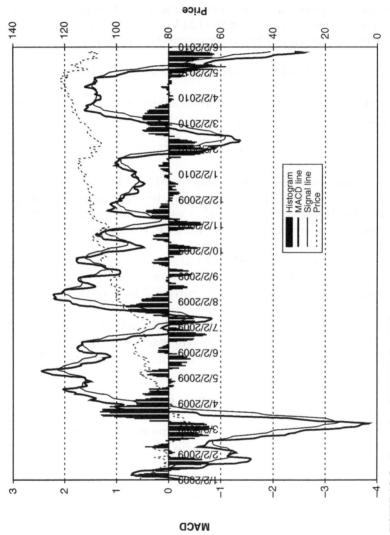

FIGURE 10.3 Example of MACD for SPY.

Typical RSI values for the overbought/oversold markets are 70/30. An example of RSI for SPY is given in Figure 10.4. For some volatile assets, RSI reaches the overbought/oversold conditions quite frequently. Then, the RSI spread may be widened to 80/20 (Kaufman 2005).

COMPLEX GEOMETRIC PATTERNS

Trends and oscillators have relatively simple visual forms and straightforward definition. However, some other popular TA patterns, while being easily recognizable with a human eye, represent a challenge for quantitative description. These include *head-and-shoulder (HaS)*, inverse HaS, broadening tops and bottoms, triangle tops and bottoms, double tops and bottoms, and others (Edwards & Magee 2001; Kaufman 2005). The main challenge in finding complex geometric patterns in a time series is filtering out noise that may produce false leads. The smoothing technique with kernel regression was successfully used for analysis of TA strategies by Lo et al. (2000) in equities and by Omrane & Oppens (2004) in FX.

Here, we describe HaS as an example. Visually, HaS is determined with five price extremes: three maxima that refer to two shoulders surrounding the head, and two valleys between the shoulders and the head (see Figure 10.5).

HaS has a neckline—the support line connecting the shoulder minima. The trading idea based on HaS is a selling signal when price breaks through the neckline from above. Inverse HaS is a mirror image of HaS in respect to the time axis. This pattern generates a buy signal when price breaks through the neckline from below.

Lo et al. (2000) have a relatively simple definition of HaS. Namely, HaS is determined with five consecutive extremes: E1, E2, E3, E4, and E5, such that
E1 is a maximum;

$$E3 > E1; \quad E3 > E5 \qquad (10.22)$$

E1 and E5 are within 1.5 percent of their average
E2 and E4 are within 1.5 percent of their average

However, Omrane & Van Oppens (2004) define HaS with nine rules including conditions for the relative heights of the head and shoulders and timings between them. Many TA experts emphasize that the trading models should not be over-fitted (e.g., Kaufman 2005; Kerstner 2003; Lo et al. 2000). The problem with overly complicated models is that they are sensitive

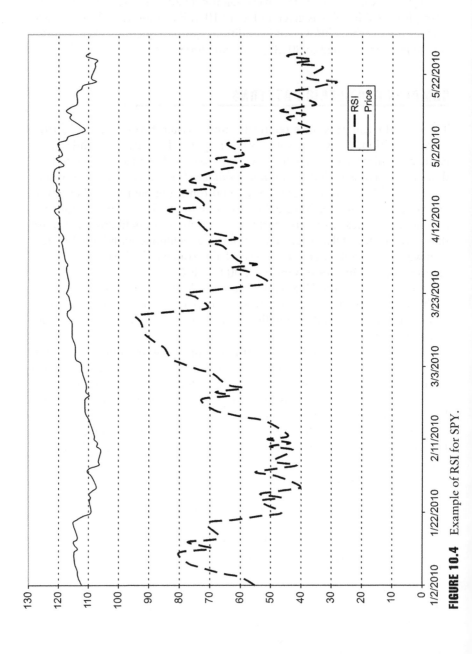

FIGURE 10.4 Example of RSI for SPY.

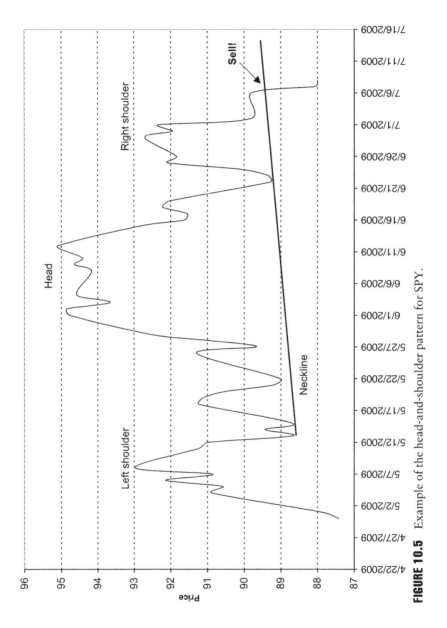

FIGURE 10.5 Example of the head-and-shoulder pattern for SPY.

to the noise present in a training data sample and as a result have poor forecasting ability. Lo et al. (2000) and Omrane & Van Oppens (2004) demonstrate potential profitability of some complex geometric patterns. However, these profits may be too small for covering transaction costs.

SUMMARY

- The general picture of TA profitability is mixed. Careful statistical analysis demonstrates that simple TA strategies might be profitable in equities and in FX until the 1980s and 1990s, respectively.
- Diversification across various TA strategies and/or instruments used within the same (or similar) TA strategies may offer new opportunities for profitable trading.
- TA strategies may be a useful complimentary tool along with fundamental analysis.
- A simple taxonomy of TA strategies includes trend strategies (filter rules, moving-averages rules, and channel breakouts), momentum and oscillator strategies (MACD, RSI), and complex geometric patterns (head-and-shoulder, tops, bottoms, triangles, and others).

CHAPTER 11

Arbitrage Trading Strategies

Accoording to the Law of One Price, equivalent assets (i.e., assets with the same payoff) must have the same price (see, e.g., Bodie & Merton 1998). In competitive markets, the price of an asset must be the same worldwide providing that it is expressed in the same currency, and the transportation and transaction costs can be neglected. Violation of the Law of One Price leads to *arbitrage*, which is risk-free profiteering by buying an asset in a cheaper market and immediately selling it in a more expensive market.

In FX, a typical example of arbitrage is so-called triangle arbitrage. It appears in case of imbalance among three related currency pairs. Namely, exchange rates for three currencies X, Y, and Z generally satisfy the condition

$$(X/Y)^*(Z/X)^*(Y/Z) = 1 \qquad (11.1)$$

An arbitrage opportunity appears if (11.1) is violated. For example, if the product $(EUR/JPY)^*(USD/EUR)$ is smaller than USD/JPY, one can buy JPY with USD, then buy EUR with JPY, and finally, make profits by buying USD for EUR.[1]

Arbitrage can continue only for a limited time until mispricing is eliminated due to increased demand and finite supply of a cheaper asset.[2] Such a clear-cut (deterministic) opportunity, which guarantees a riskless gain, is sometimes called *pure arbitrage* (Bondarenko 2003). Deterministic arbitrage should be discerned from *statistical arbitrage*, which is based on statistical deviations of asset prices from their expected values and may incur losses (Jarrow et al. 2005). Note that practitioners use this term for denoting a specific trading strategy (see the next section).

Many arbitrage trading strategies are based on hedging the risk of financial losses by combining long and short positions in the same portfolio. An ultimate long/short hedging yields a market-neutral portfolio, in which risks from having long and short positions compensate each other.

Market-neutral strategy can be described in terms of the CAPM. Indeed, since market-neutral strategy is supposed to completely eliminate market risk, the parameter β_i (8.22) for the market-neutral portfolio equals zero.

As a simple example of market-neutral strategy, consider two companies within the same industry, A and B, one of which, say A, often yields higher returns. A simple investing approach might be buying shares A and neglecting shares B. A more sophisticated strategy named *pair trading* may involve simultaneously buying shares A and short selling shares B. Obviously, if the entire sector rises, this strategy does not bring as much money as simply buying shares A. However, if the entire market falls, it is expected that shares B will have higher losses than shares A. Then, profit from short selling shares B would compensate for the loss resulting from buying shares A. One possible problem with such thinking is that the persistent inferiority of company B in respect to A implies that B may be out of business after some time. Generally, pair trading is based on the idea of *mean reversion* (Vidyamurthy 2004). Namely, it is expected that the divergence in returns of similar companies A and B is a temporary effect due to market inefficiency, which is eliminated over some time. Pair trading strategy is then opposite to what we just described above. Namely, one should buy shares B and sell shares A.

Not all arbitrage trading strategies are market-neutral: The extent of long/short hedging is often determined by the asset fund manager's discretion. The hedge fund industry has been using a taxonomy that includes not only strategy type but also instruments and geographic investment zones (Stefanini 2006; Khandani & Lo 2007).

This chapter continues with an overview of the major hedging strategies. Then, I focus on market-neutral pair trading, which has a straightforward formulation in terms of the econometric theory. Finally, recent studies of arbitrage risks are discussed.

HEDGING STRATEGIES

Long/short hedging strategies are widely used by financial institutions, most notably by the hedge funds. Detailed specifics of these trading strategies are not widely advertised for the obvious reason: The more investors target the same market inefficiency, the faster it is wiped out. Still, general directions in the long/short hedging are well publicized (see, e.g., Stefanini 2006) and are outlined next.

Let's start with *equity hedge*. Sometimes, one of two positions (e.g., the long one) is a stock index future while the other (short) one consists of all stocks that constitute this index (so-called *index arbitrage*). Pair trading and its special case, *ADR arbitrage,* also fit in this category. American depositary receipts (ADR) are securities that represent shares of non-U.S. companies traded in U.S. markets. Variations in market liquidity, trading volumes, and exchange rates may create discrepancies between prices of ADR and their underlying shares. Equity hedge may not be exactly the market-neutral one. Moreover, the ratio between long and short equity positions may be chosen depending on the market conditions. In recent years, so-called *130/30* (or more generally *1X0/X0*, where $X = 2 \div 5$) mutual funds have gained popularity. These funds have 130 percent of their capital in long positions, 30 percent of which is funded by short positions. Sometimes, these portfolios are named long/short funds. On the other hand, portfolios with *dedicated short bias* always have more short positions than the long ones.

Equity market-neutral strategy and statistical arbitrage. According to Khandani & Lo (2007), practitioners often use the term *statistical arbitrage* for describing the most challenging trading style: "highly technical short-term mean-reversion strategies involving large numbers of securities (hundreds to thousands, depending on the amount of risk capital), very short holding periods (measured in days to seconds), and substantial computational, trading, and IT infrastructure." Equity market-neutral strategy is a less demanding approach that may involve lower frequency of trading and fewer securities. Economic parameters also may be incorporated into predicting models derived under the umbrella of market-neutral strategies.

Convertible arbitrage. Convertible bonds are bonds that can be converted into shares of the same company. Convertible bonds often decline less in a falling market than shares of the same company do. Hence, the idea of the convertible arbitrage may be buying convertible bonds and short selling the underlying stocks.

Fixed-income arbitrage. This strategy implies taking long and short positions in different fixed-income securities. Using analysis of correlations between different securities, one can buy those securities that seem to become underpriced and sell short those that look overpriced. One example is *issuance-driven arbitrage,* for example, *on-the-run* versus *off-the-run* U.S. Treasury bonds. Newly issued (on-the-run) Treasuries usually have yields lower than older off-the-run Treasuries but both yields are expected to converge with time. A more generic *yield curve arbitrage* is based on anomalies in dependence of bond yield on maturity. Other opportunities may appear in comparison of yields for Treasuries, corporate bonds, and municipal bonds.

Mortgage-backed securities (MBS) arbitrage. MBS is actually a form of fixed income with a prepayment option. Namely, mortgage borrowers can prepay their loans fully or partially prior to the mortgage term, which increases the uncertainty of the MBS value. While the MBS arbitrage is similar to the general fixed-income arbitrage, there are so many different MBS that this makes them a separate field of arbitrage expertise.

The strategies listed above can be combined into the family of *relative value arbitrage*. Another group of arbitrage strategies is called *event-driven arbitrage*. A typical example here is *merger arbitrage* (also called *risk arbitrage*). This form of arbitrage involves buying shares of a company that is expected to be bought and short selling the shares of the acquirer. The rationale behind this strategy is that businesses are usually acquired at a premium, which sends down the stock prices of acquiring companies. Another event-driven arbitrage strategy focuses on financially distressed companies. Their securities are sometimes sold below their fair values as a result of market overreaction to the news of distress.

Multi-strategy hedge funds use a synthetic approach that utilizes several hedging strategies and different securities. Looking for the arbitrage opportunities across the board is technically more challenging yet potentially rewarding. *Global macro* hedge funds apply their multiple strategies to instruments traded worldwide.

Stefanini (2006) offers a general review of historical performance of different arbitrage strategies. Khandani & Lo (2007) and Avellaneda & Lee (2010) find that performance of statistical arbitrage has generally degraded since 2002.

PAIR TRADING

The general idea behind pair trading was introduced in the introduction to this chapter. *Arbitrage Pricing Theory* (APT) provides some theoretical background to this trading strategy (see, e.g., Grinold & Kahn 2000). The CAPM equation (8.23) implies that return on a risky asset is determined by a single non-diversifiable risk factor, namely by the risk associated with the entire market. APT offers a generic extension of CAPM into the multifactor paradigm. Namely, APT states that the return for an asset i at every time period is a weighed sum of the risk factor contributions $f_j(t)$ ($j = 1, \ldots, K$) plus an asset-specific random shock $\varepsilon_i(t)$:

$$R_i(t) = a_i + \beta_{i1}f_1 + \beta_{i2}f_2 + \ldots + \beta_{iK}f_K + \varepsilon_i(t) \qquad (11.2)$$

In (11.2), β_{ij} are the factor weights (betas). It is assumed that the expectations of all factor values and for the asset-specific innovations are zero:

$$E[f_1(t)] = \ldots = E[f_K(t)] = E[\varepsilon_i(t)] = 0 \qquad (11.3)$$

Also, the risk factors of the asset-specific innovations are independent and uncorrelated:

$$\begin{aligned} \text{Cov}[f_j(t), \quad f_j(t')] &= \text{Cov}[\varepsilon_i(t), \varepsilon_i(t')] = 0, \quad t \neq t'; \\ \text{Cov}[f_j(t), \quad \varepsilon_i(t)] &= 0 \end{aligned} \qquad (11.4)$$

Then, APT states that there exist such $K + 1$ constants $\lambda_0, \lambda_1, \ldots \lambda_K$ that

$$E[R_i(t)] = \lambda_0 + \beta_{i1}\lambda_1 + \ldots + \beta_{iK}\lambda_K \qquad (11.5)$$

In (11.5), λ_0 has the sense of the risk-free asset return, and λ_j is called the risk premium for the jth risk factor. APT implies that similar companies have the same risk premiums and any deviation of returns from (11.5) is a mispricing, which yields arbitrage opportunities. For example, shares of an underpriced company should be bought while shares of an overpriced company should be shorted. Alas, APT does not contain a recipe for defining risk factors. These factors can be chosen among multiple fundamental and technical parameters. APT turns out to be more accurate for portfolios rather than for individual stocks. Hence, as Grinold & Kahn (2000) note, "APT is an art, not a science."

APT offers a valuable rationale for pursuing long/short trading strategies. Yet, it should be noted that buying underpriced and selling overpriced (in respect to the APT benchmark) securities in equal cash amounts does not guarantee market neutrality of the resulting portfolio. Truly market-neutral strategies do not need outside benchmarks; they employ relative mispricing, which can be recovered with the cointegration analysis.

Cointegration and Causality

Cointegration is an effective statistical technique developed by Engle and Granger for an analysis of common trends in multivariate time series (see, e.g., Hamilton 1994 and Alexander 2001). One might think that the correlation analysis might be used in the selection of trading pairs. However, the correlation analysis can be applied only to stationary variables. Hence, it requires preliminary de-trending of prices or, in other words, can be applied only to returns.[3] Correlations are a measure of a short-term relationship that may be affected by volatility. Therefore, trading strategies based on the correlation analysis need frequent rebalancing. On the other hand, cointegration describes long-term trends that may be stable even when correlations are broken (Alexander 1999).

Two non-stationary time series are cointegrated if their linear combination is stationary. While the difference between two arbitrary prices series (the spread) may vary unpredictably, it is stationary for cointegrated series. If the spread deviates from its stationary value, it is expected that mean reversion will bring it back, or, in other words, mispricing will be eliminated. Formally, two time series $x, y \sim I(1)$ are cointegrated if there is such a constant α that

$$z = x - \alpha y \sim I(0) \tag{11.6}$$

The standard technique offered by Engle and Granger for finding if two time series are cointegrated is derivation of the linear regression

$$x_t = \alpha y_t + c + \varepsilon_t \tag{11.7}$$

The residuals ε_t are then tested for *stationarity*. Usually, the augmented Dickey-Fuller (ADF) test is used for unit roots (see e.g., Hamilton 1994). If stationarity is not rejected, then the cointegration condition (11.6) holds. In the context of the cointegrated portfolios, the residuals are sometimes called *tracking errors* (Alexander et al. 2001).[4]

The cointegration property is closely related to *Granger causality*, which implies that turning points in the direction of one series precede turning points of the other one. Consider the *error correction model* (ECM)

$$\Delta x_t = \delta_1 + \sum_{i=1}^{M_1} \beta_{1i}\Delta x_{t-i} + \sum_{i=1}^{M_2} \beta_{2i}\Delta y_{t-i} + \gamma_1 z_{t-1} + \varepsilon_{1t} \tag{11.8}$$

$$\Delta y_t = \delta_2 + \sum_{i=1}^{M_3} \beta_{3i}\Delta x_{t-i} + \sum_{i=1}^{M_4} \beta_{4i}\Delta y_{t-i} + \gamma_2 z_{t-1} + \varepsilon_{2t} \tag{11.9}$$

where Δ is the difference operator, and the coefficients δ_i, β_{ij}, and γ_i are estimated with the linear regression. The *Granger representation theorem* states that cointegration and ECM are equivalent. Namely, if x_t and y_t are cointegrated, then $\gamma_1 < 0$ and $\alpha\gamma_2 > 0$. As a result, any deviation of z from its stationary value will be corrected.

It is said that x "Granger-causes" y when x and y are cointegrated and lagged terms of one time series x are significant in the dynamics of the time series y. Granger causality is not true causality. It may be simply that both x and y depend on a common factor but have different lagging models.

The direction of Granger causality may change over time; that is, the leader and the follower may change their mutual roles. An example of such a role change can be found in the ECM analysis of futures and spot prices (Alexander et al. 2001).

Pair Selection

Vidyamurthy (2004) describes the following pair trading strategy: Buy a portfolio consisting of long shares A with log price x_t and short shares B with log price y_t (providing that (11.6) holds) when

$$x_t - \alpha y_t = c - \Delta \tag{11.10}$$

and sell the portfolio when

$$x_t - \alpha y_t = c + \Delta \tag{11.11}$$

The challenge, of course, is the selection of stocks A and B for the trading portfolio and defining the optimal value of Δ.

Within the APT framework, it is natural to pick up stocks from the same industry as their prices are expected to be determined with the same risk factors. However, the search for cointegrated pairs can be extended into entire industrial sectors (such as materials, financials, etc.) or even beyond them (Gatev et al. 2006). Several problems arise with the cointegration technique. First, there is arbitrariness in choosing an independent variable in the linear regression (11.7). In other words, two options exist:

$$p_t^A = \alpha^A p_t^B + c^A + \varepsilon_t^A \quad \text{with} \quad \alpha^A = \text{Cov}(\varepsilon_t^A, \varepsilon_t^B)/\text{Var}(\varepsilon_t^A) \tag{11.12}$$

and

$$p_t^B = \alpha^B p_t^A + c^B + \varepsilon_t^B \quad \text{with} \quad \alpha^B = \text{Cov}(\varepsilon_t^A, \varepsilon_t^B)/\text{Var}(\varepsilon_t^B) \tag{11.13}$$

Vidyamurthy (2004) suggests choosing a variable with lower volatility as the independent one.

Another problem is that ADF being a probabilistic test does not always offer an unambiguous conclusion about the stationarity of residuals. Schmidt (2008) suggested using the Johansen test, which is regarded as superior to ADF.

In general, choosing Δ in the strategy (11.10) to (11.11) should be based on an analysis of residuals ε_t. Practitioners sometimes suggest entering the market when prices diverge by more than two historical standard deviations σ (e.g., Chan 2009). Vidyamurthy (2004) advises to calculate Δ by maximizing the trading profits. If the cumulative distribution function of the spread is $Pr(\Delta)$, then the probability that profits exceed Δ equals $(1 - Pr(\Delta))$ and the profits W depend on Δ as

$$W \sim \Delta(1 - Pr(\Delta)) \qquad (11.14)$$

Minimization of the right-hand side of (11.14) yields an optimal Δ. In particular, if the spread follows the Normal distribution, the profits have a maximum when Δ is 0.75σ.

Rather than employing the Engle-Granger cointegration framework, Gatev et al. (2006) used the concept of weakly dependent stocks. Namely, they have chosen such counterparts in trading pairs that minimize the sum of squared deviations between the two normalized price series (*the distance measure*).

Another practical criterion in choosing trading pairs is that a successful outcome must be realized within acceptable time frame. Since residuals are expected to fluctuate around zero value due to mean reversion, even visual inspection of the chart ε_t may give an idea about possible round-trip execution time for a given pair. *The zero-crossing rate* of a mean-reverting process can be used as a quantitative measure of the execution time. For a stationary ARMA process, the zero-crossing rate can be determined with the Rice's equation (see Abrahams 1986, for a review).

Elliott et al. (2005) use the Ornstein-Ulenbeck equation for modeling mean reversion of the spread $X(t)$:

$$dX(t) = \rho(\mu - X(t))dt + \sigma dW \qquad (11.15)$$

In (11.15), dW is the standard Brownian motion. Elliott et al. estimate all parameters in (11.15) from an empirical time series using the Kalman filter technique. The Ornstein-Ulenbeck equation has the following standard form:

$$dZ(t) = -Z(t)dt + \sqrt{2}dW(t) \qquad (11.16)$$

The first passage time to $Z(t) = 0$ for the initial value $Z(0) = s$ has the probability density distribution[5]

$$f_{\mathrm{FPT}}(t) = \sqrt{\frac{2}{\pi}} \frac{|s|e^{-t}}{(1 - e^{-2t})^{3/2}} \exp\left(-\frac{s^2 e^{-2t}}{2(1 - e^{-2t})}\right) \qquad (11.17)$$

Elliott et al. suggest that the timing of pair trading can be based on the time that yields the maximum value of $f_{\text{FPT}}(t)$:

$$\hat{t} = 0.5\ln[1 + 0.5(\sqrt{(s^2-3)^2 + 4s^2} + s^2 - 3)] \qquad (11.18)$$

Namely, Elliott et al. choose the most likely time T when $X(T) = \mu$

$$T = \hat{t}/\rho \qquad (11.19)$$

Then, the trading strategy for a chosen value of s would be entering pair trade when the spread is higher than $\mu + s\sigma/\sqrt{2\rho}$ or lower than $\mu - s\sigma/\sqrt{2\rho}$, and later unwinding this trade at time T.

ARBITRAGE RISKS

Arbitrage traders face multiple risks. Liu & Longstaff (2004) convey this by quoting a bond trader: "So there's an arbitrage. So what? This desk has lost a lot of money on arbitrages." Indeed, an event-driven arbitrage may go wrong simply because an event does not happen (a merger may be annulled). Or, the market perceives this event in an unconventional way: for example, it does not seem that an acquirer overpaid for the purchase and its stock goes up right after the acquisition announcement. A distressed business may never recover, and the list goes on.

As for the relative-value arbitrage, past mean reversion may be broken in the future. Moreover, it has been implied that investors have unlimited patience and resources for living through times of widening spread until mean reversion brings it to zero (so-called *textbook arbitrage*). In real life, market-neutral portfolio is not self-funded as brokers who lend shares for short selling require collateral. If the spread keeps widening after the long/short portfolio was set up, an investor may receive a margin call from the broker. In the case of limited capital, this may force partial liquidation of the portfolio at a loss. For highly leveraged hedge funds, such a loss may become quite dramatic. A classical example here is the demise of a very large (and initially very successful) hedge fund LTCM (Lowenstein 2000).

Another case in point is the analysis of unprecedented losses that long/short hedge funds had in early August of 2007 (Khandani & Lo 2007). These losses were caused by forced liquidations of significant portfolio volumes, possibly due to margin calls. Initial liquidation might happen even outside the pure long/short group of hedge funds. However, it had put a pressure on entire the equity market and caused stop-loss trading and de-leveraging processes. These events are examples of significant systemic risks in modern financial markets.

Several recent accounts address the risks of widening spread and limited trading horizon in the market-neutral arbitrage (Jurek & Yang 2007; Liu & Timmermann 2009). Here, I focus on a stylized and instructive model offered by Liu & Longstaff (2004). In this model, the investment capital is split into a riskless asset R_t and an arbitrage opportunity A_t. The dynamics of a riskless asset are shown as

$$dR = rRdt \qquad (11.20)$$

where r is an interest rate. Providing the initial value R_0 is 1,

$$R_t = \exp(rt) \qquad (11.21)$$

It is assumed that A_t is described with the *Brownian bridge* process that converges to zero at some time T:

$$dA = -\frac{\alpha A}{T - t}dt + \sigma dZ \qquad (11.22)$$

In (11.22), $\alpha > 0$ determines the rate with which A converges to zero, $\sigma > 0$ is volatility, $0 \leq t \leq T$, and dZ is the standard Brownian motion. The value of A corresponds to a portfolio with a long notional amount invested in underpriced security and the same but short amount invested into overpriced security. The solution to (11.22) for $t \leq s \leq T$ is

$$A_t = \left(\frac{T-s}{T-t}\right)^{\alpha} A_t + \sigma \int_{t}^{s} \left(\frac{T-s}{T-\tau}\right)^{\alpha} dZ_\tau \qquad (11.23)$$

Within the Liu-Longstaff model, the investor's total wealth at time t equals

$$W_t = N_t A_t + P_t R_t \qquad (11.24)$$

where N_t and P_t are the numbers of the arbitrage and riskless units held in the portfolio. Assuming that there are no additional capital flows, the wealth dynamics have the following form:

$$dW = NdA + rPRdt = NdA + r(W - NA)dt$$

$$= \left[rW - \left(r + \frac{\alpha}{T-t}\right)NA\right]dt + \sigma NdZ \qquad (11.25)$$

It follows from (11.25) that

$$W_T = W_t \exp\left(\int_t^{eT} \left(r - \left(r + \frac{\alpha}{T-s}\right)\frac{NA}{W} - \frac{\sigma^2 N^2}{2W^2} \right) ds + \sigma \int_t^T \frac{N}{W} dZ \right)$$

(11.26)

If the margin requirement per unit of the given arbitrage is $\lambda > 0$, then the collateral constraint on the portfolio is

$$W_t \geq \lambda |N_t|$$ (11.27)

Liu & Longstaff (2004) maximize the expected utility function $E[ln W_T]$ in terms of the variable N_t that satisfies the constraint (11.27). The optimal values of N_t depend on the following conditions:

$$N_t = W_t/\lambda \quad \text{if} \quad A_t < -\sigma^2/[r + \alpha/(T-t)] \qquad (11.28)$$

$$N_t = \frac{r + \frac{\alpha}{T-t}}{\sigma^2} A_t W \quad \text{if} \quad |A_t| < \sigma^2/[r + \alpha/(T-t)] \qquad (11.29)$$

$$N_t = -W_t/\lambda \quad \text{if} \quad A_t > \sigma^2/[r + \alpha/(T-t)] \qquad (11.30)$$

This result implies that due to the collateral constraints, investors should take only a finite amount in arbitrage. This amount coincides with the maximum defined with (11.27) in the cases (11.28) and (11.30). However, a lower value is optimal in the case (11.29). Liu & Longstaff (2004) show also that when their optimal strategy is used, the arbitrage portfolio can experience losses prior to convergence at time T.

The drawback of the Liu-Longstaff model is that it implies that the time of mean reversion, T, is known. Jurek & Yang (2007) replaced the Brownian bridge process in the Liu-Longstaff model with the Ornstein-Ulenbeck equation, which implies uncertainty of T. Jurek and Yang also assume that investors optimize the CRRA utility function for a given horizon T. They found that equally risk-averse investors are expected to be more aggressive in pursuing arbitrage opportunities if they have a longer T. This implies that the asset fund managers who are required to report their performance less frequently may display riskier behavior. The Jurek-Yang model points also at some critical mispricing level, beyond which the amount of investment into the arbitrage should be reduced.

While the arbitrage strategies discussed in this section are market neutral, Liu & Timmermann (2009) show that a truly optimal strategy for investors with the CRRA risk aversion may yield unbalanced long and short position. Hence, risk-averse investors may want to optimize their portfolios without imposing the constraint of market neutrality.

SUMMARY

- Deterministic arbitrage is risk-free profiteering that involves buying an asset in a cheaper market and immediately selling it in a more expensive market.

- Statistical arbitrage is based on statistical deviations of prices from their expected values and may incur losses.

- Many arbitrage trading strategies are based on hedging the risk of financial losses by combining long and short positions in the same portfolio. In a market-neutral portfolio, risks from having long and short positions compensate each other.

- There are two major families of arbitrage trading strategies: (1) relative value arbitrage (e.g., equity hedge, fixed-income arbitrage, and convertible arbitrage) and (2) event-driven arbitrage (merger arbitrage, distressed equity arbitrage).

- Pair trading based on the mean reversion effect is a popular form of statistical arbitrage. Selection of pairs and times of entering/exiting the market are the main challenges for this strategy.

- Recent findings in the statistical arbitrage theory emphasize the risk of leveraging and question the need of market-neutral constraint for risk-averse investors.

CHAPTER 12

Back-Testing of Trading Strategies

"**I**t is hard to make predictions, especially about the future," reportedly noted Mark Twain. Asset management institutions translate this wisdom into the standard disclaimer: "Past investment performance does not guarantee future returns." Yet, forecasting has been widely used in economics, finance, and natural sciences (e.g., climate modeling)—arguably in every field where time series analysis is involved. The term *back-testing* implies that the forecasting models are fitted and tested using past empirical data. Usually, the entire available data set is split into two parts, one of which (earlier data) is used for *in-sample* calibration of the predicting model while the other is reserved for *out-of-sample* testing of the calibrated model. In simple models, it is usually assumed that the testing sample is variance-stationary; that is, the sample volatility is constant.

If it is expected that the optimal strategy parameters may evolve in time, *walk-forward testing* can be used. In this case, moving-window sampling is implemented. For example, if a 10-year data sample is available, the first five-year data are used for in-sample calibration and the sixth-year data are used for out-of-sample testing. Then, the data from the second to the sixth year data are used for in-sample calibration and the seventh year is tested out-of-sample, and so on.

In general, the choice of the data sample is not always determined by the rule *more is better*, as the long time series may be non-stationary. Moreover, the time series may include *regime shifts* caused by macroeconomic events or changes in regulatory policies (e.g., introduction of the Euro in 1999, changes in the uptick rule, etc.). Markov-switching models are sometimes used for a unified description of data samples with regime shifts (see, e.g., Tsay 2005). However, that sophisticated technique is beyond the scope of this overview.

There is always a danger of model over-fitting, or implementing a model with too many parameters. The result of over-fitting may be too good to be true with regard to in-sample accuracy—and disastrous when it comes to the out-of-sample outcome. In this case, the model is fitted to the in-sample noise rather than to the deterministic relationship. Several maximum likelihood-based criteria, most notably *Akaike information criterion* (AIC), may be used for choosing an optimal number of model parameters n. In the general case,

$$AIC = -2 \ln[L(n, N)]/N + 2n/N \qquad (12.1)$$

In (12.1), $L(n, N)$ is the maximized likelihood for the chosen model and N is the number of observations. In particular, for the ARMA(p, q) models with Gaussian noise,

$$AIC(p, q, N) = \ln(\sigma_{p,q}^2) + 2(p + q)/N \qquad (12.2)$$

where $\sigma_{p,q}^2$ is the maximum likelihood estimator of the sample error variance. The combination (p, q) that yields the minimal value of AIC is considered optimal. Unfortunately, Hansen (2010) has recently shown that models optimized in-sample with AIC or similar criteria may not be accurate out-of-sample.

Then, there is a general problem of *data snooping* bias.[1] Generally, this bias can appear during the testing of different strategies with the same data set. Some strategies may work much better than others on a given data set simply due to luck. A well-publicized example of data snooping is offered by Sullivan et al. (1999), who quoted Leinweber's finding that the best predictor in the United Nations database for the S&P 500 stock index is the production of butter in Bangladesh.

A general solution to the data snooping bias is data *resampling*. *Bootstrap* is arguably the most popular resampling procedure. The general idea of bootstrap was introduced by Efron (see Davidson & Hinkley 1997). In a nutshell, bootstrap implies creating multiple data sets by randomly drawing the elements of a given sample (with replacement). Other resampling techniques include *jackknife* (creating data subsets by randomly dropping sample elements), and *permutation tests*, in which the order of elements of a given sample is randomly changed.[2]

Another way to approach the problem of data snooping is resampling using the *Markov Chain Monte Carlo* (MCMC) simulations (Davidson & Hinkley 1997). Within the MCMC protocol, the original sample is used to estimate probabilities of new returns conditioned on current and past returns. These probabilities are then used for generating new samples.

Finally, one may note the *random entry protocol* being a simple resampling procedure that addresses the problem of correlations in two coupled time series (Schmidt 2009a).

This chapter starts with an overview of performance measures that are usually used in analysis of trading strategies. Then, various sampling techniques are discussed. Finally, I outline the White's (2000) protocol for comparing the performance of different trading strategies and their respective extensions by Hansen (2005), Romano & Wolf (2005), and Hsu et al. (2009).

PERFORMANCE MEASURES

Performance measures for trading strategies usually relate to a rather long time interval (at least a quarter or a year), during which a given strategy is used multiple times. Market imperfections, such as finite liquidity and the bid/ask spread are often neglected in the back-testing of trading strategies due to their uncertainty though they may have notable contributions to performance. Also, transaction fees associated with frequent trading may become a matter of concern. Hence, practical performance measures should be evaluated *after* fees.

Total return (which alas can be negative) is the ultimate performance benchmark. It is calculated over some trading period after all long and short positions in the trading portfolio are closed. In other words, it is *realized* return that matters. Note that the compounded return usually listed in asset management statements is not realized and may include dividends and reinvestment. We, however, are interested in pure trading strategy performance and hence use the same notional amount in every round-trip trade.

Sometimes, a positive gain is a result of a few extremely lucky strikes accompanied with multiple losses. Therefore, the percentage of winning trades, p, is another important performance measure. If this percentage and the ratio of the average winning amount to average losing amount, r, is assumed to be stable, one can use the Kelly's criterion for estimating the optimal fraction of trading capital, f, to be used in each trade:

$$f = (pr - 1 + p)/r \qquad (12.3)$$

It can be shown that the Kelly's criterion is equivalent to choosing the trading size that maximizes the geometric mean of outcomes. The derivation of the Kelly's criterion is described in detail by Thorp (2006).[3] Note that the Kelly's formula yields an estimate that is valid only asymptotically.

Therefore, risk-averse practitioners are advised to use a value of f lower than the Kelly's criterion suggests.

The total number of trades for a given period is also important. Indeed, frequent trading may lead to more volatile outcomes. Multiple trades with a given strategy generate a probability distribution that can be used for hypothesis testing, in particular for comparing different strategies. Hence, the average return, μ, and its variance, σ, are very important performance measures. Note that a positive return being accompanied with a high variance does not guarantee the strategy's quality. Providing the return distribution is normal, one can use the t-statistic for testing the hypothesis that the distribution mean is zero. Namely, for a given number of round-trip trades, N, one calculates the t-value:

$$ t = \frac{\mu}{(\sigma^2/N)^{1/2}} \tag{12.4} $$

Then, the t-value can be used for finding *statistical significance* (also called *p-value*) from the Student's distribution. Note that this distribution is the function of degrees of freedom, which in our case equal $(N - 1)$. Usually, the null hypothesis in an analysis of trading strategies is that the strategy return is zero. For example, if p is less than 0.05, the hypothesis of zero return can be rejected in more than 95 percent of cases.

Obviously, if two strategies have the same average return, the one with lower variance is more attractive. Providing that the return distributions are normal, two trading strategies A and B can be compared using the t-statistic:

$$ t = \frac{\mu_A - \mu_B}{(\sigma_A^2/N_A + \sigma_B^2/N_B)^{1/2}} \tag{12.5} $$

In this case, the degrees of freedom equal $N_A + N_B - 2$. The t-statistic (12.5) can also be used for analysis of profitability of a single strategy if indexes A and B refer to buy and sell signals, respectively (Brock et al. 1992).

The Sharpe ratio (8.24) is often used in performance analysis. Sometimes, the *Sortino ratio* is chosen instead. In the latter ratio, only negative returns are included in calculating the standard deviation σ. If a trading strategy (or portfolio) performance is compared with performance of an index (or buy-and-hold strategy), the *information ratio* that looks similar to the Sharpe ratio can be used:

$$ \text{IR} = (E[r_i] - E[r_0])/\sigma_{i0} \tag{12.6} $$

In (12.6), r_i is given return, r_0 is return of an index, and σ_{i0} is the tracking error (standard deviation between returns of the strategy and returns of the index[4]).

The *maximum drawdown* (MD) is another important risk measure, particularly for leveraged trades. For a process $X(t)$ on the interval $[0, T]$,

$$MD = \max[\max(X(s) - X(t)] \qquad (12.7)$$
$$t \in [0, T] s \in [0, t]$$

In other words, MD is the largest drop of price after its peak. For the general random walk with drift, estimation of MD is quite cumbersome. However, if drift can be neglected, expectation of MD has a simple analytic form (Magdon-Ismail & Atiya 2004):

$$E[MD] = 1.2533\sigma\sqrt{T} \qquad (12.8)$$

In some performance criteria, such as the *Calmar ratio*, the Sharpe ratio is modified by replacing the standard deviation of returns with MD.

Finally, no trading strategy works forever. A possible signal for dropping a strategy that used to be profitable in the past is a growing number of consecutive losing trades. Hence, this number may be handy for tracking the strategy performance.

RESAMPLING TECHNIQUES

In this section, I describe the most widely used resampling techniques: the bootstrap and MCMC. Then I address a problem of resampling a system of two coupled time series with the random entry protocol.

Bootstrap

The t-statistic can be misleading when it is applied to non-normal distributions. Brock et al. (1992) suggest using bootstrap for analyzing the performance of trading strategies. In the simple case, the bootstrap protocol is based on picking up at random an element of a given sample of size N, copying it into the new sample, and putting it back (replacement). This random selection continues until the new sample has the same number of elements as the original one. In recent literature, application of bootstrap to back-testing the trading strategies is discussed by Hsu et al. (2009) and Fusai & Roncoroni (2008).

Sometimes, blocks of several sequential elements of a given sample are picked at once (*block bootstrap*). Usually, the block bootstrap is implemented with replacement and blocks are not overlapping. Such an approach may preserve short-range autocorrelations present in the original sample. While a simple estimate of an optimal block size $L \sim N^{-1/3}$ can be used, choice of L in the general case is not trivial (Davidson & Hinkley 1997). Politis & Romano (1994) offered an expansion of the block bootstrap. This method ensures the stationarity of samples bootstrapped from the stationary data—and is called accordingly: *stationary bootstrap*. The block size L in stationary bootstrap is randomly drawn from the geometric distribution

$$Pr(L = k) = (1 - p)^{k-1} p \qquad (12.9)$$

The average block size for the stationary bootstrap case equals $1/p$, which can serve as a bridge between the size of the simple block bootstrap and the stationary bootstrap parameter p.

A more sophisticated approach implies estimating a mathematical model that fits the given sample and bootstrapping the model's residuals. Typical models used for stock prices are the random walk with drift, the AR models and the GARCH models (Brock et al. 1992). Note that residuals within this approach are assumed to be IID and must be standardized for obtaining unbiased estimates.

Consider an example with the AR(1) model for logarithmic returns $r = \log(p)$:

$$r_t = \alpha + \beta r_{t-1} + \varepsilon_t, \quad \varepsilon_t = \text{IID}(0, \sigma^2) \qquad (12.10)$$

First, the coefficients α and $\beta < 1$ in (12.10) are estimated using OLS. Then, the standardized residuals are calculated as

$$e_t = (r_t - \alpha - \beta r_{t-1})/\sigma \qquad (12.11)$$

A new sample of residuals, $\breve{e}_t$, is generated using the bootstrap and used for constructing a new sample of returns:

$$\breve{r}_t = \alpha + \beta r_{t-1} + \breve{e}_t, \qquad (12.12)$$

Then, a new price sample calculated via sampled returns, $\hat{p}_t = \exp(\breve{r}_t)$ can be used for another round of testing the trading strategy.

The number of bootstrapped samples needed for good accuracy may reach from several hundred (Brock et al. 1992) to several thousand (Schmidt 2009a). The fraction of bootstrapped samples for which a given strategy yields return that is higher than for the original sample can be interpreted as the *p*-value. If this fraction is small (a few percentage points), then either the model chosen for simulations of returns is inadequate or the return obtained with a given strategy on the given sample is the result of data snooping.

Markov Chain Monte Carlo

Markov process is a generic stochastic process determined with relationships between its future, present, and past values. Here, *discrete* Markov processes called Markov chains are discussed. In a nutshell, future value for the Markov chain of the 1st order is determined by its present value; future value for the Markov chain of the 2nd order is determined by its present value and the most recent past value, and so on. The Markov processes of the 1st order cover a very wide class of dynamic short-memory phenomena including diffusional transfer. In fact, the equation for Brownian motion can be derived directly from the definition of the Markov process.[5]

By definition, the Markov chain of the *k*th order is such a sequence of random variables $X_1, X_2, \ldots$, which satisfies the following equation:

$$
\begin{aligned}
&Pr(X_n = x | X_{n-1} = x_{n-1}, X_{n-2} = x_{n-2}, \ldots, X_1 = x_1) \\
&= Pr(X_n = x | X_{n-1} = x_{n-1}, X_{n-2} = x_{n-2}, \ldots, X_{n-k} = x_{n-k}) \quad (12.13)
\end{aligned}
$$

In other words, only *k* past values (sometimes called initial conditions) determine the present value. In particular, for $k = 1$, only one initial condition is needed:

$$
\begin{aligned}
&Pr(X_n = x | X_{n-1} = x_{n-1}, X_{n-2} = x_{n-2}, \ldots, X_1 = x_1) \\
&= Pr(X_n = x | X_{n-1} = x_{n-1}) \quad (12.14)
\end{aligned}
$$

The Markov chain is stationary (or time-homogeneous) if probability in the left-hand side of (12.13) does not depend on index *n*.

Generally, Markov variables can assume only a finite number of values (states). Stationary Markov chains of the 1st order with N states are determined with N^2 probabilities $Pr(X_n = x_k \mid X_{n-1} = x_i) = p_{ik}, i, k = 1, 2, \ldots, N$. These probabilities are called the *transition kernel*, and the complete set of values p_{ik} is called the *transition matrix*. Note that for each *k*

$$
\sum_{i=1}^{N} p_{ik} = 1 \quad (12.15)
$$

Similarly, stationary Markov chains of the 2nd order are determined with N^3 probabilities $Pr(X_n = x_k \mid X_{n-1} = x_i, X_{n-2} = x_j) = p_{ijk}$, $i, j, k = 1$, $2, \ldots, N$, and

$$\sum_{i,j=1}^{N} p_{jik} = 1 \tag{12.16}$$

In MCMC-based resampling, the transition matrix is assumed stationary and is calculated using the original sample. Then, drawings from the uniform distribution are mapped onto transition probabilities for generating new samples. For example, consider a two-state Markov chain with $p_{11} = p$, $p_{22} = q$ (which implies that $p_{12} = 1 - p$ and $p_{21} = 1 - q$). Say the current state is 1. If a drawing from the uniform distribution is less than or equal to p, then the next state is 1; otherwise, it is 2. If the current state is 2 and a drawing from the uniform distribution is less than or equal to q, then the next state is 2; otherwise, it is 1.

Since the transition matrix size grows with the Markov chain's order as the power law, the use of higher orders for multi-state models can become a computational challenge. Also, the original sample may be not long enough for reliable estimates of all transition probabilities. Luckily, financial returns do not have a long memory. Hence, low-order Markov chains should suffice for their resampling. In particular, Schmidt (2009a) found that MCMC with Markov chains of the first and second order used in resampling of FX returns on a grid with one-second timescale yielded practically the same results.

Random Entry Protocol

So far, we have discussed resampling of a single time series (i.e., returns, as far as trading strategies are concerned). In the general case, trading strategies can be determined not only by price dynamics but also by some liquidity measure(s), such as the bid/ask spread and the asset amount available at best price, which also varies with time. Depending on the problem addressed with resampling, one may either want to preserve or destroy correlations between two time series. If correlations between two samples are weak, MCMC can be implemented for both coupled samples independently, and bootstrap for coupled samples can be reduced to picking up pairs of variables at the same time. However, if both samples have autocorrelations of varying strength, choosing the bootstrap block size becomes tricky.

On the other hand, it may not be desirable to preserve all autocorrelations in some applications. A case in point is the simulation of execution costs in the global FX market where both best prices and aggregated order size at best price determine the trading strategy (Schmidt 2009a). In this strategy, a bid order was submitted at the best bid price. If this order (or its part) was not filled before the best bid increased, the order (or its unfilled part) was cancelled and resubmitted at the new best bid; pegging to the best bid continued until the order was completely filled. At first, the analysis was done with *sequential trading protocol*, which is often used in back-testing of trading strategies. In sequential trading, filling an order implies the immediate submitting of another order. Another form of sequential trading may imply that a signal of exiting long position is also the signal for entering short position and vice versa.[6] It turns out that negative autocorrelations present in returns yield a systematic bias to the expected execution costs for large orders that are filled in several transactions. Indeed, after filling the rest of the current bid order, a new bid will probably be resubmitted at a higher price due to negative autocorrelations in returns.

While analysis of this execution strategy may benefit from destroying some autocorrelations in returns, it is not clear whether persistent positive autocorrelations of the aggregated order size at best price can be neglected. A simple solution to handle correlational effects was offered by Schmidt (2009a). Namely, it was suggested to use the random entry protocol rather than sequential trading. The random entry protocol implies choosing a random time within the given sample for each new submitted order. This certainly helps to avoid the bias due to autocorrelations in returns but preserves autocorrelations in order book size. The random entry protocol is similar to the stationary bootstrap in that they both have a variable block length. The difference between the two approaches is that in the former, the block size is determined with the time intervals during which orders are filled rather than from the geometric distribution. A natural constraint of the random entry protocol is that in contrast to bootstrap and MCMC, it can yield only a limited number of distinct trade simulations m.[7] Namely, if the sample size is N and typical number of time intervals needed for filling a large order is n, then $m \approx N - n$.

The random entry protocol may also help in filtering out those trading strategies that are the result of data snooping, particularly in high-frequency trading.[8]

COMPARING TRADING STRATEGIES

So far the discussion of resampling techniques has addressed the question of whether a given trading strategy may be profitable. A more challenging problem is comparing the efficiency of several trading strategies. This section starts with a description of the pioneering approach (the so-called bootstrap reality check) offered by White (2000). Then an overview of new developments in this field is offered.

Bootstrap Reality Check

Resampling techniques (e.g., in the spirit of Brock et al. 1992) may help to decide whether a trading strategy has a positive return within a given time interval. However, this approach still does not prevent the danger of data snooping in comparative testing of multiple trading strategies on the same data sample. As Brock et al. (1992) put it, "There is always the possibility that any satisfactory results obtained may simply be due to chance rather than to any merit inherent in the method yielding the results." One reason for data snooping is that the many strategies that were unsuccessful in the past are eliminated from current comparative testing, so that only a small set of strategies is considered in the end, and the best of them is assumed to be the best among all. White (2000) illustrates this problem with a newsletter scam. A scammer sends his free forecast to a large group of potential clients, suggesting that the market will go up in one half of letters and that the market will go down in another half. The following week, the scammer sends his newsletter only to those people who got the right forecast. Again, half of them are informed that the market will go up, and the rest that the market will go down. After several such iterations, the scammer gets a group of people who received only correct forecasts and may agree to pay for future advice.

White (2000) has offered the Bootstrap Reality Check (BRC) for avoiding data snooping. It is based on the $l \times 1$ statistic

$$\bar{f} = n^{-1} \sum_{t=R}^{T} f_{t+1}(\widehat{\beta}_t) \qquad (12.17)$$

where l is the number of trading strategies, n is the number of prediction periods indexed from R to T, $T = R + n + 1$, $\widehat{\beta}_t$ is a vector of parameters that determine the trading strategies. Performance is defined via excess returns in respect to some benchmark model defined with β_0

$$f_{k,t+1}(\beta) = \ln[1 + y_{t+1} S_k(\chi_t, \beta_k)] - \ln[1 + y_{t+1} S_0(\chi_t, \beta_0)],$$
$$k = 1, \ldots, l \qquad (12.18)$$

In (12.18), X_t is the original price series, $y_{t+1} = (X_{t+1} - X_t)/X_t$, $S_k(\chi_t, \beta_k)$ and $S_0(\chi_t, \beta_0)$ are the trading signal functions that translate the price sequence $\chi t = \{X_{t-R}, X_{t-R+1}, \ldots, XT\}$ into the market positions. The trading signal functions can assume values of 0 (cash), 1 (long position), and −1 (short position). Buy-and-hold strategy or cash position are usually chosen as the benchmark models. In the latter case, β_0 is the risk-free interest rate.

The null hypothesis in BRC is that the performance of the best technical trading rule is no better than the performance of the benchmark. In terms of the average returns for each strategy k, $\bar{f}_k = E(f_k)$, this hypothesis states that

$$H_0: \max\{\bar{f}_k\} \leq 0, \quad k = 1, \ldots, l \tag{12.19}$$

Rejection of the null hypothesis implies that performance of the best technical trading is superior to the benchmark. The stationary bootstrap is used in BRC for resampling the observed values of $f_{k,t}$. This yields the average bootstrapped values $\bar{f}^*_{k,i}$ for each strategy k where $i = 1, \ldots, N$ indexes the bootstrap samples. Then, the following statistics are calculated:

$$\bar{V}^*_i = \max\left\{ \sqrt{n}\left(\bar{f}^*_{k,i} - \bar{f}_k\right) \right\}, \quad i = 1, \ldots, N$$
$$k = 1, \ldots, l \tag{12.20}$$

$$\bar{V} = \max\left\{ \sqrt{n}(\bar{f}_k) \right\}, \quad k = 1, \ldots, l \tag{12.21}$$

Finally, the percentile of $\bar{V}^*_i$ is compared with $\bar{V}$ for estimating p-value of BRC.

Sullivan et al. (1999) have investigated a wide range of technical trading strategies using BRC on 100 years (1897 to 1996) of daily data for the Dow Jones Industrial Average. They have shown, in particular, that the strategy that is the best (according to BRC) for a given sample outperforms holding cash. However, the best in-sample strategy is not superior to the benchmark when tested out of sample.

New Developments

The ideas used in BRC for avoiding data snooping were expanded further in several directions. First, Hansen (2005) has shown that BRC may have a lower power due to the possible presence of poorly performing strategies in the test. Note that the power of the statistical test relates to the ability of rejecting false null hypotheses. Hansen enhanced BRC with two contributions. The first is studentizing the performance statistics, that is, dividing

$\overline{f}_k$ by an estimator of their standard deviation σ_k. Secondly, Hansen suggested including in the test only promising strategies with performance that satisfy the condition

$$\sqrt{n}(\overline{f}^*_{k,i} - \overline{f}_k)/\sigma_k \le -(2\log(\log n))^{1/2} \tag{12.22}$$

Furthermore, Romano and Wolf (2005), and Hsu et al. (2009) suggested using a stepwise protocol for enhancing the data snooping technique. This approach is focused on the family wide error (FWE) rate that is defined as the probability of rejecting at least one correct null hypothesis. Namely, the stepwise protocol identifies the strategies that violate the null hypothesis at a predefined significance level.

In a nutshell, this protocol starts with calculating a critical value, q, for all bootstrapped strategy performances using a chosen significance level. Next, all $\overline{f}_k$ are rearranged in descending order. The top model k is rejected if its performance exceeds q. If no rejection occurs, the process stops. Otherwise, the model is eliminated and the critical value is recalculated. The process continues until no model is rejected.

An interesting result Hsu et al. (2009) obtained with the stepwise bootstrap is that technical trading strategies that used to be profitable for emerging market indices in the past have deteriorated after exchange-traded funds replicating these indexes were introduced.

SUMMARY

- Simple back-testing protocols divide available data sample into two parts, one of which is applied for in-sample model calibration, with the other one used for out-of-sample testing.

- Akaike information criterion can be used for choosing the optimal number of model parameters.

- Important trading performance measures include, among others, total return and its variance, percentage of winning trades, and maximum drawdown.

- Resampling, most notably bootstrap and MCMC, is widely used as a measure against data snooping.

- Bootstrap implies creating multiple data sets by randomly drawing the elements of a given sample (with replacement). Block bootstrap may preserve autocorrelations in samples but choosing the block size is not trivial.

- A more sophisticated form of bootstrap implies estimating a mathematical model that fits the given sample (e.g., the random walk with drift) and bootstrapping the model's residuals.

- MCMC is based on the assumption that time series is a Markov chain. In MCMC, the probabilities of given return conditioned on past returns are calculated for the original data sample. Then, new samples are generated using these conditional probabilities.

- The higher is the fraction of generated samples for which given trading strategy yields returns exceeding return for the original sample—the better is the chance that the strategy is profitable.

- White's BRC can be used for comparing the efficiency of multiple trading strategies.

- The BRC can be enhanced with studentizing performance statistics and filtering out poorly performing strategies.

- The strategy that is the best for a given sample does not guarantee superior performance in the future.

CHAPTER **13**

Execution Strategies

Trading strategies that were discussed in former chapters are derived for producing positive returns in round-trip trades. In other words, these strategies offer signals on *what* and *when* to buy and sell. Sometimes, the term *opportunistic algorithm* is used for denoting them (Johnson 2010). Another problem that traders face is reducing the losses associated with the trading process. Some of these losses, such as the brokerage fees, commissions, and taxes are fixed. Others depend on the order placement strategy and therefore may be minimized.

Perold (1988) introduced the notion of *implementation shortfall* (IS) as a measure of the total transaction costs. IS represents the difference between the actual portfolio return and the paper estimate of this return at the beginning of trading.[1] If trading of an order with size X started at price p_0 (*arrival price*) and ended at price p_N, and the order was split into N *child orders* of size x_k that were filled at price p_k, then

$$\text{IS} = \underbrace{\sum x_k p_k - p_0 \sum x_k}_{\text{execution cost}} + \underbrace{(p_N - p_0)\left(X - \sum x_k\right)}_{\text{opportunity cost}} + C \qquad (13.1)$$

In (13.1), C is the fixed cost. Note that not all child orders may be executed during the trading day. For example, submission of child orders may be conditioned on specific price behavior. The unfilled amount, $X - \Sigma x_k$, determines an *opportunity cost*.

A new field, *algorithmic trading*, focuses on making decisions *where* and *how* to trade. Note that the notion of algorithmic trading is sometimes perceived as equivalent to *black-box trading* and *quantitative trading*. However, the professional trading community attributes algorithmic trading primarily to the execution strategies (Johnson 2010). Hence, the question of *whether* to trade is beyond the scope of this chapter. It is assumed here that the decision to trade a given amount within a given time horizon has been made and we are concerned only with its implementation. The decision *where* to trade is important primarily for institutional trading. As was indicated in Chapter 2, contemporary financial markets consist of multiple liquidity providers including exchanges and ATS. Modern institutional trading systems often have *liquidity aggregators* that facilitate connections to various liquidity sources. These trading systems may use *smart routing processes* for the automatic splitting of large orders into child orders and submitting them to the markets with better price and deeper liquidity.

Here, I discuss only the theoretical basics for making decisions on *how* to trade. While the general taxonomy in this field is still evolving (see Johnson 2010, and references therein), two major families of execution algorithms are discerned: *benchmark-driven algorithms* and *cost-driven algorithms*. Obviously, any execution algorithm addresses the problem of minimizing execution costs. However, benchmark-driven algorithms are based on some simple measures of market dynamics rather than on explicit optimization protocols. Cost-driven algorithms minimize IS and are often named *implementation shortfall algorithms*. Market impact due to order execution in conditions of limited liquidity is the main culprit of trading loss. Indeed, submission of a large order may wipe out the top of the order book (and possibly several price levels behind it). Hence, large orders can move price in the adverse direction. A general way for reducing trading loss is splitting large orders into child orders and spanning their submission (scheduling) over a given time interval.

In the next section, I review several popular benchmark-driven algorithms. Then, I describe the cost-driven algorithms including risk-neutral and risk-averse frameworks. Finally, I outline the problem of choice between the maker orders and taker orders (the so-called *taker's dilemma*).

BENCHMARK-DRIVEN SCHEDULES

Time-weighted average price (TWAP). In this schedule, child orders are spread uniformly over a given time interval. Such a simple protocol has a risk of exposure of the trader's intentions to other market participants. Some *scalpers* may realize that a large order is being traded and start trading the same instrument in expectation that the large trading volume will inevitably move the price. To prevent the information leak, the TWAP schedule may be randomized in terms of size and submission time of child orders. Then, periodic execution benchmarks are implemented for following the average schedule. For example, if the trading interval is four hours,

25 percent of the trading volume must be executed each hour. Then, the child-order sizes may be adjusted deterministically on an hourly basis. In more sophisticated TWAP schedules, some adaptive algorithms based on short-term price forecast may be implemented. For example, if price is expected to increase, the buy schedule may be sped up to decrease opportunity cost.

Volume-weighted average price (VWAP). Markets often have pronounced intraday trading volume patterns (see Chapter 6). Therefore, the VWAP schedule may be more appropriate than the TWAP schedule. If an asset during some time interval has N trades with price p_k and volume v_k, its VWAP is

$$\text{VWAP} = \sum_{k=1}^{N} v_k p_k \bigg/ \sum_{k=1}^{N} v_k \tag{13.2}$$

Practical implementation of the VWAP algorithm involves calculation of the percentage of daily trading volume u_k for each trading period k using historical market data:

$$u_k = v_k \bigg/ \sum_{i=1}^{N} v_i \tag{13.3}$$

Then, the size of child order k for the order of total size X equals

$$x_k = X u_k \tag{13.4}$$

Historical estimates of u_k may have significant variation. Therefore, sophisticated VWAP algorithms have adaptive mechanisms accounting for short-term price trends and the dynamics of u_k. It should be noted that while the VWAP algorithm helps in minimizing the market impact cost, it does not necessarily yield possible price appreciation, which is, in fact, a form of opportunity cost. This becomes apparent when price has a pronounced intraday trend. Indeed, if price grows (falls) on a high volume during a day, the trader might get more price appreciation if the entire buy (sell) order is placed in the morning rather than spread over the whole day. On average, however, such an opportunity cost is compensated for buy (sell) orders on days when the price falls (grows).

The VWAP benchmark has become very popular in post-trade analysis. Many buy-side firms use vendor software that provides VWAP trading functionality. How well this software performs can be checked by comparing the realized trading cost with the true VWAP, which is calculated using available market data.

Percent of volume (POV). In this schedule, the trader submits child orders with sizes equal to a certain percentage of the total trading volume, γ. This implies that child orders have acceptable market impact (if any), and execution time is not strictly defined. In estimating the size of child order x_k, one should take into account that the child order must be included in the total trading volume X_k at time period k:

$$\gamma = x_k/(X_k + x_k) \qquad (13.5)$$

As a result,

$$x_k = \gamma X_k/(1 - \gamma) \qquad (13.6)$$

Participation weighted price (PWP). This benchmark is a combination of VWAP and POV. Namely, if the desirable participation rate is γ and the order volume is N, PWP for this order is VWAP calculated over N/γ shares traded after the order was submitted.

COST-DRIVEN SCHEDULES

While executing a large order, a risk-averse trader faces a dilemma: Fast execution implies larger child orders and hence higher market impact and higher IS. On the other hand, submitting smaller child orders consumes more time and exposes traders to the price volatility risk (market risk). For example, say that bad news comes in the middle of execution of a sell order. Obviously, the rest of the order will be sold at a price notably lower than expected. Nevertheless, volatility risk is sometimes neglected in the derivation of execution algorithms. Therefore, cost-driven schedules can be partitioned into risk-neutral algorithms and risk-averse algorithms. In the former case, the schedule is derived by minimizing market impact. In the latter case, the schedule is derived by minimizing utility function that has two components: market impact and volatility risk. An overview of both approaches is given next.

Risk-Neutral Framework

Bertsimas & Lo (1998) introduced the following model for optimal execution. In terms of the notations used in the previous section, the objective to minimize the execution cost is

$$\underset{\{x_k\}}{\text{Min }} E \left\{ \sum_{k=1}^{N} x_k p_k \right\} \qquad (13.7)$$

which is subject to the constraint

$$\sum_{k=1}^{N} x_k = X \tag{13.8}$$

It is assumed that price follows the arithmetic random walk in the absence of market impact, and market impact is permanent and linear upon volume.

$$p_k = p_{k-1} + \theta x_k + \varepsilon_k \tag{13.9}$$

In (13.9), $\theta > 0$ and ε_k is an IID process that is uncorrelated with trading and has zero mean. Bertsimas & Lo (1998) formulate the dynamic programming problem in terms of the volume remaining to be bought, w_k

$$w_k = w_{k-1} - x_k, \quad w_1 = X, \quad w_{N+1} = 0 \tag{13.10}$$

The dynamic programming protocol is based on the condition that the solution optimal for the entire sequence $\{x_1^*, \ldots, x_N^*\}$ must be optimal for the subset $\{x_k^*, \ldots, x_N^*\}$, $k > 1$. This property is expressed in the Bellman equation, which relates the optimal values of the objective at times k and $k+1$:

$$V_k (p_{k-1}, w_k) = \underset{\{x_k\}}{\text{Min}} \, E\{p_k x_k + V_{k+1}(p_k, w_{k+1})\} \tag{13.11}$$

It follows from the boundary condition $w_{N+1} = 0$ that $x_T^* = w_T$. Then, the Bellman equation can be solved recursively: first by going backward and retrieving the relationship between x_k^* and w_k, and then by going forward, beginning with the initial condition $w_1 = X$. It turns out that the simple model defined above yields a rather trivial solution:

$$x_1^* = \ldots = x_N^* \tag{13.12}$$

In other words, the order should be split into equal pieces. This result is determined by the model assumption that the permanent impact does not depend on either price or the size of the unexecuted order. More complicated models generally do not have an analytical solution. Yet, they can be analyzed using numerical implementation of the dynamic programming technique (Bertsimas & Lo 1998).

Obizhaeva & Wang (2005) expanded this approach to account for exponential decay of market impact. Recently, Gatheral (2009) described the relationship between the shape of the market impact function and the decay of market impact. In particular, Gatheral has shown that the exponential decay of market impact is compatible only with linear market impact.

Risk-Averse Framework

The risk-averse framework for optimal execution was introduced by Grinold & Kahn (2000). Almgren & Chriss (2000) expanded this approach by constructing the *efficient trading frontier*[2] in the space of possible execution strategies.

Let's apply the Almgren-Chriss model to the selling process (the buying process is assumed to be symmetrical). Our goal is to sell X units within the time interval T. Let's divide T into N periods with length $\tau = T/N$ and define discrete times $t_k = k^* \tau$ where $k = 0, 1, \ldots, N$. Furthermore, let's introduce a list $n = \{n_0, \ldots, n_N\}$, where n_i is the number of units sold during the interval $t_{i-1} < t \leq t_i$. Another list will also be used: $x = \{x_0, \ldots, x_N\}$, where x_k is the remaining number of units at time t_k to be sold; $x_0 = X$; $x_N = n_0 = 0$

$$x_k = X - \sum_{i=1}^{i=k} n_i = \sum_{i=k+1}^{i=N} n_i \qquad (13.13)$$

It is assumed that price S follows the arithmetic random walk with no drift. Another assumption is that market impact can be partitioned into the permanent part that lasts the entire trading time T, and the temporary part that affects price only during one time interval τ. Then,

$$S_k = S_{k-1} + \sigma\tau^{1/2}\, d\xi_1 - \tau g(n_k/\tau) \qquad (13.14)$$

where the function $g(n_k/\tau)$ describes the permanent market impact. The temporary market impact contributes only to the sale price of the order k

$$\hat{S}_k = S_{k-1} + \sigma\tau^{1/2}\, d\xi_1 - \tau h(n_k/\tau) \qquad (13.15)$$

but does not affect S_k. As a result, the total trading cost equals

$$
\begin{aligned}
\mathrm{IS} &= XS_0 - \sum_{k=1}^{N} n_k \hat{S}_k \\
&= -\sum_{k=1}^{N} x_k(\sigma\tau^{1/2}d\zeta_k - \tau g(n_k/\tau)) + \sum_{k=1}^{N} n_k h(n_k/\tau)
\end{aligned}
\qquad (13.16)
$$

Within these assumptions, the expected IS, $E(x)$, and its variance, $V(x)$, equal

$$E(x) = \sum_{k=1}^{N} \tau x_k g(n_k/\tau) + \sum_{k=1}^{N} n_k h(n_k/\tau) \qquad (13.17)$$

$$V(x) = \sigma^2 \tau \sum_{k=1}^{N} x_k^2 \qquad (13.18)$$

The Almgren-Chriss framework is based on minimization of the utility function

$$U = E(x) + \lambda V(x) \qquad (13.19)$$

where λ is risk aversion.[3] Both permanent and temporary market impacts are assumed to be linear upon order size:

$$g(n_k/\tau) = \gamma\, n_k/\tau \qquad (13.20)$$

$$h(n_k/\tau) = \varepsilon\, sgn(n_k) + \eta n_k/\tau \qquad (13.21)$$

Here, γ and η are constant coefficients, ε is fixed cost (fees, etc.), and *sgn* is the sign function. Then,

$$E(x) = \frac{1}{2}\gamma X^2 + \varepsilon X + \frac{\tilde{\eta}}{\tau}\sum_{k=1}^{N} n_k^2, \quad \tilde{\eta} = \eta - \gamma\tau/2 \qquad (13.22)$$

Minimization of the utility function (13.19) is then reduced to equating zero to $\delta U/\delta x_k$, which yields

$$x_{k-1} - 2x_k + x_{k+1} = \tilde{\kappa}^2 \tau^2 x_k \qquad (13.23)$$

with

$$\tilde{\kappa}^2 = \lambda\sigma^2/\tilde{\eta} \qquad (13.24)$$

The solution to (13.23) is

$$x_k = X\frac{\sinh(\kappa(T - t_k))}{\sinh(\kappa T)}, \quad k = 0, 1, \ldots, N \qquad (13.25)$$

Then, it follows from the definition $n_k = x_k - x_{k-1}$ that

$$n_k = \frac{2X\sinh(\kappa\tau/2)}{\cosh(\kappa T)}\cosh(\kappa(T - t_{k-1/2})), \quad k = 1, 2, \ldots, N \qquad (13.26)$$

where $t_{k-1/2} = (k-1/2)\tau$ and κ satisfies the relation

$$2(\cosh(\kappa\tau) - 1) = \tilde{\kappa}^2 \tau^2 \qquad (13.27)$$

When τ approaches zero, $\tilde{\eta} \to \eta$ and $\tilde{\kappa}^2 \to \kappa^2$. Note that κ is independent of T and characterizes exponential decay of the size of sequential child orders. Namely, κ^{-1} units of time (order's half-life) decrease the child order size by the factor of e. Obviously, the higher is risk aversion λ, the shorter is the order's half-life. In fact, if $\kappa^{-1} \ll T$, then the order can be executed faster than the chosen execution time T implies.

Almgren & Chriss (2000) define the efficient trading frontier as the family of strategies that have minimal trading cost for a given cost variance, that is, a curve in the space E-V defined with (13.17), (13.18), and (13.25). The properties of this frontier are described in detail by Kissell & Glantz (2003).

Recent expansions of the Almgren-Chriss framework by Huberman & Stahl (2005), Almgren & Lorenz (2007), Jondeau et al. (2008), and Shied & Schöneborn (2009) have led to models that account for time-dependent volatility and liquidity, sometimes within the continuum-time framework. All these models generally share the assumption that market impact can be represented as a combination of the permanent and short-lived transitory components. However, recent findings by Bouchaud et al. (2004) in equity markets and by Schmidt (2010a) in FX exhibit the power-law decay of market impact.

In general, market impact of the ith trade at time t_k is $F(n_i, t_k - t_i)$. We call $s_k = -F(n_k, 0)$ the *initial market impact* of a child order n_k. Note that market impact is negative in the case of selling; hence, $s_k > 0$.

The total market impact after k trades equals to

$$MI(t_k) = \sum_{i=1}^{k} F(n_i, t_k - t_i) \qquad (13.28)$$

As a result, price dynamics is

$$S_k = S_0 + \sum_{i=1}^{k} [\sigma\tau^{1/2} d\xi_i + F(n_i, (k-i)\tau)] \qquad (13.29)$$

Another drawback of the Almgren-Chriss model and its extensions in the known literature is that the kth child order is executed not exactly at price S_k but at the VWAP, $S_{\text{vwap } k}$, which for a sell order is within the interval $S_k < S_{\text{vwap } k} \leq S_{k-1}$. Let's denote the *VWAP increment* (VWAPI) in respect to S_{k-1} with $c_k(n_k)$. For selling, this equals

$$c_k(n_k) = S_{k-1} - S_{\text{VWAP } k} \tag{13.30}$$

Then, the cost of trading has the form (Schmidt 2010a)

$$\text{IS} = \sum_{k=1}^{N} n_k c_k - n_1 \sigma \tau^{1/2} \, d\xi_1 - \sum_{k=2}^{N} n_k \sum_{i=1}^{k-1} [\sigma \tau^{1/2} d\xi_i + F(n_i, (k-i)\tau)] \tag{13.31}$$

Power-law decay of market impact can be approximated in the following form:

$$c_k(n_k) = \alpha n_k \tag{13.32}$$

$$s_k(n_k) = \beta n_k \tag{13.33}$$

$$F(n_k, t) = \gamma s_k(n_k)/(t - t_k)^m, \quad t > t_k \tag{13.34}$$

where the positive coefficients α, β, γ, and m can be approximated with empirical data.

The presence of long-range memory in the market impact dramatically complicates obtaining a tractable solution for the problem of minimizing the utility function (13.19). However, if one accounts only for the $(k - 1)$th child order's impact, $F(n_{k-1}, t)$, in the double sum of (13.31), then the utility function has the following simple form (Schmidt 2010a):

$$U(x) = \sum_{k=1}^{N} (\alpha n_k^2 + \beta \gamma n_{k-1} n_k / \tau^m + \sigma^2 \tau x_k^2) \tag{13.35}$$

Minimization of the utility function (13.35) reduces the problem to solving the equation similar to (13.23):

$$x_{k-1} - 2x_k + x_{k+1} = \kappa_0^2 \tau^2 x_k \tag{13.36}$$

with

$$\kappa_0^2 = \lambda \sigma^2 / (\alpha + \beta \gamma \tau^{-m}) \tag{13.37}$$

Obviously, the slower is decay (the smaller is m) and the higher is the order half-time.

Estimation of market impact from empirical data is another non-trivial problem. Usually, the trading volume is used as predictor for market impact (Almgren et al. 2005). However, as was indicated in Chapter 6, the expected market impact may be notably higher than the realized market impact. The reason for this may be that those informed traders[4] who do not have strict constraints on execution time simply do not submit large orders at times of lower liquidity. Therefore, the expected market impact may be more appropriate for calibrating the execution models with time constraints.

THE TAKER'S DILEMMA

Let's begin with terminology. A trader is called a *maker* if he provides liquidity on *both* bid/ask sides of the market. A trader who takes liquidity on one side of the market is a *taker*. Non-marketable bid/ask orders are maker orders and buy/sell orders are taker orders. Hence, a taker (trader) can submit a maker order.

When a taker makes a decision to take a long position in the market, he has a choice between submitting a market buy order or a marketable bid order (both are taker orders), or a bid order at current best bid or lower price (maker order).[5] In limit-order markets where market orders are not permitted, taker orders are associated with marketable limit orders. Submitting a taker order usually implies immediate execution. This, however, may not be the case for limit-order markets. Indeed, during the time interval between the order submission and arrival in the market, current best price may be taken away by other traders. Bid order can have a price significantly lower than the best bid, but this makes sense only if a trader believes that the trading asset is significantly overpriced.

In general, the taker order has the advantage of fast execution but has a loss in respect to the maker order. For example, if the taker order is filled at the current best ask price and the maker order is filled at the best bid price, the taker loss equals the bid/ask spread per unit of trading asset. Hence, the taker's dilemma is in determining which order to use. Analysis of this problem in an experimental market by Bloomfield et al. (2004) shows that informed traders are inclined to submit limit orders while liquidity traders use market orders more often.

The taker's dilemma can be formulated in terms of minimization of the utility function similar to (13.19) (Schmidt 2010b). Let P, BB, and BO be the order price, the best bid, and the best offer, respectively. The bid-side distance from best price is defined as $D = BB - P$, and the offer-side distance is defined as $D = P - BO$. Let's introduce a loss function for an order of size V placed at distance D from the best price:

$$L_1(V, D, \lambda) = aV \cdot \left[\lambda \sigma \sqrt{T(V, D)} - D \right] \qquad (13.38)$$

The first term within the brackets of (13.38) is an estimate of potential loss due to volatility, σ; $T(V, D)$ is the expected order execution time and λ is the risk-aversion coefficient. The second term is the order P/L in respect to the current market best price. The scaling parameter a in (13.38) depends on the units of V and D.

Schmidt (2010b) found that in the FX market, the loss function might have minima and therefore point at optimal placement of the limit order. This approach can be expanded for the optimal slicing of large orders. Consider a large amount N partitioned into n child orders of amount V ($N = nV$). Each child order is placed immediately after the former one is filled. Within this strategy, the nth order is *on hold* during the time it takes to execute $(n - 1)$ previous orders as well as the nth order itself. Therefore, the potential loss, L_n, for the nth order is:

$$L_n(V, D, \lambda) = aV \cdot \left[\lambda \sigma \sqrt{nT(V, D)} - D \right] \qquad (13.39)$$

Then, the loss function for the total amount, N, is the sum of the individual loss functions L_1 through L_n:

$$L_{(N=nV)}(V, D, \lambda) = aV \left[\lambda \sigma \cdot \sum_{k=1}^{n} \sqrt{kT(V, D)} - nD \right] \qquad (13.40)$$

Searching the global minimum of (13.40) on the V-D plane for a given risk aversion and total order size N can define the optimal size of child orders and their price. For example, if N is 100, the minimum of (13.40) may answer the question whether to trade 10,000 units using, for example, 1,000 child orders of size 10 at the best price, or using 5 child units with size 2,000 at a price one tick behind the best price.

The critical element in calculations of optimal child order size and price using the relation (13.38) is an accurate estimation of the expected execution time $T(V, D)$. This is a complicated task. First, the values of $T(V, D)$ depend on the market volatility. Another problem is the treatment of those orders that are cancelled prior to their execution or after they are partially filled. Order cancellation can occur for various reasons. In particular, when price moves in an adverse direction, traders (or automated trading software) may decide that price will not revert within an acceptable time horizon and therefore resubmit an order at a new price (see discussion of a relevant strategy below). Cancelled orders constitute a significant percentage of submitted orders and ignoring them can notably skew the results towards shorter execution times (Lo et al. 2002; Eisler et al. 2009).

The Random Walk Model

An interesting contribution to the problem of limit-order execution time estimation was given by Lo et al. (2002). In this work, price is modeled using the geometric Brownian motion with drift

$$dP(t) = \alpha P(t)dt + \sigma P(t)dW \tag{13.41}$$

In (13.41), α and σ are constant and dW is the standard Brownian motion. Let's denote the current time and price with t_0 and P_0, respectively. Consider the time interval $[t_0; t_0 + t]$, where P_{min} denotes the lowest price observed in this interval. A bid order with price P_l will be executed within the given interval if and only if P_{min} is less than or equal to P_l. Thus, the probability of filling the bid within the interval $[t_0; t_0 + t]$ is the probability that P_{min} is less than or equal to P_l. This probability can be formulated in terms of the first-passage time (FPT). Namely,

$$P_{FPT} = \Pr(P_{min} \le P_l | P(t_0) = P_0) = 1 - \Phi\left(\frac{\log(P_0/P_l) + \mu t}{\sigma\sqrt{t}}\right)$$
$$+ \left(\frac{P_l}{P_0}\right)^{2\mu/\sigma^2} \Phi\left(\frac{\log(P_l/P_0) + \mu t}{\sigma\sqrt{t}}\right), \quad P_l \le P_0 \tag{13.42}$$

where $\mu = \alpha - \sigma^2/2$, $\Phi()$ is the standard normal cumulative distribution function. If T is the bid execution time, the cumulative distribution function $F(t)$ for T equals

$$F(t) = \Pr(T \le t | P(t_0) = P_0) = \Pr(P_{min} \le P_l) \tag{13.43}$$

The theoretical distribution $F(t)$ can be compared with empirical data for the limit-order execution time. The values μ and σ that define $F(t)$ can be calculated from a given sample of returns using the maximum likelihood estimator. Then, the histogram of the empirical limit-order execution times is computed.

Lo et al. (2002) employed the methods of survival analysis to estimate the probability that limit orders will not be cancelled by the time t. They chose a parametric survival distribution in the form of the generalized gamma distribution and approximated it using empirical data on order cancellations for the 100 largest stocks in the S&P 500 for 1994 to 1995. Then, this survival distribution was used for *censoring* the empirical distribution of the limit-order execution times. Namely, if the order cancellation and execution are independent stochastic processes, the probability that the *time to fill* (TTF) for the limit order is t equals (Eisler et al. 2009):

$$P_{\text{TTF}}(t) = \frac{P_{\text{FPT}}(t)P_{LT}(> t)}{\int\limits_{0}^{\infty} P_{\text{FPT}}(\tau)P_{LT}(> \tau)d\tau} \qquad (13.44)$$

In (13.44), $P_{LT}(>t)$ is the probability that the limit order will not be cancelled by the time t.

Unfortunately, for practical applications, Lo et al. (2002) found that the first-passage time based on the random walk model does not describe accurately the empirical limit-order execution times. This conclusion was confirmed by Eisler et al. (2009) with further analysis of empirical first-passage times, order cancellation times, and limit-order execution times. In particular, Eisler et al. have shown that the statistical distributions for all three variables follow the power law with varying scaling exponents, and the first-passage time distribution decays notably slower than the execution time distribution.

Simulations of the Execution Costs

In general, the problem of estimating the limit-order execution time cannot be reduced to estimation of first-passage time since limit orders are placed in the order book in price/time priority and hence must reside at the top of the order book prior to their execution. Therefore, the model of limit-order execution should describe the order book depletion that depends on both the filling and cancellation of orders. One such model was offered by Schmidt (2009a) for describing a maker strategy in the institutional FX market. This strategy is much more aggressive than the one described with the utility function (13.39). Namely, rather than submit a bid order at best bid price and wait until the market *comes and takes it*, it is suggested to cancel and resubmit the order each time the best bid moves in an adverse direction prior to the order execution.[6]

In simulations, historical data for best bid prices and aggregated order volumes at best bid price were used. The distribution of the order book depletion rate was estimated using empirical data on transactions and order cancellations. For EUR/USD, this distribution fits well with the gamma distribution. In the beginning of each simulation, a *virtual order* was placed at the end of the order queue present at best bid. If the new best bid was higher than the current one, the virtual order was cancelled and resubmitted at the new bid price. If the new bid was the same, the order book was depleted using the simulated depletion rate. Depending on whether the virtual order was or was not on top of the order book, the depletion rate was determined only by the order filling rate or by both the order filling and cancellation rates. Finally, if the new best bid was lower than the current one, two scenarios were considered. Namely, if the virtual order was *not* on top of the order book, it was brought on top. If the virtual order was already on top, it was depleted with a simulated depletion rate. The simulation process for a given virtual order continued until it was completely filled. Such simulations were repeated for several thousand times using the random entry protocol (see Chapter 12). Finally, the averaged execution time and loss were estimated. The main conclusion from these simulations is that the maker strategy described above has an average loss per unit of order size (i.e., the cost in respect to initial best bid) lower than the bid/ask spread, and hence, it has statistical advantage over the taker strategy. However, order execution time remains an important risk factor in this strategy.

SUMMARY

- Execution strategies focus on minimizing losses associated with the trading process.
- Implementation shortfall is the generic measure of transactional costs.
- Market impact is the main cause of execution costs.
- Execution strategies can be partitioned into the benchmark-based schedules and cost-driven schedules.
- Benchmark-based schedules (most notably VWAP) are based on simple measures of market dynamics.
- Cost-driven schedules can be formulated as risk-neutral or risk-averse protocols.
- Risk-neutral protocols minimize market impact.
- Risk-averse protocols minimize utility function that includes market impact and market risk. The latter risk is determined by volatility.
- Estimation of market impact remains a considerable challenge in deriving and implementing optimal execution strategies.

Probability Distributions

Probability distributions are used for describing the statistical properties of a financial time series. While many classical theories are based on the normal (Gaussian) distributions, it has been well documented that empirical data may follow other distributions, too. Here, an overview of probability distributions discussed in this book is provided. For a more detailed description of the material, readers can consult definitive probability courses (e.g., Ross 2007).

BASIC NOTIONS

Consider a random variable (or *variate*) X. *The probability density function* $f(x)$ defines the probability to find X between a and b:

$$Pr(a \leq X \leq b) = \int_a^b f(x)dx \qquad (A.1)$$

The probability density must satisfy the normalization condition

$$\int_{X_{\min}}^{X_{\max}} f(x)dx = 1 \qquad (A.2)$$

where the interval $[X_{\min}, X_{\max}]$ is the range of all possible values of X. We shall omit the integration limits when they cover the entire range of possible values. Several distributions widely used in finance are listed in the next section.

Another way of describing random variables is to use *the cumulative distribution function*:

$$Pr(X \leq b) = \int_{-\infty}^b f(x)dx \qquad (A.3)$$

Obviously,

$$Pr(X > b) = 1 - Pr(X \leq b) \qquad (A.4)$$

Two characteristics are used to describe the most probable values of random variables: (1) *mean* (or *expectation*), and (2) *median*. Mean of X is the average of all possible values of X that are weighed with the probability density $f(x)$:

$$m = E[X] = \int xf(x)dx \qquad (A.5)$$

Median of X is the value M for which

$$Pr(X > M) = Pr(X < M) = 0.5 \qquad (A.6)$$

Expectation of a random variable calculated using some available information I_t (that may change with time t) is named *conditional expectation*. The conditional probability density is denoted by $f(x|I_t)$. Conditional expectation equals

$$E[X_t|I_t] = \int xf(x|I_t)dx \qquad (A.7)$$

Variance, Var, and *the standard deviation,* σ, are the conventional estimates of the deviations from the mean values of X:

$$Var[X] \equiv \sigma^2 = \int (x - m)^2 f(x)dx \qquad (A.8)$$

In financial literature, the standard deviation of price is used to characterize volatility (see Chapter 8). Higher-order moments of the probability distributions are defined as

$$m_n = E[X^n] = \int x^n f(x)dx \qquad (A.9)$$

According to this definition, mean is the first moment ($m \equiv m_1$), and variance can be expressed via the first two moments, $\sigma^2 = m_2 - m^2$. Two other important parameters, *skewness* S and *kurtosis* K, are related to the third and fourth moments, respectively:

$$S = E[(x - m)^3]/\sigma^3, \quad K = E[(x - m)^4]/\sigma^4 \qquad (A.10)$$

Both parameters S and K are dimensionless. Zero skewness implies that the distribution is symmetrical around its mean value. The positive and negative values of skewness indicate long positive tails and long negative tails, respectively. Kurtosis characterizes the distribution *peaked-ness*. Kurtosis of the normal distribution (defined in the next section) equals three. The *excess kurtosis*, $K_e = K - 3$, is often used as a measure of deviation from the normal distribution. In particular, positive excess kurtosis (or *leptokurtosis*) indicates more frequent large deviations from the mean value than is typical for the normal distribution. Leptokurtosis leads to the flatter central part as well as to the so-called fat tails in the distribution. Negative excess kurtosis indicates frequent small deviations from the mean value. In this case, the distribution sharpens around its mean value while the distribution tails decay faster than the tails of the normal distribution.

The *joint distribution* of two random variables X and Y is the generalization of the cumulative distribution (A.3):

$$Pr(X \le b, Y \le c) = \int\limits_{-\infty}^{b} \int\limits_{-\infty}^{c} h(x,y)dx\,dy \qquad (A.11)$$

In (A.11), $h(x, y)$ is the joint density that satisfies the normalization condition

$$\int\limits_{-\infty}^{\infty} \int\limits_{-\infty}^{\infty} h(x,y)dx\,dy = 1 \qquad (A.12)$$

Two random variables are *independent* if their joint density function is simply the product of the univariate density functions: $h(x, y) = f(x)\,g(y)$.

Covariance between two variates provides a measure of their simultaneous change. Consider two variates X and Y that have the means m_X and m_Y, respectively. Their covariance equals

$$Cov(x,y) = \sigma_{XY} = E[(x - m_X)(y - m_Y)] = E[xy] - m_X m_Y \qquad (A.13)$$

Clearly, covariance reduces to variance if $X = Y$: $\sigma_{XX} = \sigma_X^2$. Positive covariance between two variates implies that these variates tend to change simultaneously in the same direction rather than in opposite directions. Conversely, negative covariance between two variates implies that when one variate grows, the other one tends to fall and vice versa. Another popular measure of simultaneous change is *the correlation coefficient*:

$$Corr(x,y) = Cov(x,y)/(\sigma_X \sigma_Y) \qquad (A.14)$$

The values of the correlation coefficient are within the range $[-1, 1]$. In the general case with N variates $X_1, \ldots, X_N$ (where $N > 2$), correlations among variates are described with the *covariance matrix*, which has the following elements:

$$\text{Cov}(x_i, x_j) = \sigma_{ij} = E[(x_i - m_i)(x_j - m_j)] \qquad (A.15)$$

A time series X is *strictly stationary* if the multivariate cumulative distributions $(x_i, x_{i+1}, \ldots, x_{i+k})$ and $(x_{i+\tau}, x_{i+\tau+1}, \ldots, x_{i+\tau+k})$ are identical for all i, k, and τ. All moments of strictly stationary distributions do not depend on time. In a *weakly stationary* (or *covariance-stationary*) time series, the first two moments, mean and variance, are finite and time-invariant. In this case, autocovariance, $\text{Cov}(x_i, x_{i-\tau})$, depends only on the lag τ.

A time series is named *ergodic* if the sampling average

$$m_T = (1/T) \sum_{t=1}^{T} x_t \qquad (A.16)$$

converges to the expectation (A.5) as $T \to \infty$. Ergodicity of a time series implies that its autocovariance decays quickly, In other words, ergodic processes have a short memory. It should be noted that price autocovariance decays rather slowly while return autocovariance decays fast.

FREQUENTLY USED DISTRIBUTIONS

Here, you will find several important probability distributions that are used in quantitative finance.

The Uniform Distribution

The *uniform distribution* has a constant value within the given interval $[a, b]$ and equals zero outside this interval:

$$\begin{aligned} f_U &= 0, \quad x < a \quad \text{and} \quad x > b \\ f_U &= 1/(b - a), \quad a \le x \le b \end{aligned} \qquad (A.17)$$

The uniform distribution has the following mean, skewness, and excess Kurtosis:

$$m_U = 0, \quad \sigma_U^2 = (b - a)^2/12, \quad S_U = 0, \quad K_{eU} = -6/5 \qquad (A.18)$$

The distribution with $a = 0$ and $b = 1$ is called the *standard uniform distribution*.

The Binomial Distribution

The binomial distribution is a discrete distribution for n successes out of N trials, where the result of each trial is true with probability p and is false with probability $q = 1 - p$ (so-called *Bernoulli trials*):

$$f_B(n; N, p) = C_{Nn}p^n q^{N-n} = C_{Nn}p^n(1 - p)^{N-n},$$
$$C_{Nn} = \frac{N!}{n!(N - n)!} \tag{A.19}$$

The factor C_{Nn} is called the binomial coefficient. Mean and higher-order moments for the binomial distribution are equal, respectively:

$$m_B = Np, \quad \sigma_B^2 = Np(1 - p), \quad S_B = (q - p)/\sigma_B,$$
$$K_{eB} = (1 - 6pq)/\sigma_B^2 \tag{A.20}$$

In the case of large N and large $(N - n)$, the binomial distribution approaches the *normal* (or *Gaussian*) distribution:

$$f_B(n) = \frac{1}{\sqrt{2\pi}\sigma_B} \exp\left[-(x - m_B)^2 / 2\sigma_B^2\right],$$
$$N \to \infty, \quad (N - n) \to \infty \tag{A.21}$$

The Poisson Distribution

The Poisson distribution can be considered as the limiting case of the binomial distribution in the case with $p \ll 1$. The former describes the probability of n successes in N trials assuming that the fraction of successes v is proportional to the number of trials ($v = pN$)

$$f_P(n, N) = \frac{N!}{n!(N - n)!}\left(\frac{v}{N}\right)^n\left(1 - \frac{v}{N}\right)^{N-n} \tag{A.22}$$

When the number of trials N becomes very large ($N \to \infty$), the Poisson distribution approaches the limit

$$f_P(n) = v^n e^{-v}/n! \tag{A.23}$$

Mean, variance, skewness, and excess kurtosis of the Poisson distribution are equal, respectively:

$$m_P = \sigma_P^2 = v, \quad S_P = v^{-1/2}, \quad K_{eP} = v^{-1} \tag{A.24}$$

The Normal Distribution

The *normal (Gausian) distribution* has the form

$$f_N(x) = \frac{1}{\sqrt{2\pi}\sigma} \exp\left[-(x - m)^2 / 2\sigma^2\right] \tag{A.25}$$

It is often denoted $N(m, \sigma)$. Skewness and excess kurtosis of the normal distribution equal zero. The transform $z = (x - m)/\sigma$ converts the normal distribution into the *standard normal distribution*

$$f_{SN}(x) = \frac{1}{\sqrt{2\pi}}\exp\left[-z^2/2\right] \qquad (A.26)$$

The integral over the standard normal distribution within the interval $[0, z]$ can be used as the definition of the *error function* $erf(x)$:

$$\frac{1}{\sqrt{2\pi}}\int_0^z \exp(-x^2/2)dx = 0.5\,\mathrm{erf}\left(z/\sqrt{2}\right) \qquad (A.27)$$

Then, the cumulative distribution function for the standard normal distribution equals

$$Pr_{SN}(z) = 0.5\left[1 + \mathrm{erf}\left(z/\sqrt{2}\right)\right] \qquad (A.28)$$

According to the *central limit theorem*, the probability density distribution for a sum of N independent and identically distributed random variables with finite variances and finite means approaches the normal distribution as N grows to infinity. The Box-Miller method is often used for modeling the normal distribution (see, e.g., Press et al. 1992). It is based on drawings from the uniform distribution that is available for simulations in many computer languages. Namely, if two numbers x_1 and x_2 are drawn from the standard uniform distribution, then y_1 and y_2 are the standard normal variates:

$$y_1 = [-2\ln x_1)]^{1/2}\cos(2\pi x_2), \quad y_2 = [-2\ln x_1)]^{1/2}\sin(2\pi x_2) \qquad (A.29)$$

Mean and variance of the multivariate normal distribution with N variates can be easily calculated via the univariate means m_i and covariances σ_{ij}

$$m_N = \sum_{i=1}^{N} m_i, \quad \sigma_N^2 = \sum_{i,j=1}^{N} \sigma_{ij} \qquad (A.30)$$

The Lognormal Distribution

In the lognormal distribution, the logarithm of a variate has the normal form

$$f_{LN}(x) = \frac{1}{xs\sqrt{2\pi}}\exp\left[-(\ln x - \mu)^2/2s^2\right] \qquad (A.31)$$

Mean, variance, skewness, and excess kurtosis of the lognormal distribution can be expressed in terms of the parameters s and μ:

$$m_{LN} = \exp(\mu + 0.5s^2),$$
$$\sigma_{LN}^2 = [\exp(s^2) - 1]\exp(2\mu + s^2),$$
$$S_{LN} = [\exp(s^2) - 1]^{1/2}[\exp(s^2) + 2],$$
$$K_{eLN} = \exp(4s^2) + 2\exp(3s^2) + 3\exp(2s^2) - 6$$
(A.32)

The Cauchy Distribution

The *Cauchy (Lorentzian) distribution* is an example of the stable distribution (see the next section). It has the form

$$f_C(x) = \frac{b}{\partial[b^2 + (x - m)^2]}$$
(A.33)

The specific of the Cauchy distribution is that all its moments are infinite. When $b = 1$ and $m = 0$, the distribution is called the *standard Cauchy distribution*:

$$f_C(x) = \frac{1}{\partial[1 + x^2]}$$
(A.34)

The Gamma Distribution

This distribution has the following form:

$$f_G(x) = x^{\alpha-1} \cdot \frac{\exp(-x/\beta)}{\Gamma(\alpha)\beta^\alpha}$$
(A.35)

Its mean, variance, skewness, and excess kurtosis equal

$$m_G = \alpha\beta, \quad \sigma_G^2 = \alpha\beta^2, \quad S_G = 2/\alpha^{1/2}, \quad K_{eG} = 6/\alpha$$
(A.36)

STABLE DISTRIBUTIONS AND SCALE INVARIANCE

The principal property of *stable distribution* is that the sum of variates has the same distribution shape as that of addends (see e.g., Mantegna & Stanley 2000; Bouchaud & Potters 2000). Both the Cauchy distribution and the normal distribution are stable. This means, in particular, that the sum of two normal distributions with the same mean and variance is also the normal distribution. The general definition for the stable distributions was given by Levy (hence, another name—the *Levy distribution*). Consider the Fourier transform $F(q)$ of the probability distribution function $f(x)$:

$$F(q) = \int f(x)e^{iqx}dx \qquad (A.37)$$

The function $F(q)$ is also called the *characteristic function* of stochastic process. It can be shown that the logarithm of the characteristic function for the Levy distribution has the following form:

$$
\begin{aligned}
&\ln F_L(q) = i\mu q - \gamma|q|^{\alpha}[1 - i\beta\delta\tan(\pi\alpha/2)], \quad \text{if} \quad \alpha \neq 1\\
&\ln F_L(q) = i\mu q - \gamma|q|[1 + 2i\beta\delta\ln(|q|)/\pi)], \quad \text{if} \quad \alpha = 1
\end{aligned}
\qquad (A.38)
$$

In (A.38), $\delta = q/|q|$ and the distribution parameters must satisfy the following conditions:

$$0 < \alpha \leq 2, \quad -1 \leq \beta \leq 1, \quad \gamma > 0 \qquad (A.39)$$

The parameter μ corresponds to the mean of the stable distribution and can be any real number. The parameter α characterizes the distribution peakedness. If $\alpha = 2$, the distribution is normal. The parameter β characterizes skewness of the distribution. Note that skewness of the normal distribution equals zero and the parameter β does not affect the characteristic function with $\alpha = 2$. For the normal distribution,

$$\ln F_N(q) = i\mu q - \gamma q^2 \qquad (A.40)$$

The non-negative parameter γ is the scale factor that characterizes the spread of the distribution. In the case of the normal distribution, $\gamma = \sigma^2/2$ (where σ^2 is variance). The Cauchy distribution is defined with the parameters $\alpha = 1$ and $\beta = 0$. Its characteristic function equals

$$\ln F_C(q) = i\mu q - \gamma|q| \qquad (A.41)$$

The important feature of the stable distributions with $\alpha < 2$ is that they exhibit the power-law decay at large absolute values of the argument x:

$$f_L(|x|) \sim |x|^{-(1+\alpha)} \qquad (A.42)$$

The distributions with the power-law asymptotes are also called the *Pareto distributions.*

Unfortunately, the moments of stable processes $E[x^n]$ with the power-law asymptotes (i.e., when $\alpha < 2$) diverge for $n \geq \alpha$. As a result, the mean of a stable process is infinite when $\alpha \leq 1$ and variance of a stable process is infinite when $\alpha < 2$. Therefore, the normal distribution is the only stable distribution with finite mean and finite variance. The stable distributions have an advantage of the flexible description of peakedness and skewness. However, their infinite variance at $\alpha < 2$ restricts their usage in financial applications. The compromise that retains the flexibility of the Levy distribution yet yields finite variance is known as *truncated Levy flight.* This distribution can be defined as

$$
\begin{aligned}
f_{TL}(x) &= 0, \quad |x| > \ell \\
f_{TL}(x) &= Cf_L(x), \quad -\ell \leq x \leq \ell
\end{aligned}
\tag{A.43}
$$

In (A.43), $f_L(x)$ is the Levy distribution with index α and scale factor γ, ℓ is the cutoff length, and C is the normalization constant. Sometimes, the exponential cut-off is used at large distances:

$$
f_{TL}(x) \sim \exp(-\lambda|x|), \quad \lambda > 0, \quad |x| > \ell \tag{A.44}
$$

Since $f_{TL}(x)$ has finite variance, it converges to the normal distribution according to the central limit theorem.

Elements of Time Series Analysis

The methods of time series analysis are the main tools used for analysis of price dynamics, as well as for formulating and back-testing trading strategies. Here, we present an overview of the concepts used in this book. For more details, readers can consult Alexander (2001), Hamilton (1994), Taylor (2005), and Tsay (2005).

THE AUTOREGRESSIVE MODEL

First, we consider a univariate time series $y(t)$ that is observed at moments $t = 0, 1, \ldots, n$. The time series in which the observation at moment t takes place depends linearly on several lagged observations at moments $t - 1, t - 2, \ldots, t - p$

$$y(t) = a_1 y(t - 1) + a_2 y(t - 2) + \ldots + a_p y(t - p) + \varepsilon(t), \quad t > p \quad \text{(B.1)}$$

is called the *autoregressive process* of order p, or $AR(p)$. The white noise $\varepsilon(t)$ satisfies the following conditions:

$$E[\varepsilon(t)] = 0; \quad E[\varepsilon^2(t)] = \sigma^2; \quad E[\varepsilon(t)\,\varepsilon(s)] = 0, \quad \text{if} \quad t \neq s \quad \text{(B.2)}$$

The *lag operator* $L^p = y(t - p)$ is often used in describing time series. Note that $L^0 = y(t)$. Equation (B.1) in terms of the lag operator,

$$A_p(L) = 1 - a_1 L - a_2 L^2 - \ldots - a_p L^p \quad \text{(B.3)}$$

has the form

$$A_p(L)y(t) = \varepsilon(t) \quad \text{(B.4)}$$

It is easy to show for AR(1) that

$$y(t) = \sum_{i=0}^{t} a_1^i\, \varepsilon(t - i) \tag{B.5}$$

Obviously, contributions of old noise converge with time to zero when $|a_1| < 1$. As a result, AR(1) does not drift too far from its mean. Hence, AR(1) with $|a_1| < 1$ is a mean-reverting process. Mean and variance of AR(1) equal, respectively,

$$E[y(t)] = 0, \quad \mathrm{Var}[y(t)] = \sigma^2/(1 - a_1^2), \tag{B.6}$$

The process AR(1) with $a_1 = 1$ coincides with the random walk

$$y(t) = y(t - 1) + \varepsilon(t) \tag{B.7}$$

In this case, (B.5) reduces to

$$y(t) = \sum_{i=0}^{t} \varepsilon(t - i) \tag{B.8}$$

The noise contributions to the random walk do not weaken with time. Therefore, the random walk does not exhibit mean reversion.

Now, consider the process that represents the first difference:

$$x(t) = y(t) - y(t - 1) = \varepsilon(t) \tag{B.9}$$

Obviously, past noise has only transitory character for the process $x(t)$. Therefore $x(t)$ is mean-reverting. Some processes must be differenced several times (say d times) in order to exclude non-transitory noise shocks. These processes are named *integrated of order d* and denoted with $I(d)$.

The *unit root* is another notion widely used for discerning the permanent and transitory effects of random shocks. It is based on the roots of the characteristic polynomial for the AR(p) model. For example, AR(1) has the characteristic polynomial

$$1 - a_1 z = 0 \tag{B.10}$$

If $a_1 = 1$, then $z = 1$ and it is said that the AR(1) characteristic polynomial has the unit root. In the general case, the characteristic polynomial roots can have complex values. It is said that the solution to (B.10) is outside the unit circle (i.e., $z > 1$) when $a_1 < 1$. It can be shown that AR(p) is stationary when absolute values of all solutions to the characteristic equation

$$1 - a_1 z - a_2 z^2 - \ldots - a_p z^p = 0 \qquad (B.11)$$

are outside the unit circle.

If the process $y(t)$ has a non-zero mean value m, then the AR(1) model can be presented in the following form:

$$y(t) - m = a_1[y(t-1) - m] + \varepsilon(t); \quad y(t) = c + a_1 y(t-1) + \varepsilon(t) \quad (B.12)$$

In (B.12), intercept c equals

$$c = m(1 - a_1) \qquad (B.13)$$

The AR(p) model with a non-zero mean has the following form:

$$A_p(L)y(t) = c + \varepsilon(t), \quad c = m(1 - a_1 - \ldots a_p) \qquad (B.14)$$

THE MOVING AVERAGE MODEL

Another popular model of a time series process is the *moving average model* MA(q):

$$y(t) = \varepsilon(t) + b_1\varepsilon(t-1) + b_2\varepsilon(t-2) + \ldots + b_q\varepsilon(t-q) \qquad (B.15)$$

MA(q) can be presented in the form

$$y(t) = B_q(L)\,\varepsilon(t) \qquad (B.16)$$

where $B_q(L)$ is the MA polynomial in the lag operator

$$B_q(L) = 1 + b_1 L + b_2 L^2 + \ldots + b_q L^q \qquad (B.17)$$

The moving average model does not depend explicitly on the lagged values of $y(t)$. Yet, it is easy to show that this model implicitly incorporates the past. Consider, for example, the MA(1) model

$$y(t) = \varepsilon(t) + b_1\varepsilon(t-1) \qquad (B.18)$$

with $\varepsilon(0) = 0$. For this model, the general result for MA(1) has the form

$$y(t)\,(1 - b_1L + b_1L^2 - b_1L^3 + \ldots) = \varepsilon(t) \tag{B.19}$$

Equation (B.19) can be viewed as the AR(∞) process, which illustrates that the MA model does depend on the past.

It is said that the MA(q) model is *invertible* if it can be transformed into an AR(∞) model. It can be shown that MA(q) is invertible if all solutions to the equation

$$1 + b_1z + b_2z^2 + \ldots + b_qz^q = 0 \tag{B.20}$$

are outside the unit circle. In particular, MA(1) is invertible if $|\,b_1\,| < 1$.

MA(q) can have the intercept

$$y(t) = c + B_p(L)\varepsilon(t), \quad c = m \tag{B.21}$$

Note that the mean of MA(q) coincides with its intercept because the mean of the white noise is zero.

THE ARMA MODEL

A model that contains both lagged observations and lagged noise is named an *autoregressive moving average model* of order (p, q), or simply ARMA(p, q):

$$\begin{aligned} y(t) &= a_1y(t - 1) + a_2y(t - 2) + \ldots + a_py(t - p) + \varepsilon(t) \\ &+ b_1\varepsilon(t - 1) + b_2\varepsilon(t - 2) + \ldots + b_q\varepsilon(t - q) \end{aligned} \tag{B.22}$$

Sometimes, modeling of empirical data requires AR(p) with a rather high number p. Then, ARMA(p, q) may be more efficient in that the total number of its terms $(p + q)$ needed for given accuracy is lower than the number p in AR(p). ARMA(p, q) can be expanded into the integrated model, ARIMA(p, d, q).

The *autocorrelation function* (ACF) for a process $y(t)$ equals

$$\rho(k) = \gamma(k)/\gamma(0) \tag{B.23}$$

where $\gamma(k)$ is the *autocovariance* of order k:

$$\gamma(k) = E[y(t) - m)(y(t - k) - m)] \tag{B.24}$$

The autocorrelation functions may have typical patterns for various processes, which can be used for identification of empirical time series (Hamilton 1994). The obvious properties of ACF are

$$\rho(0) = 1, \ -1 < \rho(k) < 1 \quad \text{for} \quad k \neq 0 \tag{B.25}$$

ACF is closely related to the ARMA parameters. In particular, for AR(1),

$$\rho(1) = a_1 \tag{B.26}$$

The ACF of the first order for MA(1) equals

$$\rho(1) = b_1/(b_1^2 + 1) \tag{B.27}$$

Note that the right-hand side of (B.27) has the same value for the inverse transformation $b_1 \to 1/b_1$. For example, two processes,

$$x(t) = \varepsilon(t) + 2\varepsilon(t - 1)$$
$$y(t) = \varepsilon(t) + 0.5\varepsilon(t - 1)$$

have the same $\rho(1)$. Note, however, that $y(t)$ is an invertible process while $x(t)$ is not.

ARMA modeling is widely used for forecasting. Consider a forecast of a variable $y(t+1)$ based on a set of n variables $x(t)$ known at moment t. This set can be just past the values of y, that is: $y(t), y(t - 1), \ldots, y(t - n + 1)$. We denote the forecast with $\hat{y}(t+1|t)$. The quality of forecast is usually defined with some loss function. The *mean squared error* (MSE) is the conventional loss function in many applications:

$$\text{MSE}(\hat{y}(t + 1|t)) = E[(y(t + 1) - \hat{y}(t + 1|t)^2] \tag{B.28}$$

The forecast that yields the minimum of MSE turns out to be the expectation of $y(t + 1)$ conditioned on $x(t)$:

$$\hat{y}(t + 1|t) = E[y(t + 1)|x(t)] \tag{B.29}$$

In the case of linear regression,

$$y(t + 1) = b'x(t) + \varepsilon(t) \tag{B.30}$$

MSE is reduced to the *ordinary least squares* (OLS) estimate for b. For a sample with T observations,

$$b = \sum_{t-1}^{T} \mathbf{x}(t)y(t+1) \bigg/ \sum_{t=1}^{T} \mathbf{x}(t)\mathbf{x}'(t) \qquad (B.31)$$

Another important concept in the time series analysis is the *maximum likelihood estimate* (MLE). Consider the general ARMA model (B.22). The problem is how to estimate the ARMA parameters on the basis of given observations of $y(t)$. The idea of MLE is to find such a vector $r' = (a_1, \ldots, a_p, \ldots, b_1, \ldots, b_q, \sigma^2)$ that maximizes the likelihood function for the given observations $(y_1, y_2, \ldots, y_T)$:

$$f_{1,2,\ldots,T}(y_1, y_2, \ldots, y_T; r') \qquad (B.32)$$

The likelihood function (B.32) has the sense of probability of observing the data sample $(y_1, y_2, \ldots, y_T)$. In this approach, the ARMA model and the probability distribution for the white noise should be specified at first. Often, the normal distribution leads to reasonable estimates even if the real distribution is different. Furthermore, the likelihood function must be calculated for the chosen ARMA model. Finally, the components of the vector r' must be estimated. The latter step may require the sophisticated numerical optimization technique. Details of the implementation of MLE are discussed by Hamilton (1994).

TRENDS AND SEASONALITY

Finding trends is an important part of the time series analysis. The presence of trend implies that the time series has no mean reversion. Moreover, mean and variance of a trending process depend on the sample. It is said that the time series with trend is *non-stationary*. If a process $y(t)$ is *stationary*, its mean, variance, and autocovariance are finite and do not depend on time. This implies that autocovariance (B.24) depends only on the lag parameter k. The definition given above is named also *covariance-stationarity* or *weak stationarity* because it does not impose any restrictions on the higher moments of the process. *Strict stationarity* implies that higher moments also do not depend on time. Note that any MA process is covariance-stationary. However, the $AR(p)$ process is covariance-stationary only if the roots of its polynomial are outside the unit circle.

It is important to discern *deterministic trend* and *stochastic trend* as they both have different natures, yet their graphs may sometimes look very similar. Consider first the AR(1) model with the deterministic trend:

$$y(t) - m - ct = a_1(y(t-1) - m - c(t-1)) + \varepsilon(t) \qquad (B.33)$$

Let us introduce $z(t) = y(t) - m - ct$. Then, (B.33) has the solution

$$z(t) = a_1^t z(0) + \sum_{i=1}^{t} a_1^{t-i} \varepsilon(t) \qquad (B.34)$$

where $z(0)$ is a pre-sample starting value of z. Obviously, the random shocks are transitory if $|a_1| < 1$. The trend incorporated in the definition of $z(t)$ is said to be deterministic when $|a_1| < 1$. However, if $a_1 = 1$, then (B.33) has the form

$$y(t) = c + y(t-1) + \varepsilon(t) \qquad (B.35)$$

The process (B.23) is named the *random walk with drift*. In this case, (B.34) is reduced to

$$z(t) = z(0) + \sum_{i=1}^{t} \varepsilon(t) \qquad (B.36)$$

The sum of non-transitory shocks in the right-hand side of (B.36) is named stochastic trend. Both the deterministic trend model with $m = 0$

$$y(t) = at + \varepsilon(t)$$

and the stochastic trend model with the same parameter a

$$y(t) = a + y(t-1) + \varepsilon(t), \quad y(0) = 0$$

may sometimes look very similar, but they also can deviate for a long time.

Stochastic trend implies that the process is $I(1)$. Then, the lag polynomial (B.3) can be represented in the form

$$A_p(L) = (1 - L)\, A_{p-1}(L) \qquad (B.37)$$

The standard procedure for testing the presence of the unit root in a time series is the augmented Dickey-Fuller method (Hamilton 1994).

Seasonal effects may significantly affect the properties of a time series. Sometimes, there is a need to eliminate these effects in order to focus on the stochastic specifics of the process. Various differencing filters can be used for achieving this goal. In other cases, seasonal effect itself may be the object of interest. The general approach for handling seasonal effects is introducing *dummy parameters* $D(s, t)$, where $s = 1, 2, \ldots, S$; S is the number of seasons. For example, $S = 12$ for modeling the monthly effects. Then, the parameter $D(s, t)$ equals 1 at a specific season s and equals zero at all other seasons. The seasonal extension of an ARMA(p, q) model has the following form:

$$y(t) = a_1 y(t - 1) + a_2 y(t - 2) + \ldots + a_p y(t - p) + \varepsilon(t)$$
$$+ b_1 \varepsilon(t - 1) + b_2 \varepsilon(t - 2) + \ldots + b_q \varepsilon(t - q) + \sum_{s=1}^{S} d_s D(s, t) \quad \text{(B.38)}$$

Note that forecasting with the model (B.38) requires estimating $(p + q + S)$ parameters.

MULTIVARIATE TIME SERIES

Sometimes, the current value of a variable depends not only on its past values but also on past and/or current values of other variables. Then, it is said that the dynamic interdependent variables constitute *multivariate time series*.

A multivariate time series $y(t) = (y_1(t), y_2(t), \ldots, y_n(t))'$ is a vector of n processes that have data available for the same moments of time. Usually, it is supposed that all these processes are either stationary or have the same order of integration. In practice, the multivariate moving average models are rarely used. Therefore, we focus on the *vector autoregressive model* (VAR). Consider a bivariate VAR(1) process

$$y_1(t) = a_{10} + a_{11} y_1(t - 1) + a_{12} y_2(t - 1) + \varepsilon_1(t)$$
$$y_2(t) = a_{20} + a_{21} y_1(t - 1) + a_{22} y_2(t - 1) + \varepsilon_2(t) \quad \text{(B.39)}$$

that can be presented in the matrix form

$$\mathbf{y}(t) = \mathbf{a}_0 + \mathbf{A}\mathbf{y}(t - 1) + \boldsymbol{\varepsilon}(t) \quad \text{(B.40)}$$

In (B.40), $y(t) = (y_1(t), y_2(t))'$, $a_0 = (a_{10}, a_{20})'$, $\varepsilon(t) = (\varepsilon_1(t), \varepsilon_2(t))'$, and

$$\mathbf{A} = \begin{pmatrix} a_{11} a_{12} \\ a_{21} a_{22} \end{pmatrix}$$

The right-hand sides in the example (B.40) depend on past values only. However, dependencies on current values can also be included (the so-called *simultaneous dynamic model*). The simultaneous dynamic models can also be represented in the VAR form. For example, the following simultaneous system

$$y_1(t) = a_{11}y_1(t - 1) + a_{12}y_2(t) + \varepsilon_1(t)$$
$$y_2(t) = a_{21}y_1(t) + a_{22}y_2(t - 1) + \varepsilon_2(t) \tag{B.41}$$

can be represented as

$$\begin{pmatrix} y_1(t) \\ y_2(t) \end{pmatrix} = (1 - a_{12} a_{21})^{-1} \begin{pmatrix} a_{11} & a_{12} a_{22} \\ a_{11} a_{21} & a_{22} \end{pmatrix} \begin{pmatrix} y_1(t - 1) \\ y_2(t - 1) \end{pmatrix}$$
$$+ (1 - a_{12} a_{21})^{-1} \begin{pmatrix} 1 & a_{12} \\ a_{21} & 1 \end{pmatrix} \begin{pmatrix} \varepsilon_1(t) \\ \varepsilon_2(t) \end{pmatrix} \tag{B.42}$$

In the general case of n-variate time series, VAR(p) has the form

$$y(t) = a_0 + A_1 y(t - 1) + \ldots + A_p y(t - p) + \varepsilon(t) \tag{B.43}$$

where $y(t)$, a_0, and $\varepsilon(t)$ are n-dimensional vectors and A_i ($i = 1, \ldots, p$) are $n \times n$ matrices. Usually, the white noises $\varepsilon(t)$ are mutually independent. Let us introduce

$$\overline{A}_p(L) = I_n - A_1 L - \ldots - A_p L^p \tag{B.44}$$

where I_n is the n-dimensional unit vector. Then, (B.43) can be presented as

$$\overline{A}_p(L)y(t) = a_0 + \varepsilon(t) \tag{B.45}$$

Two covariance-stationary processes $x(t)$ and $y(t)$ are jointly covariance-stationary if their covariance $\text{Cov}(x(t), y(t - s))$ depends on lag s only. The condition for the covariance-stationary VAR(p) is the generalization of (B.11) for AR(p). Namely, all values of z satisfying the equation

$$|I_n - A_1 z - \ldots - A_p z^p| = 0 \tag{B.46}$$

must lie outside the unit circle. Equivalently, all solutions of the equation

$$|I_n \lambda^p - A_1 \lambda^{p-1} - \ldots - A_p| = 0 \tag{B.47}$$

must satisfy the condition $| \lambda | < 1$.

Notes

CHAPTER 1 Financial Markets: Traders, Orders, and Systems

1. Obviously, these profits are not guaranteed (see below).
2. See Hull (2006) for a definitive description of the options theory and its applications.
3. Harris (2002) combines informed traders and technical traders into the same group of *speculators*, which seems to be at odds with contrasting speculators and informed value investors (see, e.g., Graham & Dodd 2008).
4. Harris (2002, 297) suggests that uninformed traders should minimize their trading in order to avoid losses. One can debate, however, the meaning of *informed trader* beyond being an insider.
5. This term should not be confused with the pricing the financial instruments called derivatives (see, e.g., Hull 2002).
6. The following notation, 100@10.25, is used to indicate that the order size is 100 and the price of one unit is $10.25.

CHAPTER 2 Modern Financial Markets

1. There were several other regional exchanges in the past. However, the financial market landscape has been dramatically changed in recent years due to mergers and acquisitions. In particular, Boston and Philadelphia regional exchanges were acquired by NASDAQ in 2007, and one of the primary markets, the American Stock Exchange, was acquired by NYSE Euronext in 2008.
2. The closing process is actually more complicated than the classical auction (Hasbrouck 2007).
3. Currently, the NYSE electronic market is named NYSE Arca.
4. The Instinet's agency brokerage was spun out into a separate business and sold to Nomura Holdings in 2007.
5. ADV is also called *turnover*. In this section, all estimates of the ADV for FX instruments worldwide and in the United States are taken from the Bank for International Settlements (2010) and New York Federal Reserve (2010), respectively.
6. Notable exclusion is exchange of the U.S. and Canadian dollars (USD/CAD), for which settlement takes one business day.
7. FX swap is a contract that simultaneously agrees to buy (sell) an amount of currency at an agreed rate and to resell (repurchase) the same amount of currency for a later value date to (from) the same counterparty, also at an agreed rate.

8. Outright forward is a contract to exchange a predetermined amount of one currency for another at an agreed date in the future, based upon a rate of exchange determined at the trade date of the contract.
9. FX option is a contract that gives the buyer the right, but not the obligation, to exchange one currency for another at a predetermined exchange rate on or until the maturity date.
10. NDF is similar to outright forward, but there is no physical settlement of two currencies at maturity. Rather, based on the movement of two currencies, a net cash settlement will be made by one party to the other—usually in U.S. dollars.
11. In a currency swap, the interest and principal in one currency are exchanged for the interest and principal in another currency.
12. Most FX retail brokerages even drop transaction fees and use the bid/ask spread and margin interest as the main sources of revenues.
13. At the time of editing this book (March 2011), NYSE Euronext and Deutsche Burse, as well as London and Toronto stock exchanges, were publicly discussing their possible mergers.

CHAPTER 3   Inventory Models

1. Poisson process is described in Appendix A. This process is routinely used for description of order dynamics (see, e.g., Farmer et al. 2005).
2. Note that the Walrasian paradigm is questioned in information-based models (see Chapter 4).
3. For a description of the gambler's ruin problem, see Ross (2007).
4. The capital asset pricing model (CAPM) is one of the bedrocks of classical finance. We outline this model in Chapter 8.
5. See Chapter 8 for the formal definition of return.
6. Applications of dynamic programming to finance are reviewed by O'Hara (1995).

CHAPTER 4   Market Microstructure: Information-Based Models

1. The following relations for two normally distributed random variables X and Y are used in derivation (4.8): $E(Y|X = x) = E(Y) + (\text{Cov}(Y, X)/\text{Var}(X))(x - E(X))$; $\text{Cov}(Y, X) = E(XY) - E(X)E(Y)$.
2. One may expect that insiders trade as much as possible in order to benefit from their private information. Then, however, this information is quickly incorporated into price.
3. The process of incorporating new information into the variables of interest using the Bayes' rule is called Bayesian learning. See more on Bayes' rule in, for example, O'Hara (1995) and Ross (2007).
4. Price cannot be strongly efficient in the Glosten-Milgrom model since informed traders possess private information unavailable to others. See more about market efficiency in Chapter 7.

CHAPTER 5 Models of the Limit-Order Markets

1. In this context, opportunity cost manifests in paying a higher price in the future due to procrastination in the bull market.
2. We call this problem *taker's dilemma* (see Chapter 13).
3. The first passage times in equity and FX markets were discussed by Eisler et al. (2009) and Schmidt (2010a), respectively.
4. See more about *volatility* in Chapter 9.
5. FKK perceive impatience as an emotional component of trader behavior and state that traders in their model are risk neutral. However, the cost of execution delay has rational meaning in terms of volatility risk. Then, this cost implies risk aversion (see Chapter 13).

CHAPTER 6 Empirical Market Microstructure

1. Glosten and Harris account for rounding price to the nearest tick (which was $0.125 in the early 1980s), but we neglect this detail.
2. Actually, Glosten and Harris are very cautious in their conclusions. They just state that their results "do not reject" the conclusion made using the information-based models.
3. While the information-based market impact may be persistent at intermediate time horizons, Hasbrouck (2002) assumes that the random walk stays in the background of the structural models at longer (e.g., monthly) time intervals.
4. VAR is described in Appendix B.
5. In the case with $a = 1$, trading volume cannot be presented in the autoregressive form (Hasbrouck 1991).
6. Emrich (2009) defines *turnover* as the daily traded volume divided by the total number of shares outstanding for each stock.
7. In this section, we follow the literature on market microstructure and use the term *order flows* for denoting trading volumes. See more in the paragraph following (6.17).
8. Recall the difference between *hits* and *quotes* described in Chapter 2.

CHAPTER 7 Statistical Distributions and Dynamics of Returns

1. The notion of *ergodicity* is defined in Appendix A.
2. The definition (7.1) neglects possible dividend payments at time t.
3. Price can react unpredictably even in the case of *expected* news. For example, if a good company's performance report is widely expected, it can be priced in the stock value prior to the reporting date. Then, the rule *buying on gossip, selling on news* may take an effect after the report comes out.
4. Recall the findings in behavioral finance described in Chapter 3.
5. An introductory review of applications of the fractal theory in finance is given by Peters (1996) and Schmidt (2004).

CHAPTER 8   Volatility

1. Small autocorrelations in squared returns do not necessarily mean that there is no volatility clustering. If there are outliers in the sample that lead to high values of skewness and kurtosis, they may lower autocorrelations. If these outliers are removed from the sample, volatility clustering may become apparent (Alexander 2001).
2. See the definition of the *autoregressive process* (AR) in Appendix B.
3. The notation *plim* denotes convergence in probability.
4. Kernel regression estimators are a popular technique for smoothing noisy data. In particular, they were used in a sophisticated analysis of technical trading strategies (Lo et al. 2000).
5. The term *profits and losses* is generally used in risk management for referring to institutional portfolio. Here, we consider one asset at a time and equate this notion with return.
6. ETL is sometimes called *expected shortfall* or *conditional* VAR.

CHAPTER 9   Agent-Based Modeling of Financial Markets

1. Some structural models do permit persistent impact of trading on price. See, however, note 3 for Chapter 6.
2. Log price in the left-hand side of (9.16) may be a better choice in order to avoid possible negative price values (Farmer & Joshi 2002).

CHAPTER 10   Technical Trading Strategies

1. Edwards and Magee (2001) is the classical introduction to TA. The sheer number of books devoted to TA is overwhelming: A search on Amazon.com using the key words *technical analysis* for new books that were printed between January 2001 and September 2010 yielded 468 entries.
2. Menhkoff and Taylor (2007) primarily discuss applications of TA in FX and indicate that FX traders may have an additional rationale for choosing TA as a tool for trading decisions. Namely, defining fair values of exchange rates is more complicated than fair values for equities. Still, the popularity of TA among many equity traders seems to be as strong as in FX.
3. For example, as we shall see below, parameters of the trend strategies may be chosen to depend on volatility.
4. Little has been published in academic literature regarding the profitability of TA on the intraday scale (Park & Irwin 2007). One may expect that the noise-to-signal ratio is prohibitively high for the TA strategies at sub-minute timescales.
5. Note that in portfolio management, look-ahead bias is closely related to *survival bias*. Namely, some companies included in a portfolio or in an index that being the portfolio benchmark in the beginning of the reporting period may be excluded (e.g., due to bankruptcy) later (see, e.g., Baquero et al. 2005).
6. Note that sometimes EMA in RSI is defined with $\beta = 1/n$ rather than with (10.8).

CHAPTER 11   Arbitrage Trading Strategies

1. An accurate evaluation of the triangle arbitrage should account for the bid/ask spreads.
2. Market regulations may maintain potential arbitrage opportunities for an indefinite time: an example is the difference in pricing of drugs in the United States and Canada.
3. Here we assume that price follows the random walk; that is, it is an integrated process I(1). See more about integrated processes in Appendix B.
4. This definition of the tracking error contradicts the one that is used in portfolio management and refers to the variance (or standard deviation) of residuals between an equity index and tracking portfolio (Grinold & Kahn 2000).
5. Cf. with the first passage time for the Brownian motion (5.2).

CHAPTER 12   Back-Testing of Trading Strategies

1. Sometimes, data snooping is equated with data mining. The latter term, however, is widely used for denoting a generic field that comprises various methods for extracting patterns from data.
2. Application of the permutation method for back-testing is described by Aronson (2006).
3. Poundstone (2006) offers a popular account on the history and controversies surrounding the Kelly's criterion.
4. Note that the notion of *tracking error* here differs from that used in Chapter 11.
5. See e.g., Schmidt (2004), where two other derivations of the Brownian motion equation are also described.
6. The term *sequential trading* is used also for denoting *one trade at a time* in information-based market microstructure models (see Chapter 4).
7. In practical implementation, simulations started too close to the end of a sample, and hence unable to fill the order (or complete round-trip trade), may be simply ignored.
8. In my experience with back-testing high-frequency technical strategies in FX, beginning trading several minutes earlier/later in the morning might completely ruin (or make up) daily return.

CHAPTER 13   Execution Strategies

1. Sometimes, the cost of delay between the time when the decision to trade was made and the beginning of trading is included in IS (Kissell & Glantz 2003).
2. Almgren & Chriss (2000) used the term *efficient frontier*, which can be confused with the same term used in the portfolio management theory. We follow Kissell & Glantz (2003) in using the term *efficient trading frontier*.

3. Note that the linear relation (13.19) differs from typical exponential utility functions used in economics (see Chapter 3). The advantage of (13.19) is that it notably simplifies construction of the efficient trading frontier.
4. In this context, the qualifier *informed* relates to those traders who receive updates of the order book structure in real time.
5. Analysis of a short position is symmetric.
6. Here again, only the bid side is considered as the offer side is assumed to be symmetric.

References

Abrahams, J. 1986. "A survey of recent progress on level-crossing problems for random Processes." In *Communications and networks: A survey of recent advances*, edited by I. F. Blake and H. V. Poor, 6–25. Berlin: Springer-Verlag.

Admati, A. R., and P. Pfleiderer. 1988. "A theory of intraday patterns: Volume and price variability." *Review of Financial Studies* 1, 3–40.

Aite Group. 2008. *U.S. electronic fixed income trading platforms: The world ain't standing still.*

———. 2009a *New world order: The high frequency trading community and its impact on market structure.*

———. 2009b *Dark pools 2009: Not so dark anymore . . .*

———. 2009c *European multilateral trading facilities: Post-MiFid exchange landscape.*

———. 2010. *High frequency in FX: Open for business.*

Ait-Sahalia, Y., P. A. Mykland, and L. Zhang. 2005. *Ultra high frequency volatility estimation with dependent microstructure noise.* NBER Working Papers 11380.

Akerlof, G. A., and R. J. Shiller. 2010. *Animal spirits: How human psychology drives the economy, and why it matters for global capitalism.* Princeton, NJ: Princeton University Press.

Alexander, C. 1999. "Optimal hedging using cointegration." *Philosophical Transactions of the Royal Society* A357, 2039–2058.

———. 2001. *Market models: A guide to financial data analysis.* New York: John Wiley & Sons.

Alexander, C., I. Giblin, and W. Weddington, III 2001. *Cointegration and asset allocation: A new active hedge strategy.* ISMA Discussion Papers in Finance.

Aldridge, I. 2009. *High-frequency trading: A practical guide to algorithmic strategies and trading systems.* Hoboken, NJ: John Wiley & Sons.

Almgren, R., and N. Chriss. 2000. "Optimal execution of portfolio transactions." *Journal of Risk* 3(2): 5–39.

Almgren, R., and J. Lorenz. 2007. "Adaptive arrival price." In *AlgorithmicTrading III*, edited by B. R. Bruce, 59–66. New York: Institutional Investor.

Almgren, R., C. Thum, E. Hauptmann, and H. Li. 2005. "Equity market impact." *Risk, July*: 57–62.

Amihud, Y. 2002. "Illiquidity and stock returns: Cross-section and time-series effects." *Journal of Financial Markets* 5: 31–56.

Amihud, Y., and H. Mendelson. 1980. "Dealership markets: Market making with inventory." *Journal of Financial Economics* 8: 31–53.

Andersen, T. G., T. Bollerslev, F. X. Diebold, and P. Labys. 2000. "Great realizations." *Risk* 13(3): 105–108.

Aronson, D. 2006. *Evidence-based technical analysis: Applying the scientific method and statistical inference to trading signals*. Hoboken, NJ: John Wiley & Sons.

Artzner, P., F. Delbaen, J.-M. Eber, and D. Heath. 1999. "Coherent measures of risk." *Mathematical Finance* 9: 203–228.

Avellaneda, M., and J.-H. Lee. 2010. "Statistical arbitrage in U.S. equities market." *Quantitative Finance* 10: 761–782.

Bank of England. 2009. *FXJSC paper on the foreign exchange market*. http://www.bankofengland.co.uk/markets/forex/fxjsc/fxpaper090923.pdf.

Bank for International Settlements. 2010. *Triennal central bank survey*.

Barndorff-Nielsen, O. E., P. R. Hansen, A. Lunde, and N. Shephard. 2008. "Designing realised kernels to measure the ex-post variation of equity prices in the presence of noise." Available at SSRN: http://ssrn.com/abstract=620203.

Barndorff-Nielsen, O. E., and N. Shephard. 2002. "Economctric analysis of realized volatility and its use in estimating stochastic volatility models." *Journal of the Royal Statistical Society B, Part 2*, 64: 253–280.

Baquero, G., J. ter Horst, and M. Verbeek. 2005. "Survival, look-ahead bias, and the persistence of the hedge fund performance." *Journal of Financial and Quantitative Analysis* 40: 493–517.

Beja, A., and M. B. Goldman. 1980. "On the dynamic behavior of prices in disequilibrium." *Journal of Finance* 35: 235–248.

Berger, D. W., A. P. Chaboud, S. V. Chernenko, E. Howorka, R. S. Krishnasami Iyer, D. Liu, and J. H. Wright. 2005. *Order flow and exchange rate dynamics in electronic brokerage system data*. International Finance Discussion Papers N830. Federal Reserve System Board of Governors.

Biais, B., D. Martimort, and J. C. Rochet. 1995. "An empirical analysis of the limit order book and the order flow in the Paris bourse." *Journal of Finance* 50: 1655–1689.

Black, K., and S. Baruch. 2004. "Information in securities markets: Kyle meets Glosten and Milgrom." *Econometrica* 72: 433–465.

Bloomfield, R., M. O'Hara, and G. Saar. 2004. "The make-or-take decision in an electronic market: Evidence on the evolution of liquidity." *Journal of Financial Economics* 75: 165–199.

Bodie, Z., and R. C. Merton. 1998. *Finance*. Upper Saddle River, NJ: Prentice-Hall.

Bondarenko, O. 2003. "Statistical arbitrage and securities prices." *Review of Financial Studies* 16: 875–919.

Boni, L., and C. Leach. 2004. "Expandable limit order markets." *Journal of Financial Markets* 7: 145–85.

Bouchaud, J.-P., Y. Gefen, M. Potters, and M. Wyart. 2004. "Fluctuations and response in financial markets: The subtle nature of 'random' price changes." *Quantitative Finance* 4: 176–190.

Bouchaud, J.-P., J. Kockelkoren, and M. Potters. 2006. "Random walks, liquidity molasses and critical response in financial markets." *Quantitative Finance* 6, No.2: 115–123.

Bouchaud, J.-P., and M. Potters. 2000. *Theory of financial risks: From statistical physics to risk management*. Cambridge: Cambridge University Press.

Brock, W. A., and C. H. Hommes. 1998. "Heterogenous beliefs and routes to chaos in a simple asset pricing model." *Journal of Economic Dynamics and Control* 22: 1235–1274.

Brock, W. A., J. Lakonishok, and B. LeBaron. 1992. "Simple technical trading rules and stochastic properties of stock returns." *Journal of Finance* 47: 1731–1764.

Calvet, L., and A. Fisher. 2002. Multi-fractality in asset returns: Theory and evidence. *Review of Economics and Statistics* 84: 381–406.

Campbell, J. Y., A. W. Lo, and A. C. MacKinlay. 1997. *The econometrics of financial markets*. Princeton, NJ: Princeton University Press.

CFTC-SEC. 2010. *The market events of May 6, 2010*. http://financialservices.house.gov/FinancialSvcsDemMedia/file/key_issues/StaffFindingsregardingtheEventsofMay6.pdf.

Chaboud, A. P., S. V. Chernenko, E. Howorka, R. S. Krishnasami Iyer, D. Liu, and J. H. Wright. 2004. *The high-frequency effects of U.S. macroeconomic data releases on prices and trading activity in the global interdealer foreign exchange market*. International Finance Discussion Papers N823. Federal Reserve System Board of Governors.

Chan, E. P. 2009. *Quantitative trading: How to build your own algorithmic trading business*. Hoboken, NJ: John Wiley & Sons.

Chiarella, C., R. Dieci, and X. He. 2009. Heterogeneity, market mechanisms, and asset price dynamics. In *Handbook on financial markets: Dynamics and evolution*, 277–344. Elsevier.

Chiarella, C., and X. He. 2001. "Asset pricing and wealth dynamics under heterogeneous expectations." *Quantitative Finance* 1: 509–526.

Cohen, K. J., S. F. Maier, R. A. Schwartz, and D. K. Whitcomb. 1981. "Transaction costs, order placement strategy, and bid-ask spread." *Journal of Political Economy* 89: 287–305.

Cooper, M. J. 1999. "Filter rules based on price and volume in individual security overreaction." *Review of Financial Studies* 12: 901–935.

de Jong, F., and B. Rindi. 2009. *The microstructure of financial markets*. Cambridge: Cambridge University Press.

Dacorogna, M. M., R. Gencay, U. Müller, R. B. Olsen, and O. V. Pictet. 2001. *An introduction to high-frequency finance*. San Diego, CA: Academic Press.

Davidson, A. C., and D. V. Hinkley. 1997. *Bootstrap methods and their applications*. Cambridge: Cambridge University Press.

Donefer, B. S. 2010. "Algos gone wild: Risk in the world of automated trading strategies." *Journal of Trading* 5, No.2: 31–34.

Dowd, K. 2002. *An introduction to market risk measurement*. Hoboken, NJ: John Wiley & Sons.

Dunis, C., J. Laws, and P. Naim, ed. 2003. *Applied quantitative methods for trading and investment*. Hoboken, NJ: John Wiley & Sons.

Easley, D., and M. O'Hara. 1987. "Price, trade size, and information in securities markets." *Journal of Financial Economics* 19: 69–90.

———. 1992. "Time and the process of security price adjustment." *Journal of Finance* 47: 576–605.

Edwards, R. D., and J. Magee. 2001. *Technical analysis of stock trends.* AMACOM. 8th edition.

Eisler, Z., J. Kertesz, F. Lillo, and R. N. Mantegna. 2009. "Diffusive behavior and the modeling of characteristic times in limit order executions." *Quantitative Finance* 5: 547–563.

Elliott, R. J., J. Van der Hoek, and W. P. Malcolm. 2005. "Pairs trading." *Quantitative Finance* 5: 271–276.

Emrich, S. 2009. "Using smarter algorithms vs. smarter use of algorithms." *A Guide to Global Liquidity II. Institutional investors journals*: 40–51.

Fabozzi, F. J. 2005. *The handbook of fixed income securities.* New York: McGraw-Hill.

Fabozzi, F. J., S. M. Focardi, and P. Kolm. 2006. *Trends in quantitative finance.* Research Foundations of CFA Institute.

Farmer, J. D., A. Gerig, F. Lillo, and S. Mike. 2006. "Market efficiency and the long-memory of supply and demand: Is price impact variable and permanent or fixed and temporary?" *Quantitative Finance* 6, No.2: 107–112.

Farmer, J. D., and S. Joshi. 2002. "The price dynamics of common trading strategies." *Journal of Economic Behavior & Organization* 49(2): 149–171.

Farmer, J. D., P. Patelli, and I. I. Zovko. 2005. "Predictive power of zero-intelligence in financial markets." *Proc. Nat. Acad. Sci. USA* 102: 2254–2259.

Feller, W. 1968. *Introduction to probability theory and its applications.* Vol. 1, 3rd Edition. New York: John Wiley & Sons.

Fleming, M., and B. Mizrach. 2009. *The microstructure of a U.S. treasury ECN: The BrokerTec platform.* Working Paper. New Jersey: Rutgers University.

Foucault, T. 1999. "Order flow composition and trading costs in a dynamic limit order book." *Journal of Financial Markets* 2: 99–134.

Foucault, T., O. Kadan, and E. Kandel. 2005. "Limit order book as a market for liquidity." *The Review of Financial Studies* 18: 1171–1217.

Frydman, R., and M. D. Goldberg. 2007. *Imperfect knowledge economics: Exchange rates and risk.* Princeton, NJ: Princeton University Press.

Fusai, G., and A. Roncoroni. 2008. *Implementing models in quantitative finance: Methods and Cases.* Berlin: Springer-Verlag.

Gabaix, X. 2009. "Power laws in economics and finance." *Annual Review of Economics* 1: 255–293.

Gabaix, X., P. Gopikrishnan, V. Plerou, and H. E. Stanley. 2003. "A theory of power-law distributions in financial market fluctuations." *Nature* 423: 267–270.

Garman, M. 1976. "Market microstructure." *Journal of Financial Economics* 3: 257–275.

Gatev, E., W. N. Goetzmann, and K. G. Rowenhorst. 2006. "Pairs trading: Performance of a relative-value arbitrage." *The Review of Financial Studies* 19: 797–827.

Gatheral, G. 2010. "No-dynamic-arbitrage and market impact." *Quantitative Finance* 10: 749–759.

Gencay, R., F. Selcuk, and B. Whitcher. 2001. *An introduction to wavelets and other filtering methods in economics and finance.* San Diego, CA: Academic Press.

Glosten, L. R., and L. E. Harris. 1998. "Estimating the components of the bid/ask spread." *Journal of Financial Economics* 21: 123–142.

Glosten, L., and P. Milgrom. 1985. "Bid, ask and transaction prices in a specialist market with heterogeneously informed traders." *Journal of Financial Economics* 14: 71–100.

Goettler, R., C. Parlour, and U. Rajan. 2005. "Equlibrium in a dynamic limit order market." *Journal of Finance* 60: 2149–2192.

Gomber, P., and U. Schweickert. 2002. *The market impact—liquidity measure in electronic securities trading.* Deutsche Bourse. http://deutsche-boerse.com/dbag/dispatch/en/binary/gdb_content_pool/imported_files/public_files/10_downloads/31_trading_member/10_Products_and_Functionalities/40_Xetra_Funds/30_Xetra_Liquidity_Measure/liq_wph.pdf.

Graham, B., and D. Dodd. 2008. *Security analysis.* 6th Edition. New York: McGraw-Hill.

Grinold, R. C., and R. N. Kahn. 2000. *Active portfolio management.* New York: McGraw-Hill.

Hamilton, J. D. 1994. *Time series analysis.* Princeton, NJ: Princeton University Press.

Hansen, P. R. 2005. "A test for superior predictive ability." *Journal of Business and Economic Statistics* 23: 365–380.

———. 2010. *A winner's curse for econometric models: On the joint distribution of in-sample fit and out-of-sample fit and its implications for model selection.* Palo Alto, CA: Stanford University Press.

Hansen, P. R., J. Large, and A. Lunde. 2008. "Moving average-based estimators of integrated variance." *Econometric Reviews* 27: 79–111.

Harris, L. 2002. *Trading and exchanges: Market microstructure for practitioners.* Oxford University Press.

Hasbrouck, J. 1991. "Measuring the informational content of stock trades." *Journal of Finance* 46: 179–207.

———. 2002. "Stalking the 'efficient price' in market microstructure specifications: An overview." *Journal of Financial Markets* 5: 329–339.

———. 2007. *Empirical market microstructure: The institutions, economics, and econometrics of securities trading.* Oxford University Press.

Hasbrouck, J., and D. J. Seppi. 1999. *Common factors in prices, order flows and liquidity.* Available at SSRN: http://ssrn.com/abstract=159698.

Hashi, Y., and T. Ito. 2009. *Effects of Japanese macroeconomic announcements on the dollar/yen exchange rate: High-resolution picture.* NBER Working Paper No. w15020.

Hashimoto, Y., T. Ito, M. Ohnishi, H. Takayasu, M. Takayasu, and T. Watanabe. 2008. *Random walk or a run: Market microstructure analysis of the foreign exchange rate movements based on conditional probability.* NBER Working Paper 14160.

Hendershott, T., and P. C. Moulton. 2009. *Speed and stock market quality: The NYSE's hybrid.* Working Paper. Haas School of Business, University of California, Berkeley.

Ho, T., and H. R. Stoll. 1981. "Optimal dealer pricing under transactions and return uncertainty." *Journal of Financial Economics* 9: 47–73.

———. 1983. "The dynamics of dealer markets under competition." *Journal of Finance* 38: 1053–1074.

Hommes, C. H. 2006. Heterogeneous agent models in economics and finance. In *Handbook of Computational Economics, Vol. 2: Agent-Based Computational Economics*, edited by Hans Amman, David Kendrick, and John Rust, 1109–1186. North-Holland.

Hong, H. G., and J. Wang. 2000. "Trading and returns under periodic market closures." *Journal of Finance* 55: 297–354.

Hora, M. 2006. *Tactical liquidity trading and intraday volume.* Available at SSRN: http://ssrn.com/abstract=931667.

Hsu, P.-H., and C.-M. Kuan. 2005. "Reexamining the profitability of technical analysis with data snooping checks." *Journal of Financial Econometrics* 3: 606–628.

Hsu, P.-H., Y.-C. Hsu, and C.-M. Kuan. 2009. "Testing the predictive ability of technical analysis using a new stepwise test without data snooping bias." Available at SSRN: http://ssrn.com/abstract=1087044.

Huberman, G., and W. Stahl. 2005. "Optimal liquidity trading." *Review of Finance* 9: 165–200.

Hull, J. C. 2006. *Options, futures, and other derivatives.* 6th Edition. Upper Saddle River, NJ: Prentice Hall.

Ito, T., and Y. Hashimoto. 2006. "Intraday seasonality in activities of the foreign exchange markets: Evidence from the electronic broking system." *Journal of Japanese International Economics* 20: 637–664.

Jarrow, R. A., M. Teo, Y. K. Tse, and M. Warachka. 2005. "Statistical arbitrage and market efficiency: Enhanced theory, robust tests and further applications." Available at SSRN: http://ssrn.com/abstract=659941.

Johnson, B. 2010. *Algorithmic trading and DMA: An introduction to direct access trading strategies.* 4Myeloma Press.

Jondeau, E., A. Perilla, and M. Rockinger. 2008. *Optimal liquidation strategies in illiquid markets.* Swiss Finance Institute Research Paper No. 09-24. Available at SSRN: http://ssrn.com/abstract=1431869.

Jorion, P. 2000. *Value at risk: The new benchmark for managing financial risk.* New York: McGraw-Hill.

Jurek, J. W., and H. Yang. 2007. "Dynamic portfolio selection in arbitrage." Available at SSRN: http://ssrn.com/abstract=882536.

Kahneman, D., and A. Tversky, ed. 2000. *Choices, values and frames.* Cambridge University Press.

Kaufman, P. J. 2005. *New trading systems and methods.* Hoboken, NJ: John Wiley & Sons.

Kerstner, L. 2003. *Quantitative trading strategies: Harnessing the power of quantitative techniques to create a winning trading program.* New York: McGraw-Hill.

Khandani, A. E., and A.W. Lo. 2007. "What happened to the quants in August 2007?" Available at SSRN: http://ssrn.com/abstract=1015987.

Kissell, R., and M. Glantz. 2003. *Optimal trading strategies. AMACOM.*

Kyle, A. 1985. "Continuous auctions and insider trading." *Econometrica* 53: 1315–1335.

LeBaron, B. 2001. "Stochastic volatility as a simple generator of apparent financial power laws and long memory". *Quantitative Finance*, 1, 621–631.

———. 2006. "Agent based computational finance." In *Handbook of Computational Economics,Vol. 2: Agent-Based Computational Economics* edited by Hans Amman, David Kendrick, and John Rust, 1187-1234. North Holland.

LeBaron, B., W. B. Arthur, and R. Palmer. 1999. "The time series properties of an artificial stock market." *Journal of Economic Dynamics and Control* 23: 1487–1516.

Levy, M., H. Levy, and S. Solomon. 2000. *The microscopic simulation of financial markets: From investor behavior to market phenomena.* San Diego, CA: Academic Press.

Liu, J., and F. A. Longstaff. 2004. "Losing money on arbitrages: Optimal dynamic portfolio choice in markets with arbitrage opportunities." *Review of Financial Studies* 17: 611–641.

Liu, J., and A. G. Timmermann. 2009. "Risky arbitrage strategies: Optimal portfolio choice and economic implications." Available at SSRN: http://ssrn.com/abstract=1356397.

Lo, A. W. 2004. "Adaptive market hypothesis: Market efficiency from evolutionary perspective." *Journal of Portfolio Management* 30: 15 –29.

Lo, A. W., and A. C. MacKinlay. 1999. *A non-random walk down Wall Street.* Princeton, NJ: Princeton University Press.

Lo, A. W., C. MacKinlay, and J. Zhang. 2002. "Econometric models of limit order execution." *Journal of Financial Economics* 65: 31–71.

Lo, A. W., H. Mamaysky, and J. Wang. 2000. "Foundations of technical analysis: Computational algorithms, statistical inference, and empirical implementation." *Journal of Finance* 55: 1705–1770.

Lowenstein, R. 2000. *When genius failed: The rise and fall of Long-term capital management.* New York: Random House.

Lux, T. 1998. "The socio-economic dynamics of speculative markets: interacting agents, chaos, and the fat tails of return distributions." *Journal of Economic Behavior and Organization* 33: 143–165.

———. 2001a"Power laws and long memory." *Quantitative Finance* 1: 560–562.

———. 2001b"Turbulence in financial markets: The surprising explanatory power of simple cascade models." *Quantitative Finance* 1: 632–640.

Lux, T., and M. Marchesi. 2000. "Volatility clustering in financial markets: A micro-simulation of interacting agents." *International Journal of Theoretical and Applied Finance* 3: 675–702.

Lyons, R. K. 2001. The microstructure approach to exchange rates. Cambridge, MA: The MIT Press.

Magdon-Ismail, M., and A. F. Atiya. 2004. "Maximum drawdown." *Risk* 17(10): 99–102.

Malinova, K., and A. Park. 2009. *Intraday trading patterns: The role of timing.* Working paper 335. University of Toronto, Canada.

Malkiel, B. G. 2003. *A random walk down Wall Street.* New York: W. W. Norton & Company.

Mandelbrot, B. B. 1997. *Fractals and scaling in finance.* Berlin: Springer-Verlag.

Mantegna, R. N., and H. E. Stanley. 2000. *An introduction in econophysics: Correlations and complexity in finance.* Cambridge University Press.

Menkhoff, L., and M. P. Taylor. 2007. "The obstinate passion of foreign exchange professionals: Technical analysis." *Journal of Economic Literature* 45: 936–972.

Mizrach, M., and C. Neely. 2009. "The microstructure of the U.S. Treasury market." In *The Encyclopedia of Complexity and System Science,* 9565–9577. New York: Springer-Verlag.

Neely, C., D. E. Rapach, J. Tu, and G. Zhou. 2010. *Out-of-sample equity premium prediction: Economic fundamentals vs. moving-average rules.* Federal Reserve Bank of St. Louis Working Paper No. 2010-008A.

Neely, C. J., P. A. Weller, and J. M. Ulrich. 2009. "The adaptive markets hypothesis: Evidence from the foreign exchange market." *Journal of Financial and Quantitative Analysis* 44: 467–488.

New York Federal Reserve. 2010. *The foreign exchange and interest derivatives markets: Turnover in the United States.*

NYSE Group. 2006. *NYSE hybrid FAQ.*

Obizhaeva, A. A., and J. Wang. 2005. *Optimal trading strategy and supply/demand dynamics.* NBER Working Paper No. W11444 92005. Available at SSRN: http://ssrn.com/abstract=752022.

O'Hara, M. 1995. *Market microstructure theory.* New York: John Wiley & Sons.

Ohnishi, T., H. Takayasu, T. Ito, Y. Hashimoto, T. Watanabe, and M. Takayasu. 2008. Dynamics of quote and deal prices in the foreign exchange market. *Journal of Economic Interaction and Coordination* 3, No.1: 99–106.

Omrane, W. B., and H. Van Oppens. 2004. *The predictive success and profitability of chart patterns in the euro/dollar foreign exchange market.* IAG Working Paper No. 95–03. Available at SSRN: http://ssrn.com/abstract=484384.

Okunev, J., and D. White. 2002. "The profits to technical analysis in foreign exchange markets have not disappeared." In *Advanced trading rules,* 2nd Edition , edited by A. E. Askar and S. Satchell. Elsevier.

Osler, C. L. 2010. "Foreign exchange microstructure: a survey of the empirical literature." *In Springer encyclopedia of complexity and systems science* (forthcoming).

Park, C.-H., and S. H. Irwin. 2007. "What do we know about profitability of technical analysis?" *Journal of Economic Surveys* 21: 786–826.

Parlour, C. A. 1998. "Price dynamics in limit order markets." *Journal of Financial Studies* 11: 789–816.

Parlour, C. A., and D. J. Seppi. 2008. "Limit order markets: A survey." In *Handbook of financial intermediation and banking,* edited by A. W. A. Boot and A. V. Thakor, 61–96. Elsevier.

Patterson, S., K. Scannell, and G. Rogow. 2009. "Ban on flash orders is considered by SEC." *Wall Street Journal,* Aug. 5.

Perold, A. F. 1988. "The implementation shortfall: Paper versus reality." *Journal of Portfolio Management* 24: 4–9.

Peters, E. 1996. *Chaos and order in capital markets.* New York: John Wiley & Sons.

Politis, D. N., and J. P. Romano. 1994. "The stationary bootstrap." *J. Amer. Statist. Assoc.* 89: 1303–1313.

Poon, S.-H., and C. W. J. Granger. 2003. "Forecasting volatility in financial markets." *Journal of Economic Literature* 41: 478–539.

Poundstone, W. 2006. *Fortune's formula.* New York: Hill and Wang.

Press, W. H., B. P. Flannery, S. A. Teukolsky, and W. T. Wetterling. 1992. *Numerical recipes: Art of scientific programming.* Cambridge University Press.

Roll, R. 1984. "A simple implicit measure of the effective bid-ask spread in an efficient market." *Journal of Finance* 39: 1127–1139.

Romano, J. P., and M. Wolf. 2005. "Stepwise multiple testing as formalized data snooping." *Econometrica* 73: 1237–1282.

Ross, S. M. 2007. *Introduction to probability models.* 9th Edition. San Diego, CA: Academic Press.

Rosu, I. 2008. *Dynamic model of the limit order book.* Working Paper. Booth School of Business, University of Chicago.

Sarno, L., and M. P. Taylor. 2006. *The economics of exchange rates.* Cambridge: Cambridge University Press.

Schied, A., and T. Schöneborn. 2009. "Risk aversion and the dynamics of optimal liquidation strategies in illiquid markets." *Finance Stochast* 13(2): 181–204.

Schiereck, D., and C. Voigt. 2008. *Intraday pattern of principal and agent account trading: An empirical investigation.* Available at SSRN: http://ssrn.com/abstract=1123649.

Schmidt, A. B. 1999. "Modeling the demand-price relations in a high-frequency foreign exchange market." *Physica* A271: 507–514.

———. 2000. "Modeling the birth of a liquid market," *Physica* A283: 479–485.

———. 2002. "Why technical trading may be successful: A lesson from the agent-based modeling." *Physica* A303: 185–188.

———. 2004. *Quantitative finance for physicists: An introduction.* Elsevier.

———. 2009a "Simulation of execution costs in the global FX market." *Journal of Trading* 4, No.4: 62–68.

———. 2009b "Detrending the realized volatility in the global FX market." *Physica* 388: 1887–1892.

———. 2010a "Optimal execution in the global FX market." *Journal of Trading* 5, No.3: 62–68.

———. 2010b "Microstructure and execution strategies in the global spot FX market." In *Econophysics approaches to large-scale business data and financial crisis.* 2010. Berlin: Springer-Verlag, 49–63.

———. 2008. *Pairs trading: A cointegration approach.* Thesis. University of Sydney, Australia.

Schulmesister, S. 2009. *Technical trading and trends in the dollar-euro exchange rate.* Austrian Institute for Economic Research.

Shephard, N., ed. 2005. *Stochastic volatility*. Selected readings. Oxford: Oxford University Press.

Stefanini, F. 2006. *Investment strategies of hedge funds*. Hoboken, NJ: John Wiley & Sons.

Stoll, H. R. 1978. "The supply of dealer services in securities market." *Journal of Finance* 33: 1133–1151.

Subrahmanyam, A. 1991. "Risk aversion, market liquidity, and price efficiency." *Review of Financial Studies* 4: 417–442.

Sullivan, R., A. Timmermann, and H. White. 1999. "Data-snooping, technical trading rule performance, and the bootstrap." *Journal of Finance* 54: 1647–1691.

Taylor, S. J. 2005. *Asset price dynamics, volatility, and prediction*. Princeton, NJ: Princeton University Press.

Timmermann, A. 2006. "Forecast combinations." In *Handbook of economic forecasting*, edited by G. Elloiott, A. G. W. Granger, and A. Timmermann, 135–196.

Thorp, E. O. 2006. "The Kelly criterion in blackjack sports betting and the stock market." In *Handbook of asset and liability management, Volume 1: Theory and methodology*, edited by S. A. Zenios and W. T. Ziemba, 385–428. North Holland, 2006.

Tsay, R. S. 2005. *Analysis of financial time series*. Hoboken, NJ: John Wiley & Sons.

Vidyamurthy, G. 2004. *Pair trading: Quantitative methods and analysis*. Hoboken, NJ: John Wiley & Sons.

Weber, P., and B. Rosenow. 2005. "Order book approach to price impact." *Quantitative Finance* 5: 357–364.

White, H. 2000. "A reality check for data snooping." *Econometrica* 68: 1097–1126.

Wilcox, C., and E. Crittenden. 2005. "Does trend following work on stocks?" www.blackstarfunds.com/files/Does_trendfollowing_work_on_stocks.pdf.

Zhang, L., P. A. Mykland, and Y. Ait-Sahalia. 2005. "A tale of two time scales: Determining integrated volatility with noisy high-frequency data." *Journal of the American Statistical Association* 100: 1394–1411.

About the Author

Dr. Anatoly B. (Alec) Schmidt holds an M.S. and Ph.D. in physics from Latvian University. His research on statistical physics, chemical physics, and biophysics has been summarized in the monograph, "Statistical thermodynamics of classical plasmas" (Energoatomizdat, Moscow, 1991) and in more than 40 academic papers.

Dr. Schmidt has been working as a quantitative analyst in the financial industry since 1997. He has published several papers on agent-based modeling of financial markets, market microstructure, and algorithmic trading as well as a book entitled *Quantitative Finance for Physicists: An Introduction* (Elsevier, 2004). Dr. Schmidt also teaches in the financial engineering program of Stevens Institute of Technology.

Index

Printed and bound by CPI Group (UK) Ltd, Croydon, CR0 4YY

23/04/2025